WITHDRAWN
NDSU

Between Exile and Asylum

BETWEEN EXILE AND ASYLUM
An Eastern Epistolary

BY
PREDRAG MATVEJEVIĆ

TRANSLATED
FROM THE CROATIAN
BY
RUSSELL SCOTT VALENTINO

Central European University Press
Budapest   New York

© 2004 by Predrag Matvejević
English translation © 2004 by Russell Scott Valentino

First published in Serbo-Croatian as *Istočni epistolar* in 1994
by CERES, Zagreb

English edition published in 2004 by

Central European University Press

An imprint of the
Central European University Share Company
Nádor utca 11, H-1051 Budapest, Hungary
Tel: +36-1-327-3138 or 327-3000
Fax: +36-1-327-3183
E-mail: ceupress@ceu.hu
Website: www.ceupress.com

400 West 59th Street, New York NY 10019, USA
Tel: +1-212-547-6932
Fax: +1-212-548-4607
E-mail: mgreenwald@sorosny.org

All rights reserved. No part of this publication may be
reproduced, stored in a retrieval system, or transmitted,
in any form or by any means, without the permission
of the Publisher.

ISBN 963 9241 85 7 cloth

Library of Congress Cataloging-in-Publication Data

Matvejević, Predrag, 1932–
  [Istočni epistolar. English]
  Between exile and asylum: an eastern epistolary / by Predrag Matvejević;
translated by Russell Scott Valentino.
   p. cm.
  ISBN 9639241857 (hardbound: acid free)
  1. Soviet Union—Description and travel. 2. Matvejevic, Predrag, 1932–
Correspondence. I. Title.
  DK29.M3613 2004
  947.084—dc22
                                                                2004015796

Preprint by Attributum Stúdió, Budapest
Printed in Hungary by Akaprint Nyomda

Contents

Acknowledgments	vii
A Note on Source Texts	ix
A Note on the Transliteration of Russian	xi

BOOK ONE • HEROIDES

To My Forebears	3
Seven Thousand Days in Siberia	24
Sinyavsky-Daniel	27
Brodsky	30
Eurasian Letters – Continued	31
The Gulag Archipelago	55

BOOK TWO • STELES

Soviet Itineraries – Continued	61
On Letters, Open and Closed	86
Kolyma	90
To Varlam Shalamov	92
Russian Letters – Continued	95
Hostage to the Truth	112
Cause for Dismissal	114
Yellow Star, White Star	120
Confession	122

BOOK THREE • EPITAPHS

Rehabilitations	127
Nikolai Bukharin	131
Kropotkin – The Dark Prince	136
Maxim Gorky	139
Lev Trotsky	144
Goli Otok – Another Gulag	148

BOOK FOUR • APOLOGIAS 153	
Mikhail Bulgakov	156
Nadezhda Mandelshtam	161
Ariadna Efron	164
Kruzhok	166
Portraits of Stalin	168
On the Perestroika of Writers	174
For Mikhail Sergeevich Gorbachev	177
Archives and Memory	181
For a New Dissidence	183
An Interrogation	186
Our Disappointments – To Brodsky	188
Final Letters	192
Heirs without Heritage	193
Emigration and Dissidence	195
The Collapse of the Intelligentsia	198
Okudzhava's Response	201
A Perverted Slavicism	204
The Gulag So Long Ago	207
To Franjo Tuđman	208
Afterword – An Open Letter to the Reader	213
Name Index	219

Acknowledgments

The translation of this book into English was facilitated by a 2002 National Endowment for the Arts Literature Fellowship. A portion of Part Four, "An Interrogation," appeared previously in *91st Meridian* (Volume 2, Number 2). I thank the editors for their permission to reprint it here.

A Note on Source Texts

With the permission and encouragement of the author, I have used three separate editions as the basis for the present translation: the Croatian *Istočni epistolar* (Zagreb: CERES, 1994); the French *Entre asile et exil: épistolaire russe* (Paris: Stock, 1995), translated by Mireille Robin and Mauricette Begic; and the Italian *Tra asilo ed esilio: romanzo epistolare* (Roma: Meltemi, 1998), translated by Leonello Costantini.

The reason for such a collectivist approach was indicated by the author himself, who, sending me three books when we had agreed that I would translate one, suggested I should "start with the Italian as it had come out last." Each of the later texts, it turns out, differs from the supposed "original" in substantive ways, though they are both called translations. To make matters more complex, the several Russian language letters that were translated by the author into French for the French edition (there is no mention of them in the Italian edition) were lost in the destruction of the city of Mostar during the war in Bosnia-Herzegovina. The very notion of "original" is therefore frustratingly inadequate in dealing with this work.

To address the issue, I have followed the author's advice and used the Croatian edition as a foundation to which the different translations, into French and Italian, relate as something like redactions of a medieval manuscripts, where intermediate textual steps have been lost or destroyed. In several cases, entire chapters have been added to the French and Italian editions. I have indicated where this is the case in endnotes.

Parenthetical glosses are provided for all the Russian words used in the work. First names of writers are given upon first mention only, unless the author has repeated them in subsequent references.

A Note on the Transliteration of Russian

The Library of Congress standard has been used for all words and non-translated titles. The same system has been used for names and toponyms except for the following:

- -ый/ий — y: Bely/Dostoevsky, Yevgeny

- -ой — oy: Tolstoy

- ь (omited): Gorky, Suzdal

- я/ю — ya/yu: Zamyatin, Tolstaya/Yury, Tyutchev

- ё — yo/o: Fyodor, Gumilyov/Kruchonykh

- initial e — ye: Yefim

- ье/ьё/ьи — ye/yo/yi: Leontyev/Solovyov/Ilyich

- certain names with time-honored transliterations: Herzen, Tchaikovsky, Scriabin, Meyerhold, Eisenstein, Khrushchev, Gorbachev etc.

Book One
HEROIDES

To My Forebears

I wrote my first letters from Russia to a man born in Odessa at the beginning of the twentieth century. By heritage Ukrainian, by language and culture Russian, he was an ecumenical Christian, neither "white" nor "red." He feared the unrest in Russia and understood the nature of his country. He emigrated at the age of twenty, embarking for Istanbul from the Crimea with the retreating White Guard in 1921. He left the Tsar's army in Turkey and found asylum in the Kingdom of Yugoslavia. There he fell in love, married, and remained for the rest of his life. He accepted exile as his destiny without taking part in the delusions of other émigrés. He felt himself a citizen of the world, whom the world had deprived of a homeland. He remained a foreigner even though he did everything he could not to be one. His name was Vsevolod Nikolaevich Matveevich. He was my father.

He read parts of this epistolary in Zagreb's Vinogradski Hospital in 1972, where, having undergone an operation for cancer of the larynx, he lay with a cannula through his throat, unable to talk, hearing little. But he could read, and I wrote him letters. I was returning from a trip to Russia, and I told him what I had seen and learned: of the family whose traces I had managed to uncover, of his relatives who had disappeared in the gulag, of the country of his birth, which he had never ceased to love. From him I learned the Russian language and learned to love Odessa.

Danilo Kiš also read some of these letters, while he worked on A Tomb for Boris Davidovich. *He was interested in the labor camps of the USSR. He had lost his father in Auschwitz. Some letters I likewise read (or reported) to Miroslav Krleža: he interrupted me often; it bothered him to hear about such things. For many years I could not publish them. It was dangerous for those whose names they contained.*

During four journeys to Russia and Ukraine, to the European and Asian Soviet Union, my desires and experiences confronted reality, my fears and suspicions, the truth.

Moscow, June 28, 1972

It's difficult to write about Russia to someone who knew it like you. Everything has changed since your ship set sail from the Crimea. In writing these letters I fear generalities. I remember young Anton Chekhov's parody: "The English live along the English coast, use English salt, smoke English cigarettes, pass away in the English manner. Rich Persians sit on carpets, poor ones on straw." This is common in writing about Russia. I'm traveling with a "delegation of the Writers' Union of Yugoslavia." Unfortunately it's the only practical way for me to travel to the Soviet Union.

We arrived at Moscow's Sheremetyevo Airport on June 28, 1972. I tried to remain as calm as possible in my "encounter" with the Russian land. I've heard that some Southern Slavs fall to their knees and kiss the ancient Slavic soil with tears in their eyes. I too was not unmoved, because of you. And them.

The airport formalities did not surprise me. At the passport control, an official in uniform and cap with an officer's insignia lowered a short metal bar between each passenger, verifying documents. It took forever. A lover of quotes would recall here the words of Custine. It used to be just like that! Let's leave it.

We were met by official representatives of the Writers' Union, Ivan Akimovich Kharitonov, cultural attaché for Yugoslavia, and "Comrade Sheskin," one of the Writers' Union's many secretaries (I didn't hear either his name or his patronymic). Neither of them is a writer, but we didn't expect writers. They don't usually do this sort of thing well. We proceeded towards Moscow in a Volga. All around everything was green but the birches. "Silver birches," remember? We stopped for a moment and they pointed at the line up to which the Germans had advanced in 1941: "Here Moscow was defended." They've put up a monument.

I was somewhat moved entering Moscow for the first time. We crossed the ring of streets towards Gorky Street, formerly Tver' Boulevard, and arrived at the Hotel Sovetskaya. Before the Revolution, the restaurant *Yar* was there, and people (Aleksandr Pushkin and so on) drank and enjoyed themselves to the dancing and singing of beautiful Gypsy women. Formalities once more: you must leave your passport at the hotel reception and receive a stamped pass in exchange; officials from the front desk accompany each person to his room individually. By the stairwell on our floor sits a person who observes people coming and going. I knew it would be this way.

In the evening we walked along the river toward the old Arbat. I wondered how much here was still Russian and how much Soviet. We walked for a long time in the sun, which slowly sank. It was still hot and we got thirsty, but nowhere was there a café in which to sit and cool off. People were standing in a line on the street for a glass of *kvas*, a drink I'd never tried, though I'd read about it. It did quench my thirst.

First we visited the Kremlin and Red Square. Saint Basil's looked different than in pictures. There was a long line in front of Lenin's mausoleum but we went first. The word "delegation" functions in this country like a turnkey. While I was prepared to meet the embalmed Lenin, I still felt uneasy walking past the mummy. Next to the Kremlin wall was a bust of Stalin, transferred here from inside the mausoleum. I watched the ceremonial changing of the guard—the rigid soldiers and their impassive faces and protracted steps. I failed to see what this had to do with the revolutionary movement.

Before I fell asleep, my phone rang. "Is Mr. X X-ovich there?" I'd heard about such calls to hotel rooms so I was not surprised. They were checking. "No," I said, "there's somebody else here and he's getting ready for bed. *Spokoinoi nochi* ('Good night')." I put down the receiver. Let them do what they will with that. I had a hard time falling asleep despite being dead tired.

The next day we each got sixty rubles at the Writers' Union, the average monthly salary here. Yugoslavs change money on the black market and are loaded with rubles. I meet them in restaurants, strutting like little upstarts. They get on my nerves. Our guides from the Writers' Union expect us to pay for everything as they have no money, but then they feel uncomfortable that we're paying. At the *Slavyansky bazar*, some of my colleagues waxed enthusiastic about the "true Russian cuisine." I'd had better. I thought about the *zakuski* (appetizers) of once upon a time in places like the *Yar* for instance, and wondered whether any of that remained.

They allowed us a visit to the monastery of Zagorsk. They bring foreigners to this sanctuary, which is in a wide "circle" where you can move around without special permission. They've restored several other churches lately in Novgorod, Pskov, Suzdal, even two or three in Moscow and Leningrad. Mostly we met old people. At the "holy font," before an enormous cross, they drew jugs of water and filled smaller vessels in order to carry it to the farthest reaches of Russia, to the Kuban River Valley or into Siberia, to the Don or the Yenisei. I started a conversation with a tall, broad-shouldered old man with blue eyes and a deep voice, from far away. "I've covered five thousand kilometers," he said. "I brought a holy epistle with everything written in it. Philosophy today has lost its bearings." He had a son he loved, for whom he wanted a life better than his own. A *starets* (venerable monk).

A woman from a group with kerchiefs in their hair told us she was a *kolkhoznitsa* (collective farm worker). She'd walked five hundred kilometers to get here. A priest appeared, blessed the people, and the women stood aside to let him pass. One had not seen him, and instead of going around he made a sign for her to move. She stepped aside deferentially. There was a bag in front of her, and the priest indicated with his finger that she should move it. The rite of kissing the feet is still observed. I had to look away. The Church here has remained behind itself. Not surprising as it has suffered so much. I looked at a gold-encased icon for a long time and wanted to hear a choir, an old Russian liturgy, one like you used to love to sing before you lost your voice. Probably we just hadn't come at the right time.

Yasnaya Polyana, June 30, 1972

A pilgrimage to Lev Tolstoy's home. Near Tula on our way to Yasnaya Polyana, our Writers' Union Volga breaks down on the wide, empty road. We get out to wait for them to fix it. I go into a little tavern on the town's edge, disorganized and dusty, with mostly empty shelves. The only person inside is a tipsy old man. He boasts of having been a captain and known Chkalov, Tolstoy's personal secretary, and of having a large "personal" pension. All around are wooden hovels and peasant huts (*izby*), women carrying buckets of water across their shoulders with a pole called a *koromyslo*, which means there are no water pipes or baths or anything of the sort. The road is unpaved. The mud from the autumn rains or during the spring thaw must be horrendous. How primitive it all is! Tula was once known for making the finest samovars, the most beautiful candelabras and sabers. Mikhail Lermontov and Ivan Turgenev and Tolstoy were born here. What remains of it all? This is my first encounter with the Russian interior, and I hear Pushkin's words, uttered on his reading the first pages of Nikolai Gogol's *Dead Souls*: "Lord, how sad our Russia is!" The words accompany me to Yasnaya Polyana.

The curator has been waiting for us in Tolstoy's house: an elderly, mild, agreeable man, who speaks differently from others. He mentions Pushkin, Chekhov, Vladimir Korolenko. He remembers Boris Pasternak, whose name is still better left unspoken. He takes us to a mound overgrown with weeds, where Lev Nikolaevich Tolstoy was buried according to his own wishes. He repeats "*Slava Bogu*" (thank God), several times. Apparently it's allowed in this place. People who come to Yasnaya Polyana already know Tolstoy was a Christian.

I was afraid of hearing more about "Tolstoy, the mirror of the Russian Revolution." I try to talk to the curator about Tolstoy's anarchism, which was not discussed. Some Christian thinkers oppose his religious anarchism, I say, and see it as too impersonal and individualistic. They say the writer imitated his own hero Platon Karataev. Was there in Tolstoy's Christianity the *sobornost* (collectivity) of Vladimir Solovyov, or was it kept in check? Had the author of *War and Peace* really wanted to become "simple" like the peasantry (*poprostet*)? Dostoevsky hadn't. What did he think about the differences between the two writers?

The good man answers me rather pathetically: "Tolstoy is great and his contradictions are great." The curator of Yasnaya Polyana cannot read treatises on such subjects, which are written mostly outside Russia and are inaccessible here. He is there to do what's expected of him. He looks at me sadly. He reminds me of the goodhearted character from classic Russian literature. I feel ashamed: perhaps I've simply provoked him with my pretentious questions.

We have lunch nearby, in a rather folkloric restaurant near a picturesque pond. The waitress, a pretty woman in her thirties with long blond hair, refuses to take tips. Her gesture restores my faith for a moment, but I immediately ask myself, faith in what? We return to Moscow "without incident," as one of our guides reports, smiling. Such expressions from the military or Party activities are common in everyday speech. I'm growing used to "Soviet Russian."

I shall have two more days in Moscow, then on to Leningrad. I take a walk with Kasim Prohić, a taciturn, erudite colleague from Bosnia. At *Manezhnaya Square* we get on a bus and experience our first "incident." A young man in a peasant blouse, or *rubashka*, with a national slogan knitted on it and ruddy cheeks has cornered a passenger, another young man with black, curly hair, thin lips, and an upturned nose. "Who are you with," he yells, "us or Israel? We know your kind. Hypocrites! Get the hell out!"

I move closer and say, "Shame on you!" In the meantime the bus has started to move. The other passengers look at me. "I'm a foreigner here. I wouldn't have believed such a thing was possible in a place where people have suffered so much. You should be ashamed." The Jew looks at me in surprise, even more afraid than before.

The youth in the *rubashka* isn't used to such reactions and draws back. "Are you a Jew too?"

"What difference does it make?" I say, loud enough for the others to hear. "Actually, no, I'm not, but as long as there are people like him here, I feel like a Jew too."

He gets off at the next stop, adding a final observation, "We all know who's responsible for the turn to the left." Kasim Prohić is uncomfortable. I feel offended. More and more are such young people turning "back to the people." More and more frequent are the manifestations of anti-Semitism, say those I've spoken with.

For Danilo Kiš I note: Nadezhda Mandelshtam's manuscript about her life with her husband Osip has been circulating through Moscow for more than a year. Before putting together these notes, I read several pages, in which she explains that the founder of the nationalist group *Otechestvo* (Fatherland), a man named Palevsky, called the poetry of Osip Mandelshtam "a Jewish scar on the beautiful body of Russian poetry." Interchangeable systems are fixed in the Stalinist and nationalist texts— Stalinists turn into nationalists. It is such a travesty.

We were given an official reception at the Writers' Union, with the president of the Commission on External Relations, Fyodorenko. A sinologist, he was in his sixties, spoke English, and distinguished himself from the majority of those we met by his urbanity. Our guide Lyudmila was there too, along with Ivan Akimovich Kharitonov (whom the Slovene writer Ciril Kozmaš affectionately dubbed "Akaky Akakievich"), as well as Sheskin and other officials and writers who normally get together on such occasions. We ate lunch inside the Writers' Union, in the hall of the Trubetskoy Palace, perhaps the very one described in *War and Peace*. We traded toasts, drank a lot of vodka. Fyodorenko was in a hurry but invited me for a meeting the next day. As our "delegation" dispersed, a number of lesser-known writers who often came to this relatively prestigious restaurant sat down at the table, while all around sat guests from "socialist neighbor" countries. My turn came to make a toast. I tried to get out of it by saying I hated making speeches and I'd written a whole book against "occasional poetry" and so on, but they would have none of it. I stood, rather tipsy myself, and said something like this: "There are people of various nationalities here, from countries connected to the USSR. They don't like Russians. We Yugoslavs don't depend on the USSR and have no reason to hate you. They think their links to your country cost them too much and that is the reason they live poorly. Maybe that's so. But it's also true that people in Russia live worse than they do. I know how you live. You are worse off. Let's drink to that bitter truth."

A writer whose name I didn't know came up and kissed me three times. A young woman sitting to one side stood and broke into tears, saying, "God protect you, Predrag Vsevolodovich!" I was embarrassed. These were my first days in Russia.

When I returned to the hotel, I noticed my suitcase had been opened and my things searched; the papers on which I'd sketched these impressions were not in the order I'd left them. Someone at the police station was going to have a lot of work from my manuscript. In the future I would be more careful.

I met Secretary Fyodorenko. I suspected someone had acquainted him with my little speech at the Writers' Union, though I couldn't tell anything from his face. Did he know I had asked for the release of Sinyavsky and Daniel? Had the "Yugoslav authorities" even allowed that letter to reach the Soviet Embassy the year before? Would the Soviet Embassy have sent it on to Moscow? To the Writers' Union?

Fyodorenko wanted to hear my thoughts about Yugoslav-Soviet cultural relations. What could I say? I told him I saw few books by Yugoslav authors in their stores, especially in comparison with, say, those by Bulgarian authors. But several important Russian authors are also absent, I added, smiling to soften my criticism. Authors with little importance in Yugoslavia are translated, but some of the most important are untouched, which gives a false picture of literature itself. Miroslav Krleža is excluded because of his pre-war conflict with the Left, as if there had never been a Twentieth Party Congress here condemning Stalinism.

He interrupted me by saying he didn't understand what I meant by Stalinism. The Twentieth Party Congress had condemned the "cult of personality," which wasn't the same thing. Then he returned diplomatically to Krleža: some of his works had been translated, others would be in the future, perhaps even part of my *Conversations with Krleža*. He asked about Krleža's health, his relationship with Tito. "Is it true Tito values him so much?" I explained how, after the war, Tito saved him from the revenge of those with whom he had argued previously. Krleža was grateful. He didn't want to create trouble, which Tito had enough of in such a complex federation.

"What are the impressions of those in your delegation?"

I said we had more contact with institutions than literature. Unfortunately, writers aren't meeting writers, though I know that's how it is when Soviet delegations visit Yugoslavia too. He asked me whom I'd like to meet, and I said I had read several of the *Kolyma Tales* of Varlam Shalamov. I'd heard the author had been rehabilitated and was in Moscow.

"Unfortunately, he's seriously ill."

I would gladly meet Vladimir Soloukhin. Would it be possible to get a copy of his *Letters from the Russian Museum*?

He would try on my behalf. (I did not receive it.)

I wanted to turn the conversation to something more meaningful, to avoid the generalities that usually dominate such meetings (print runs, translations, authorial royalties). I said that at the beginning of the century Russian culture was in a position to examine itself seriously, make judgments about itself. Are there sufficient opportunities for self-reflection today? If so, how does it take place?

Fyodorenko did not take up the thread but gave the impression that he found such questions interesting. He asked me whether I had any particular wishes. I did. Would it be possible to travel for two or three days to Odessa? I wanted to write something about the Mediterranean quality of the Black Sea. He would call to let me know. It was difficult to get plane tickets right now for the South because of the summer holidays. I added one more "wish": could I visit Nikita Khrushchev's grave? "We'll see."

The next day, with two colleagues and a guide, I visited the grave of Nikita Khrushchev in the Novodevichy Cemetery and placed several flowers there. This did not please the Writers' Union functionaries, as the one-time Party leader had fallen into disfavor. They spoke of his memoirs as a falsification, a betrayal. "Our opinion of him is different," they said.

Mine too, I said. I considered Khrushchev superficial and crude. When he was in power, it seemed to me that he was trying in vain to reconcile populism and Bolshevism, his personal position with the Party line. But the Twentieth Congress was his doing, bold and astonishing. Despite everything, it produced a split between the Party and ideology, between what was "necessary" and what was true, between the regime and justice. That was why I put flowers on his grave.

Candles had been lit all around, old women were praying. There was a monument by the sculptor Ernst Neizvestny above Khrushchev's grave.

POSTSCRIPT – *I met Neizvestny ten years later in New York. Arthur Miller presented his works in a University Hall near the Village. Afterward, at the sculptor's home, he showed me grandiose projects, sketches, and designs for several hours. He seemed wise and interesting. I wished him success in not becoming completely Americanized but also in not remaining confined to the ghetto of Russian émigrés, which often happens to non-cosmopolitan dissidents. It has been a long time since I heard anything about him.*

Moscow, July 4, 1972

The night before departing for Leningrad, I made several notes about the divisions within Russian literature and literary life. The conversations and meetings of the preceding days served to fill in my knowledge and reinforce my assumptions.

No other European literature has experienced the divisions of Russia's. At the beginning of the century came the rupture between pre- and post-revolutionary literature; then another within each of these between revolutionary and "counterrevolutionary"; and another between the literature that remained and that which emigrated. Part of the writers supported the Soviets, part opposed them. A literature of the regime appeared, and another that attempted to distance itself, officially and otherwise, "Socialist Realism" and "something else." Such divisions were of course more political than literary. On one side was the literature that "passed" and was printed without great difficulties (besides the mundane one: lack of paper); on the other was the literature that waited and encountered obstacles. Between them was situated the *promezhutochnaia literatura* (intermediate literature) which, depending on the circumstances, passed with greater or lesser difficulty or was less and sometimes more critical of the regime. It is usually assumed that what is between is in the center, but in this case such an assumption would be mistaken.

Anti-regime literature, which is called dissident outside the USSR, is either hidden away in a drawer or circulates secretly in manuscript. The part that is reproduced inside the country is called *samizdat* (self-published), that which comes out *tam* (over there) is called *tamizdat*, and that which appears in neither is *neizdat* (unpublished). There are also topographical indications: *prisoiuznaia* (inter-republic) *Literatura*, for example, is closest to the Writers' Union and its leadership. It "waits" the shortest time and receives the greatest support from the *Litfond (*Literary Fund). People call one of its subdivisions "secretarial literature," as it comprises works by the leaders of authorial organizations, institutes, academies, and the like. It is considered inappropriate to mention such phenomena in the presence of Writers' Union functionaries.

One can pass from one category to another (some writers appear simultaneously in legal editions and in samizdat). People bandy about the reproach, "They publish you," or "Your books can be printed." I learned of Mandelshtam's ironic response to a young writer who'd complained his work wasn't being published: "You think they published Sappho? Did they print Jesus Christ?" Some of the ones who don't get published aren't really worth publishing. In the literature that does not "pass" there are many works that shouldn't. Amidst "dissident literature" (it's hard to admit sometimes) there is often more dissidence than literature. All this is not simply a part of literature but also of the spiritual forces which produce it.

The literature of the Russian emigration has split as well: the smaller portion continues, in spite of everything, to try and satisfy the exigencies of literature as such (from Bunin and Nabokov to Brodsky and Sinyavsky—there are many); the other places itself in the political camps of the emigration, or at least in those the emigration supports.

But despite all this, Russian literature has survived, although it has paid a high price.

People often talk of its being inspired by prophetic visions: it gave warnings, anticipated danger, and predicted apocalypse. Pushkin glimpsed "the Russian rebellion, without sense or mercy", Lermontov the "black year," filled with "blood and death", Dostoevsky "demons" who threatened to overrun Russia. Russian literature foresaw nearly everything but its own fate: that it would be fragmented into as many pieces as it has been. But perhaps even of that it had a presentiment. In an essay of

1921 entitled "I fear," Yevgeny Zamyatin wrote: "I am afraid the future of Russian literature might be only its past."

Questions are being asked once again: Is Soviet literature dying? Did it ever really exist? Isn't it only the alienated or appropriated portions of individual national literatures? It is difficult to establish to what extent it really existed and, if so, whether it is now dying. As far as Russian literature is concerned, what is most important is whether, in the end, despite all of its fissures and divisions, it will become one.

POSTSCRIPT – *While writing these notes in my room in the Hotel Sovetskoe I did not have at hand the works of Yevgeny Zamyatin, in which answers may be found to several of these questions: "True literature can exist only where it is created by lunatics, hermits, heretics, dreamers, rebels, and skeptics, not by well-paid and conformist bureaucrats." Abroad, and now in Russia itself, I have met members of the intelligentsia, who, confronted with all that has happened to their country, respond proudly that despite it all they had a literature—of Pushkin, Tolstoy, Dostoevsky. They say it exclusively in the past tense. Perhaps the intelligentsia will go "to the past" just as it once went "to the people."*

As regards a unity at its center, in the amalgam of Russian culture as a whole, my father often recalled the words of George Florovsky, whom he met in Belgrade on the eve of the Second World War. That extraordinary thinker and theologian, today largely forgotten, was born in Odessa eight years before my father. Having emigrated from the Crimea at approximately the same moment, he wandered the globe, teaching the "spiritual history" of Russia at the Institute of Saint Sergius in Paris and the Institute of Saint Vladimir in New York. Florovsky saw Russian culture as an inspired heretic: "The history of Russian culture is characterized by sudden and unexpected shocks, paroxysms, renunciations or acts of caprice and infatuation, of disillusionment and betrayal, of rupture and explosion... The most diverse and incompatible contortions of the spirit, from different periods of time, manage to exist together in the same time and strengthen one another. But splicing (srostok) *is not the same thing as synthesis. It is precisely synthesis that has never succeeded."*

But is synthesis of this kind needed at all in literature?

It was late at night on July 4, 1972 when I noted down a portion of these observations in my room in the Hotel Sovetskoe, trying to bring closure to an unfinished letter.

Moscow–Leningrad, July 5, 1972

Traveling to Leningrad on the night express, the "Red Arrow" of which the locals are so proud. It covers the distance between the two capitals in eight hours. The poet Brana Petrović, who can't ever keep still, made a discovery in the neighboring compartment: the screenwriter of *Ballad of a Soldier*, his young, film-actress wife, and her co-star in one or another film, a handsome youngster, who, I later learned, had played the role of Raskolnikov in *Crime and Punishment*. We moved to their compartment and began to talk.

The two young people did not hide the fact that they were lovers. They looked each other in the eye, held hands, and kissed. The husband sat next to them and drank glassfuls of vodka. The wife drank too. Her mother had been an actress as well. Just before the war she had met an American diplomat and fallen in love. She'd paid for her love with exile: ten years in Siberia. She had given birth to her daughter "there," in a camp somewhere beyond the Ural Mountains; not even she knew exactly where.

The young actress has beautiful round lips that she bites from time to time. She tosses back the chestnut hair that falls onto her face. Her skin is pale, her expression melancholic. She seems prepared to ruin herself and everything around her. The film they're making is "stupid." "You know what kind of films they make here. Only war movies. It's absurd!" Her husband adds that the majority of his films are "shameful." The young actor says nothing.

There's another man in the compartment, near the window. He's fiftyish, with glasses and a wrinkled, thought-worn face. I don't know whether he belongs to the group or is a chance companion. We get into a conversation about the Russian intelligentsia, what it once was and what's left of it. I realize my interlocutor has read many books that are illegal here. He cites religious thinkers from the nineteenth and twentieth centuries, the 1909 collections *Vekhy* (Landmarks) and the 1921 *Smena vekh* (A Changing of Landmarks). Afterward I noted down our conversation without always distinguishing clearly between his words and mine.

The Russian intelligentsia was the product of a people that did not see itself as a nation, and it refused—perhaps the only such case in Europe—to formulate the nationality of its own people. The nation-state relation was dubious in Russia: the two elements did not become unified. The intelligentsia did more to impede such unification than to realize it. History had created a despotic regime, against which the intelligentsia exhausted itself in battle, despite history, until the very ground beneath its feet had disappeared.

The distancing of the intelligentsia from the government, their refusal, or *otshchepenstvo*, to collaborate in the national project, led to anarchism or populism, mysticism or revolution. At the turn of the twentieth century, the intelligentsia reminded Aleksandr Blok of "a sick multitude divorced from its surroundings." On one side he saw 150 million culture-less souls, on the other, several hundred thousand more or less cultivated individuals who were "incapable of agreeing about fundamental issues." The "people" not only had no culture but also harbored an entire series of prejudices about culture. The points of support on which the intelligentsia could depend were weak or absent altogether. In most cases its members were without practical sense, while their material interest lay elsewhere. They took the position of being "opposed" at all costs. They lacked not capacity but the real possibility of applying it, as if history simply didn't want to put them to use. In such a state Russian literature was born in all its greatness, a unique, though insufficient, point of support.

The *Russian idea* was more religious than national, more messianic than ideological—a topic on which much has been written. The most significant Christian thinkers, Vladimir Solovyov for instance, wanted the Russian messianic spirit to be universal. Dostoevsky was perhaps the first to understand that even socialism in Russia was more religious than historical: the intelligentsia's messianic desire to save humanity without divine assistance.

Nor was there unity in the history of Russia: Kievan *Rus*, Muscovite *Rus* before and after the Tartar epoch, the Russia of Peter the Great, and the Russia after him, Imperial Russia, and the Soviet Union—each such period denied more than upheld what preceded it. Frequently it began from scratch. Perhaps one day it will do so again.

The eastern and western elements, the Asiatic and the European, did not harmonize in Russian existence. It did not find a "third place, above the principles of east and west. Russia is a vast Orient-Occident according to divine intent, and a rash, failed Orient-Occident in actual reality." (The words of Nikolai Berdyaev, whom my interlocutor quoted often, I subsequently filled in using printed sources.) The majority of Russia's revolutionaries were Asiatic by temperament and westerners and Europeans by education. It was a contradiction that left lasting marks on the people.

The people were a "victim of the country's immenseness." They experienced the byzantinism of the powers that be as "a yoke." The state bent before tsarist despotism. The idea of the tsar held the parts together but did not strengthen the whole. "Holy Russia" and the Russian Empire contradicted each other at every pass. The Christian Tolstoy set himself in opposition to the tsar. The "symphony" of faith and the regime was a fraud. The letter of Filofei to Ivan III, in which he declared Moscow the "Third Rome," was pure myth: it flattered Russian vanity and was accepted by those parts of Europe that knew Russia only poorly or feared her. "Orthodoxy did not engender historical enterprise and civilization," Berdyaev maintained. Populism did not give a thought to the creation of a modern nation or state. Its most radical portion helped those destroying first the state and then the nation.

Spread across a vast territory without the factors of national or state unity, lacking an ideology or ideologues capable of creating and promoting such factors, with the enormous resistance represented by its own immenseness and inertia, its backwardness and mysticism, Russia was incapable of facing modernity and accepted only in part the forms of humanistic culture, without developing the rule of law either in society or the government and without recognizing secularism and "religious neutrality." It did not accept rationalistic forms of knowledge, and it "rejected formal logic."

Russian history did not know the forms of courtly society or knightly courtesy. The boyars were not real nobles. Nor was there any real bourgeois culture, even if the bourgeoisie was earnestly attacked. Russian works of the greatest value are characterized by an aristocratic spirit, even though the confrontation with the aristocracy was extremely brutal. The carriers of authentic peasant culture were the well to do of the countryside, the kulaks, denounced as the worst of enemies and driven from the land. Perhaps the revolution was needed, but it should have taken a different course. If the Russian Empire deserved such an end, Russia did not. The members of the intelligentsia wanted to be the instruments of history, but Russian history was so fragmented and contradictory that it was incapable of making use of them. Perhaps this explains all of the haste and necessity, real and utopian at the same time, for history itself to be advanced, pushed ahead.

One more thing we discussed: the intelligentsia as a form of *raskol* (schism), a monastic brotherhood, a sect. Its condition is difficult to compare with that of intellectuals in other parts of Europe. The member of the *intelligentsia* had two extremes of choice were: on the one hand, passivity and verbalism, "Oblomovitis" and superfluity, and on the other, anarchy or radical nihilism. Russian culture did not conceptualize "law as a value." The greater part of the intelligentsia held that moral values were sufficient unto themselves, an illusion for which they would pay dearly. In this belief, Slavophiles and Westernizers were in essential agreement, and their attitudes vis-à-vis Russia were never as different as they are often portrayed. The Slavophiles considered it "like a mother," the Westernizers "like a child." I should add here the well-known formula: "a child in need of supervision." To create an authentic national consciousness it would have been necessary to overcome both Slavophilism and Westernism and to dominate the very opposition that separated them. I understand that generalizations of this sort cannot hope to explain all the singular phenomena, but without such generalizations historical thought is impossible. How does one think about Russian history? Is today's Russian intelligentsia thinking? Does it even exist anymore?

We've separated from the others in the compartment and, like the tipsy characters of Dostoevsky, we talk about anything and everything, persuading each other of our beliefs, bringing to bear the sources of our thoughts, filling them out, sermonizing, alas, in the old Russian manner. I don't know my interlocutor's surname. Someone called him Pavel. He avoids contemporary topics, and I don't insist. We continue our discussion.

Stalinism forcibly fused the intelligentsia with the government, thereby destroying individual intellectual *otshchepenstvo* (nay-saying). Doubtless Lenin played a part in this as well, perhaps without intuiting where it would lead. I continue to believe that several of his compatriots (Bukharin, Trotsky, Lunacharsky) considered it simply a "temporary measure." The intelligentsia was preparing its own destruction. Later there would be no choice: ideology would grow stronger than ideas, the Party would take the place of the Soviets.

Our conversation went on for a long time. We spoke quietly, out of habit or prudence. The lovers still held hands, now with their eyes closed in semi-sleep. Perhaps they were happy. The husband continued to drink, calm apparently, resigned. The Red Arrow flew towards Leningrad.

I returned to the delegation's compartment next door but did not sleep.

Leningrad, July 5, 1972

They put us up at the Hotel Rossiya. I don't intend to describe the city. That's been done. I walk through the famous sites, looking for what might be left of old "*Piter*." Historical monuments: Saint Isaac's Cathedral, the Church of the Holy Savior, Kazan Cathedral, the spire of the Admiralty, the Peter and Paul Fortress, the Cruiser Aurora, the Stroganov Palace. The whole city is a monument. Anna Akhmatova died six years ago. Who can know all that she suffered here: the execution of Nikolai Gumilyov, the deportation of her son, the countless insults—"And Russia with its frightened face contorted beneath the boot." Toward the end of her life she became a believer again. In which of these churches did she pray?

At noon (it is Wednesday) in the Cathedral of St. Nicholas they sing the liturgy. At last I hear a real Russian choir. I had wanted to buy gifts on Nevsky Prospect for friends. People pointed me toward the "Beryozka" store, where, for foreign currency, one could buy "something better." The passersby heard us speaking a foreign language and offered to change money at higher than the official rate. It made me feel awful, and I found myself thinking of Pushkin's words about "poor Russia" again.

Not long ago I learned that Joseph Brodsky was exiled from the USSR. I try to find out more about him. In the sixties Akhmatova and Dmitry Shostakovich sought his release from prison. Some friends suggest I speak with Professor Yefim Etkind, who spoke on his behalf in court, but I'm unable to make contact. I am told he too is in disfavor. In the Leningrad Writers' Union they are afraid to talk about it. They nod but are clearly uncomfortable. They're subordinate to Moscow through and through. Leningrad is more provincial than I expected.

I made a brief visit to the Hermitage in the company of Alla Konstantinovna Borisova, an attractive, intelligent guide from the Writers' Union. I asked about the works kept in special collections, in particular about paintings by Kazimir Malevich, which were supposed to be housed there. I received an ambiguous response: "They're here but not now."

Alla Konstantinovna gave me good news: I'd been granted permission to go to Odessa. They were looking for a plane ticket, but now was vacation time and everything was full. Would I mind going by train? Would I mind! Before rejoining the delegation in Moscow, I would spend only a day and a half in the city of my father's birth, a city I had heard so much about, imagined in so many different lights, a city I had seen through the eyes of its writers, Konstantin Paustovsky, Valentin Kataev, and especially Isaak Babel. Which of these Odessas would I be visiting?

It's a thirty-one-hour train ride.

In the train that very evening. I jotted down in my notebook that it was the 7th, but it might have still been the 6th. I've lost all sense of time: I'm traveling into real and imaginary space at the same time, the present and the past, my own and someone else's. Half the car is empty. Why did they say there were no tickets? "It'll fill up," says the conductor. "Don't worry." I do anyway. I might finally discover what happened to my family. Was anyone still alive? Grandfather, no, but maybe Grandmother or Uncle Kostya or my aunts...

During the ride I worried more than I saw. I remember only two or three stations. Women selling *kartofelochki*, boiled and roasted potatoes wrapped in newspaper, sour cherries with the stems two by two. Country roads stretching in all directions with tire tracks and tractor treads. It had rained recently. Mud. A man in boots leaving deep prints behind.

We passed through Vitebsk, even sadder than Tula. I thought of Marc Chagall, how he had seen this place, his home, as a youngster. I recalled our conversation about the "Vitebsk years" at the Yugoslav art exhibition in Paris the year before. He'd given me an unusual drawing: an eye, with which he must have looked on all of this. And what was left? The products of an ideology based not on reality but on the representation of how reality ought to be. Everyday life dominated by banalities, from which the same jokes derived, the little double entendres, hidden allusions, trite irony, secret criticism, and all too passive, or quite dangerous, resistance. Brezhnev's Soviet Union.

Odessa, July 8, 1972

At last in Odessa! Members of the local Writers' Union chapter welcomed me. We immediately take care of all the formalities, and I tell them I want to visit friends. But they already know I have relatives here. I set off for the address I received from the Red Cross, 22 Lev Tolstoy Street, the home of Konstantin Mikhailovich Grigorashenko, a retired engineer, my father's first cousin.

His wife Yelena opens the door. I introduce myself and she's taken aback. Konstantin Mikhailovich comes forward, also surprised. I pull a photograph from my billfold and point to it: this is Vsevolod

Nikolaevich Matvejevich. I am his son. As if I want to vindicate myself, convince them of something.

"Yes," he says, "that is Vsevolod. Seva. Fifty years ago." The old man breaks into tears.

I don't know where to start in the little time we have, what to say to him. "Uncle Kostya" served as a military engineer and became a colonel in the Red Army. He built roads and laid train tracks. That was what saved him. "We needed engineers."

His use of the word "we" disturbs me. It's the way officials talk here. "I wasn't in politics," he says, as if in justification. "Vladimir Nikolaevich, your father's brother, disappeared at the end of the thirties, but later he was rehabilitated. Your Uncle Nikolai Ivanovich came back alive. My sister Nataliya, Tusya, she knows more of the details about all that. She can tell you everything. We don't see each other much. She's a little eccentric." In the end he adds, "And we were afraid."

I did not stay long at 22 Lev Tolstoy.

Nataliya Mikhailovna Grigorashenko, "Meshkova" from the husband she divorced, "Aunt Tusya," lives in apartment 11 at number 4 Mikoyan Street, not far from the old Moldovanka quarter, where my father's classmate once played his violin with fervor, the "young genius," Jascha Heifetz. But the Moldovanka does not resemble what I heard about. The Jewish quarter from Babel's *Stories of Odessa* is nowhere to be seen. I look for Tusya's room in the building marked Number Four but don't find it inside. There is a shed made of stone and boards in the courtyard. Tusya lives there, in a single, narrow room some fifteen feet in length, cramped, filthy. She rises with difficulty from the bed. She hardly moves at all, her swollen legs cause her pain. We kiss. She starts to cry. So do I. Her mind is still lucid, her face bright, her voice much younger than her years. "See where I live," she says.

They give her a small disability pension, thirty rubles per month (with which one can barely afford a pair of shoes). She says, "They didn't count the years I worked before the war. The Odessa archive burned down, and I didn't worry myself about collecting all the documents." She served four years of forced labor at the camp in Karaganda. Her health suffered, her marriage was destroyed. She had no children.

"The neighbors give me a hand," she says. "And sometimes I get up and go outside. To think I dreamed of being a singer. That sure didn't work out."

I hear her words and see the misery in which she lives and can hardly control myself. The room's floor is wooden; the walls are yellow or yellowish-brown from moisture and smoke. Along one wall stands an iron bed with rusted ribs, next to that something resembling a nightstand with a burned candle in a plate on top. Further on is a little table, scratched and stained, with a full washbowl or dish, it's hard to say which. Next to the bed is a pair of house slippers that can also be used for walking through the snow to the toilet in the courtyard (the toilet is in the courtyard). On one shelf, next to a stack of old sheet music, is a narrow, greenish-blue flask, which, judging by its markings, could have come from the beginning of the century. It's the only personal item in the room, the only private object, hardly a luxury.
(POSTSCRIPT – *I did not tell my father about the conditions in which I found Tusya. It would have been too hard for him. This portion of the epistolary appeared only after his death.*)

I hold her slack, swollen hand and recall my father's stories about his "beautiful cousin Tusya," whom he'd accompanied at the piano, and about her father, Mikhail Afanasievich, "Uncle Misha," a respected physician who used to take them to his box at the opera. Over and over she repeats, "You're one of us, our Seva's son, Predrag Vsevolodovich. God keep you safe."

I tell her I've been to see Kostya. "I never see them," she says. "They've lived a different life from ours."

Haltingly, she begins to tell me about Uncle Vladimir, once an esteemed professor of Russian literature, who spoke French fluently and was open and fearless in expressing his thoughts. He fell in love with an opera singer whose husband was politically influential. She divorced her husband for him and had two sons. He loved her very much, but it wasn't a happy relationship. Her ex-husband, an elderly man, lived with them in the same apartment. One day someone denounced Volodya for speaking ill of the Party, for having "contacts abroad" ("his brother Vsevolod has emigrated"), for being a Trotskyite, in short, using the usual formulas of the time. They came for him one night and took him away. He did not return. Later we learned he had perished in Siberia, perhaps at Kolyma. Because of him they arrested his father, my grandfather, Nikolai Ivanovich, who spent five years in Alma-Ata. "When he came back," says Tusya, "his wife, Neonila Petrovna, whom we called Nina, had already lost her mind. She died soon after." She tells me there's a woman in

Odessa, Olga Ivanovna Antonovich, who lived with Grandfather during his last years. She's very old but remembers everything. Tusya suggests I visit her and tells me how to get there. "It's not far." I resolve to find her.

I don't know how long I remained sitting on Aunt Tusya's bed, holding her hand, or what I managed to say or how I behaved. Nor do I recall how I reached Olga Antonovich's, on the ground floor of the house where my father was born and where he spent his childhood. The house was surely different then. Now it holds a communal apartment, where various families have been assigned a room each, everything else being shared. Olga Ivanovna is near ninety. Her hair is thin, tied into a bun at the crown of her head. Her once bright blue eyes have grown dull. There is a goiter on her neck. To make a little money she watches after a neighbor's child. Her memory is clear, and she speaks distinctly. Her voice is weak but pleasant. She lost her fiancé in the First World War and chose to remain faithful to him forever. She was a nurse in the second war, her three brothers were killed, her family dispersed. Uncle Nikolai found her wounded at the Odessa train station and brought her home to treat her. "I'll take care of you now," he said. "You take care of me when I'm old." She recovered, cleaned up the apartment, deloused it, and mended and cleaned his clothes. At the time they had two rooms.

I ask whether my grandmother had already died then. "She had died of unhappiness," says the old woman with commiseration. "She'd lost one son in the first war, another in a camp, the third, your father, she had no news from. They'd taken her husband away. How could she not go crazy?"

Grandfather saved himself at the camp in Alma-Ata by chance: he knew how to tune pianos. There were officers and functionaries in Alma-Ata who wanted their daughters to play, but the old pianos requisitioned after the revolution often went out of tune. Nikolai Ivanovich repaired them, and by eating a little something in the houses where he worked he managed to survive. He came back just before the war started. Without his wife, his children, he was all alone and had nothing else to lose. During the siege of Odessa he went from trench to trench carrying a cross, helping the soldiers, giving them courage. Death was still not ready for him. When the Germans cut the water supply and occupied the town, they didn't suspect him, an old man who'd spent years in the camps. He hid partisan fighters in his house. After the war he was decorated for that. He didn't like to talk about it. Tusya knows. "This icon belonged to your grandfather, now it's your father's. Take it." I left the icon with Olga Ivanovna: she prays before it.

* * *

I could not compose myself for a long time after. I had learned too many things all at once. I left the house and walked without knowing where I was going. I sat against a fence, waiting, and then began to cry, which helped. People walked by and looked, but I paid no attention. Someone asked me what was wrong. I don't know what I said. I didn't care. All of a sudden I felt the need to latch onto something ordinary, fixed, solid, to calm myself. I went to the beach. The sea was the same as when our family had lived here, as when my father had set sail. The street I walked down afterward is still named Deribasovskaya. The famous Odessa steps of the old port are still there as well. I took hold of some such certainties. Back at the Writers' Union, I did not want anyone to see my face and guess what had happened. They didn't even look at me.

The rest of the journey, the return to Moscow, and the departure for Yugoslavia were insignificant. I saw nothing else and remembered nothing. I stopped writing these letters.

Seven Thousand Days in Siberia

I met Karlo Štajner in Zagreb at the end of the 1970s. He had known my uncle, Vladimir Nikolaevich, in a Siberian concentration camp. It brought us together. Štajner spent twenty years in camps in the Solovetsky Islands, Norilsk, the White Sea, and Maklakovka.

He returned from the USSR *to Yugoslavia in 1956. Tito, it seems, had asked Nikita Khrushchev to locate his boyhood friend. They found him among the survivors and let him go. On returning, Štajner wrote a moving account of his camp experiences, which for many years could not be published. Two copies disappeared from the files of the Party committee assigned the task of determining whether such a work should or should not appear in print. The author had kept an additional copy. But after all he had lived through, he did not dare provoke a scandal in the land whose leaders had freed him from Siberia.*

At the end of 1970, the editor of the Belgrade weekly Nin, *Frane Barbieri, sent me several excerpts from Štajner's manuscript and asked me to write a review: he was trying to get it published and needed support. I wrote him a letter, and in the winter of 1971, under the title* Seven Thousand Days in Siberia, *they began publishing excerpts from Štajner's memoirs. The entire book was published in Zagreb in 1972. Then something of a miracle took place. The selection committee for one of the most prestigious literary awards, named for the Croatian poet and partisan soldier Ivan Goran Kovačić, approved my nomination of Štajner. Not even in Yugoslavia could such a decision have been made without considerable difficulty. The editorial board of the journal* Vjesnik, *which sponsored the prize, did not take the decision well. They reminded the committee members that Tito would be traveling to Moscow for a meeting with Brezhnev at exactly the time that the award would be announced: the Soviet leadership might take it as a provocation. I asked the committee not to give up but to "seek the Marshal's opinion." The response came that Štajner could be awarded the prize but the announcement should not be made until the official portion of his meeting with Brezhnev was complete. Clearly Tito was more astute than his courtiers.*

The book enjoyed incredible success and went through twenty editions in Yugoslavia alone. It came out before Aleksandr Solzhenitsyn's Gulag Archipelago, *but Štajner was constrained not to give his permission for translations into other languages until later. If the manuscript had not lingered for so long, Štajner would be much better known than he is.*

I traveled with him to various cities. I spoke about the work, he spoke about the gulag. Danilo Kiš wrote the preface for the French and American editions. I expanded my letter to Nin *and published it as the afterword to Štajner's book* A Hand from the Grave. *It appears here in its original version. This, in truth, marks the beginning of this epistolary.*

Zagreb, November 1970

I already knew of the manuscript to *Seven Thousand Days in Siberia*: parts of it in Russian and German (languages the author knew better than Serbo-Croatian) had been circulating in Zagreb and Belgrade for some time. I was afraid it might turn out to be the kind of memoir retired politicians often write. But happily, literary ambition is alien to Štajner. "I will not enter into an analysis of the events. I state the bare facts." This is the book's great advantage, for such testimonials are most often spoiled by the pretense of making them literary.

Štajner is obsessed with a different calling. "I carried within me but one desire: to live through it all and recount to the whole world, but especially to my partisan friends and comrades, the horrors we endured. This is a small part of what happened. To recount everything that happened to me and the tens of thousands of others with me during twenty years of Soviet camps and prisons would require a superhuman memory." Luckily Štajner's memory is indeed superhuman. He recalls what many another would as well forget.

He was born into a humble Jewish family on the outskirts of Vienna. His father was killed on the Galician front in World War I. He joined Austria's Communist Youth. During a demonstration, he nearly bled to death on the sidewalk of Hoerlgasse Street after being hit by a police bullet. His companions sent him to Yugoslavia, where the Party put him to work in Zagreb. In 1933 he moved to Moscow to work for the Comintern in the *Otdel mezhdunarodnykh otnoshenii* (Foreign Relations Division).

Before he was arrested during the purges of 1936, he met a sixteen-year-old girl, Sofya Yefimovna Moiseeva—Sonya. He spent twenty years—seven thousand days—in the camps of the Solovetsky Islands, Norilsk, the most northern reaches of Siberia. Sonya waited for him. She lost the child who'd been born in his father's absence; she worked and hid, in a state of constant anxiety. If we were speaking of literature or history, this would be the moment to recall the wives of the Decembrists or the heroines of classic Russian novels.

Štajner survived exile and the gulag and returned. *Seven Thousand Days in Siberia* is not the first book to describe the camps and their victims. We have read the testimony of Antun Ciliga (1938) and Živojin Pavlović's *Balance of the Soviet Thermidor* (1940). We know the works of Dal and Nikolaevsky, of Buber-Neumann and Kravchenko, as well as Lev Trotsky's *Crimes of Stalin*. But such a work as Štajner's has never been seen. Štajner entered the last circle of hell and remained there for twenty years, condemned to every form of punishment, even to death by firing squad, and to a life worse than death. "It's impossible to put into words," he kept saying at our first meeting in Zagreb in 1970.

The attitude of some ex-communists is well known (it's been well described by Isaac Deutscher). When they stop defending communism, they turn to defending humanity from communism on the same basis, seeing themselves as infallible in the same manner as they previously saw their Party. There is nothing of the sort in Štajner. His rehabilitation, to himself and to others, came about not just through the piece of paper he received from the USSR but through this work, which tells us who he is and what he is worth.

I am incapable of presenting all the virtues of his manuscript in a letter: no form of anti-Stalinist propaganda could furnish an equivalent critique of Stalinism. Publish it as soon as possible. When excerpts come out in journals, the book will surely follow. I shall do everything in my power to ensure that Štajner's book is received as it ought to be. In the battles in which only the losers are victorious, Štajner has become a hero of our time. And more still: he has brought us to a new understanding of heroism itself.

POSTSCRIPT – *We already knew about the camps when this letter was composed, though Solzhenitsyn's work had not yet appeared. Many writers were then under arrest or had been forced to emigrate. I began writing letters in their defense, sending them openly to those in power.*

Sinyavsky-Daniel
To Leonid Brezhnev

Zagreb, Spring 1971

From year to year we await the release of Andrei Sinyavsky and Yury Daniel, condemned in 1966 to years of servitude—the first to seven, the second to five—in forced-labor concentration camps. They were tried for literary works that they were unable to publish in their own country and that were published abroad under the pseudonyms Avram Terts and Nikolai Arzhak. Only supporters of the regime were present at the trial, which was announced publicly. The prosecutors identified the defendants' social criticism as "enemy propaganda," reducing literature to politics: it is not the first time and it is not accidental.

The hopes aroused by the Twentieth Party Congress and the condemnation of the "cult of personality" have been extinguished. Neither the way of life nor the forms of repression have changed in the USSR. The intelligentsia remains subordinate to the Party, culture to ideology.

We believed that a true "thaw" in literature and the arts would begin, that the excesses of the Zhdanov period would not be repeated. But instead we see that the bureaucracy continues to interfere in literary and artistic questions, to hinder diversity of thought, to persecute dissidence.

We expected that the USSR Writers' Union would cleanse itself of bureaucracy and begin to serve writers and their work. Instead, bureaucrats continue to dominate it and the authentic representatives of literature are excluded. We believed that Socialist Realism would free itself of the ideology and Party-mindedness that had been forced upon it. But it remains the official line, the only recognized method, even though the finest creators avoid it and disparage it. The text "On Socialist Realism" published by Sinyavsky abroad, and to which the tribunal attributes special significance, does not express his ideas alone.

We expected that censorship—along with the self-censorship that accompanies it—would become more tolerable and less injurious. But its effects still weigh heavily on the arts, on literature especially, and on public life in general. We believed that literature would re-obtain the right and possibility to engage in satire and social criticism. The condemnation of Sinyavsky and Daniel shows how little prepared Soviet society is for that, and how ill disposed to it is Soviet power. Mikhail Zoshchenko's testimony of the pains that await the writer of satire, even the most harmless, has retained all of its force today.

We expected a concession to the Czechs and Slovaks, the Poles and Hungarians, the East Germans and all the others, so that they might be able to decide for themselves which path to follow into "the happy future," but despite everything, the Soviet leadership continues to impose its own way as the only correct one, the sole possibility. We believed that never again would soldiers of the Red Army cross the borders of its "friendly, brother countries." After Budapest, Soviet tanks entered Prague and now control Warsaw as well as Berlin, preventing the USSR's "allies" from living as they want to live.

We expected that the number of Soviet labor camps would decrease and that their administration would change. But we see new arrests and, in some cases, the use of special psychiatric treatments. We believed that the Soviet legal system would come into accordance with its own professed norms. Instead, a new penal code has been introduced, which contains articles (190, nos. 1 and 3) that punish the crime of thought and deny the right of citizens' free association.

Since the trial of Sinyavsky and Daniel, which was more effective than any conceivable anti-Soviet propaganda, the following individuals have been tried, interrogated, and/or imprisoned: Anatoly (Tolya) Marchenko, Vladimir (Volodya) Bukovsky, Aleksandr (Alik) Ginzburg, Andrei (Andryusha) Amalrik, Eduard (Edi) Kuznetsov, and former Red Army General Pyotr Grigorenko. Other detainees deserve equal mention, women such as Nataliya (Natasha) Gorbanevskaya, Larisa (Lara) Bogoraz, and Vera Lashko, members of the *Russian Word* editorial committee, the "Berdyaev Circle," and the demonstrators who, on August 25, 1968, gathered before St. Basil's Cathedral on Red Square, prepared to sacrifice themselves out of shame at knowing that soldiers from their country had occupied the ancient Czech capital.

In a similar manner, intellectuals and writers have been persecuted and silenced in the countries of Eastern Europe, obliged to toe a common political line and adopt analogous measures: Milan Kundera, Josef Škvorecký, Václav Havel, Pavel Kohout, Tadeusz Konwicki, and many more.

You declared a poet of Joseph Brodsky's talent a "hooligan and parasite." I do not cite all their names—names of which you are no doubt aware—but nor do I forget them.

I hope that the present letter, which I am sending to the Embassy of the USSR in Belgrade, will be forwarded to the appropriate responsible individuals, if possible directly to the General Secretary. It expresses what can be understood as the manner in which "the intelligentsia of friendly socialist countries" views the place of "the first socialist country."

Brodsky
To Leonid Brezhnev
c/o the Embassy of the USSR
in Belgrade, Yugoslavia

Zagreb, August 1972

The young poet Joseph Brodsky has been exiled from the Soviet Union. This punishment is too severe for him. He has already spent time in prison and in the labor camps. He did not wish to emigrate: his place lies in the midst of the Russian language, inside the culture of Russia.

Little of his poetry has made it to us, but what we have read testifies to a new and extraordinary body of work. He continues along the path of Mandelshtam and Akhmatova. You must not cut him off from Russian language and culture.

Brodsky is one of those poets who know only how to write poetry. The tribunal proclaimed him a vagabond and parasite. Allow him to do the only thing he can. Russia has few poets of his talent. Russian language and culture have need of him.

I add my voice to the prayers of those who have already spoken out on his behalf: Anna Akhmatova, Dmitry Shostakovich, and many others.

Free the poet from this too burdensome punishment.

Postscript – *Immediately following his expulsion from the Soviet Union, Brodsky sent a similar letter to Leonid Brezhnev (June 4, 1972): "In leaving Russia against my will, I venture to address this prayer to you... Allow me to remain in Russia's literary world, at least as a translator... Even if I lose my Soviet citizenship, I will not cease to be a Russian writer... I belong to the Russian language."*

I did not know of his letter when I wrote mine. I knew only that he "belonged to the Russian language" and appealed to that certainty.

Eurasian Letters
— Continued —

Once more I am in the USSR. I shall be in Russia, Ukraine, Armenia, and Georgia for nearly a month.

Mihajlo Mihailov made a similar journey in 1963. I often recall his experience: he was severely condemned in Yugoslavia after the publication of his diary, A Moscow Summer, *and the KGB conducted an investigation of all the intellectuals he mentioned in the Soviet Union. I must be careful not to let my letters fall into their hands.*

Again I set aside the pages for Vsevolod Nikolaevich. Some I send to Danilo Kiš. Some I recount to Krleža.

Moscow, November 10, 1973

Sheremetyevo Airport once more, and all the same formalities. Things change slowly here. I am housed at the Hotel Rossiya, in the center of town. I'll be staying in Moscow for several days. The weather is dark but not yet cold.

I'm surprised by the guide they've chosen for me at the Writers' Union. His name is Nikolai Kiselev, "Kolya." He looks like a Russian university student from the late nineteenth century. By profession he is an art historian. He writes articles on South Slavic art for the *Soviet Encyclopedia*. He is taciturn, wears thick glasses, and speaks slowly, without a trace of political lexicon. He is pleased that I know Russian. This way he won't have to translate for me, "only help." I was told to be wary of these types especially, for "they all work for the KGB." I disregard the warning. We become friends.

I've received permission to work in the Lenin Library. At my lecture at Lomonosov State University, I make an effort to include references to the conflicts of the Left, "Trotskyism," surrealism, and so on. The students seem to have never heard of such things. During the Revolution they dreamed of making the university the central meeting place of ideas and dialogue, of education and renewal. What was not promised in the name of the Revolution! I meet many officials with various distinctive decorations on their chests: fetishes. What sort of consciousness corresponds to this brand of political fetishism? A revolutionary consciousness?

I try to guess the meanings of acronyms: CHEKEBU, CHIKI, VUFKU, GLAVBUM, SLON, and so on. Impossible. Language has suffered here. It's clearer now why Mandelshtam wanted philology to become a "moral conception." But it has not been possible to apply such a therapy. The formalist Boris Tomashevsky once warned, "One cannot use a journalistic style with impunity." The punishment has been merciless: the majority of books are written in precisely that "style," not just works on politics but also scientific publications and the masses of various "pamphlets." Moreover, publishers use glue that emits a terrible stench, detectable the moment one steps foot in a bookstore. It seems to me the odor of books and bookstores. "Dead words stink" (*Durno pakhnut mertvye slova*), wrote Gumilyov not long before his death. I am surprised not so much by the phenomenon itself as by its pervasiveness, its presence in "objective reality." In a used bookstore I found a collection of Ivan Bunin's works, edited by Aleksandr Tvardovsky, which had been published during the "Thaw," in 1965. Tvardovsky claims that Bunin suffered from the illness of *beziazykost'* (privation of language). An exact diagnosis, but not only of Soviet literature.

I search the used bookstores in vain for works of certain "progressive critics" of the tsarist epoch. It seems that Pyotr Chaadaev's *Philosophical Letters* have not been published in years, perhaps decades. I don't know how many used bookstores I looked in; they are not to be found. Apparently the Party does not want young people reading the author's critical expressions of 1836: "To all our misfortunes we must add one more, that of the false impression we have of ourselves... We belong to none of the great civilizations. We are neither of the West, nor of the East... Nor has the general enlightenment of humanity reached us. We grow but do not mature. We move forward but along a tortuous road that leads nowhere..." Schoolchildren everywhere memorize Pushkin's *Ode to Chaadaev*, but no one has the possibility of reading what Chaadaev wrote. In his time he was declared insane. Today, dissidents are shut away in psychiatric wards, the so-called *psikhushka*.

At the theater I recognize a manner of speaking that corresponds to written journalistic style. The Bolshoi and Khudozhestvennyi have become theater-museums. I could not get a ticket for the Taganka, where Lyubimov works differently, like Efros at the Malaya Bronnaya, and Tovstonogov in Leningrad. The difference consoles me. In Russia one always finds a way to console oneself.

Practically at random I purchase the poetry collections of various authors. I flip through them, read some. They are awful. Russian poetry was always characterized by a great deal of "occasional verse." Now it's practically all occasional. Space flight—salvos for the successes of Soviet cosmonauts. A Party congress—odes in honor of its "wise leadership." They are examples of what is called "publicistic poetry" here. In fact, they are a form of verbal delirium in which poor prosody unites with worse ideology. It is no accident that the drunk, official poet of Bulgakov's *Master and Margarita* is named Bezdomnyi (homeless). Few have managed to save themselves. Yevgeny Yevtushenko paid his debt to journalism. It seemed to me a decade ago that audacity would pull him through, but that did not happen: he is audacious as long as it suits him. Andrei Voznesensky is aware of the dangers to Russian poetry and has managed to distance himself. But he too has paid a price: at times he is constrained to grimace. Bela Akhmadulina is both authentic and gifted, but she is running out of breath. Brodsky went to the limit, but they exiled him. I am sorry I never particularly liked Tvardovsky's poetry, although I esteem the man and his work as editor of *Novyi mir*. Pasternak translated more than he wrote, which was not the worst choice he could have made. And his poetry is better than his prose. The sung poetry of Bulat Okudzhava and Vladimir Vysotsky is an interesting phenomenon. Singing allows them to find a register that does not depend on the impersonality, the *beziazykost'*, that has taken hold of the language. All of Russia listens to them in secret. Perhaps what hinders them most is their popularity itself.

After the conference at Moscow State, I saw an announcement for a poetry reading to be held in the same room that evening. Bulat Okudzhava, Yury Levitansky, Registan (I don't know his first name), the parodist Ivan Ivanov, and Bela Akhmadulina were scheduled to take part. I waited in the student cafeteria until evening, watching the groups of young people, imagining the poetic gatherings of the time of Sergei Yesenin and Vladimir Mayakovsky: the "slap in the face of public taste," their reading tours and recitals, the cafes in which they declaimed, their love affairs and scandals.

Bela Akhmadulina did not show up. She is drinking a great deal lately, and her health has suffered. The papers attack her from all sides. They won't forgive her for having kissed Solzhenitsyn in front of everyone after his address to the Writers' Union. Okudzhava sings his "Ballad," in the spirit of François Villon: "Lord, my God, my green-eyed." Applause. He explains how he was criticized for that "God." He is not religious. He wrote the work when his wife was ill. More applause. All of Yury Levitansky's words and gestures are imbued with nonconformism. He has trouble talking. It's clear he drinks too. Lisyansky, the emcee, says of him that he is "not in state service." Someone adds, "He's not even in the Party." The students applaud him. Levitansky is as poetic when he reads as is Okudzhava when he sings in his trembling voice, all hunched over his guitar. I cannot judge them differently here: poetry is not in books alone. In the Russian tradition, a special poetics has divorced itself from literature.

It is the turn of Registan, author of the words to the Soviet national anthem, "*Soiuz nerushimyi narodov svobodnykh*" ("The Indestructible Union of Free Peoples"). He stands and recites something like this: "I forgive. I forgive my mother everything, for she is my mother. It was hard for her. She is Russia. ...I am a realist. I believe in Russia." (I cite from memory). Then he reads some verse entitled "Dark Man." (An older man calls out from the crowd, "You're the dark man!") He makes some other patriotic, pathetic remarks. "I glimpse a spark in my son's eye. He too will fight when the time comes," and so on. The students applaud him too. I'm disappointed. I ask Kolya why they do it. "They've been reared that way," he says. They haven't worked out their own criteria. How long will it take them to free themselves from what they've been taught? The satirist Ivanov wittily targets the "Russifying tendency," and once more I have occasion to console myself.

The youth sitting next to me is nervous, impatient. He keeps turning around. Probably he's waiting for someone. Towards the end of the evening a girl in a blue scarf arrives and sits down next to him. They start talking. Where has she been all this time? "In line. I've wanted a blue scarf for so long. It was a long line." It's an ordinary scarf. Long lines are an absolutely normal fact of life in this country. I interrupt: "The scarf looks very good on you." The two of them smile and make up. The incident of the blue scarf brings the evening to a close.

The next day I'm leaving for Armenia. I look for Mandelshtam's memoirs of his journey there but can't find them anywhere. I don't know exactly when they were printed or where. No one else seems to either. I don't know whom to ask. The weather worsens. Kolya encourages me by saying it will be warmer in Yerevan than in Moscow. He too is happy we're leaving. Such trips are expensive for "normal Soviets."

Moscow–Yerevan, November 15, 1973

Domodedovo Airport. The flight is delayed "indefinitely" because of bad weather. Many young soldiers, their hair cropped and their belts cinched, are waiting for flights to the Far East. A variety of physiognomies—redheads and blonds, with slanted eyes, some tall, some short. Elderly Armenians and Georgians sleep on the seats. I wait in line for a little *kefir*. All around are television screens. They're showing Tito's departure from Kiev, where his meeting with Brezhnev took place. I explain to Kolya my sorrow when the Yugoslav leadership changed its position toward the Soviet Union after 1956. I understand there were reasons of state, and the dangers of Soviet aggression have still not subsided. We saw what happened in Budapest in 1956, in Prague in '68, and before that in Berlin and Warsaw.

Nevertheless, we should have maintained a more severe attitude in speaking of them, without recognizing in the USSR any "socialism," or "positive heritage," or "friendship." I'm considering writing to Tito, not only about this. I value his work during the war and in the resistance against fascism, in the conflict with Stalin, but it is time for him to leave power to others. Yugoslavia is not proceeding along the best path, younger people must be found, more capable—than those who surround the president—of making social, economic, cultural decisions. Tito needs to withdraw in time. Otherwise he risks compromising his own work.

Kolya looks at me. He's a little surprised. Yugoslavia seems to him a better place than it actually is. He begins to confide in me. His father was a communist and did not allow either his two sons or his daughter to be baptized. Not long ago he decided to be. His wife Natasha, daughter of a Soviet admiral, now the military attaché to Cuba, followed his example. They had their daughter Ksyusha baptized too. Soon they will be married in church. His spirit has been reborn in Christianity. But he's stayed in the Komsomol. If he left the organization, the consequences would be severe. He doesn't feel he is contradicting his own faith, because the Komsomol is "a ridiculous thing." Ninety percent of the young people forced to join feel the same way. "They can't offend us any longer by simply pointing at us, showing that we're believers. There are more and more of us." He is working to develop and perfect himself spiritually. The ritual bothers him a little, and he tries to minimize it. A group of believers has begun meeting at Professor Lazarev's institute. They read Solovyov, Leontyev, Berdyaev, and, of their contemporaries, Sergei Averintsev. He is sorry that, because of the Soviet sins, "everyone hates the Russians."

My confession surprises him. He is amazed to learn that I'm an agnostic and that, being Croat on my mother's side, I was educated in the Catholic faith, not the Orthodox. His amazement is still greater, and perhaps tinged with disappointment, at my defense of "socialism with a human face." I try to explain my position. "Real socialism" is a lie, Stalinism a tragedy. But there are other socialist traditions. The horrors perpetrated in the Soviet Union cannot be justified by any "objective difficulties," but this is not the only road to socialism. The possibilities that carried the germ of Stalinism were not the only ones: founding a state does not have to mean state terror; establishing a central power does not necessarily mean centralism; giving authority to a government, especially in a country threatened by anarchy, does not necessarily mean authoritarianism; the police that protect citizens' freedoms do not need to become dictatorial; the administration that links institutions must not perforce be an administrative bureaucracy; the impulse to create culture does not have to be the cultural monopoly of the Party. In the radicalism of Russian social thought, from Herzen to Lenin, there were certainly other possibilities beyond those that were later realized in the USSR. There is no sin in seeing that they were there, provided one does not use them to justify what actually came to pass. I realize my judgments have ended in wordplay, or in suppositions that can be neither proven nor disproved. I break off. Sometimes rhetoric is out of place.

Kolya closes up when he talks about such things, drawing himself inward into a sort of mystical attitude. I don't know whether he's following me or whether he's listening at all. I want to tell him, as far as Orthodoxy is concerned, that I'm afraid of what Berdyaev called the "metaphysical hysteria of the Russian character," the "tendency to rage over something," God knows what, the "expectation of miracle" typical of Russians. We've seen where "miracles" can lead. One rage should not substitute for another. "Savage capitalism" cannot save Russia. People here have always opposed capitalist accumulation, Christians and revolutionaries, populists and anarchists, Slavophiles and Westernizers. The merchant who had grown wealthy sought to atone for his wealth by creating a charitable endowment, going on a pilgrimage, becoming a monk. Russian religious thinkers have always looked on commerce and trade with diffidence. Sergei Bulgakov preached the economy of "Sophia"; Leontyev disdained the mercantile spirit; Dostoevsky considered that the Russian people's economic capacity was subordinate to its moral capacity. The people themselves created the expression *kupecheskaia dusha* (commercial soul). It is a position closer to Christ driving the merchants from the temple than it is to Marx. The peasant believed the land was God's gift to him, not his property, while in the very concept of happiness, giving was more important than having. All true reforms in Russia, if and when they come about, must take this fact into account. There is no place in Russia for "classical capitalism" as it exists elsewhere. I don't know what kind of socialism is possible there. Perhaps there is a third way.

We've been waiting for eight hours at Domodedovo, thinking aloud or to ourselves. We meet, among others, a group of singers of musical comedy from Yugoslavia. They're on the way to Khabarovsk. They talk about how cold it is there, minus thirty degrees Celsius, but say you make good money. They can take the rubles out and exchange them for dinars. I think about all that has been taken from this country and sold in the world, how many icons and art works, gold and precious objects. Everyone has taken and sold—the state, individuals, the *nomenklatura*, émigrés. What is left?

The fog lifts at last. We take off. Gradually I form an image of the expanse of this country. It seems to me that one can recognize various parts of the world from the color of the earth. Here no. We make out Mount Ararat before us. I wonder to what extent the Caucasus is Asia. I don't know. Nor will I remain here long enough to know.

Yerevan, November 16, 1973

We are met by a woman from the Armenian division of the Writers' Union, Metakse, a poet. She's an interesting person. She talks about the sadness of the Armenians, about the Turkish massacre of ethnic Armenians in 1915. She points to Ararat, a symbol of elevation and humiliation. It belongs to Armenia but lies in Turkey. The landscape has a biblical aspect, lacking only a desert.

We visit ancient temples constructed out of huge stone blocks. Inside one Metakse joins her hands together and sings an old religious hymn. Christianity was accepted early here, and the Armeno-Gregorian ritual is still observed. The head of the church is called the *Katolikos*. National and religious museums are situated next to his domicile. Inside there are icons from the first centuries after Christ, ancient manuscripts, a piece of "wood from Noah's ark." Myth and history. It is a people with its own identity, its own traumas: in this case the traumas are the nature of the identity. The Armenians are sensitive and hardworking. Given the chance, they would be wealthier and would live better. Does the Soviet Union hinder or help? They say it protects them.

Soviet monuments can be seen at the crossroads: a clumsy statue of Lenin rises as usual atop the central square. The divisional Writers' Union office has five secretaries. Book publishing is similar to that in Russia, only in smaller proportions. Every year, twenty-some works by Armenian authors are published in Russian. They attach great importance to being translated. I don't see any signs of anti-Sovietism. "They're the only ones who don't detest us," says Kolya.

On the eighteenth of November we head north to Lake Sevan. Located six thousand feet above sea level, it is considered one of the world's great wonders for the way it changes colors in the course of the day: its bottom is formed of volcanic stone, which reflects light and shadow in a variety of ways from dawn to dusk. It is blue, gray, and dark green by turns. The water is very clear and drinkable. All around are rocks, beaches, boats. We dine on trout prepared in traditional Armenian fashion at some sort of rest home. An Indian man named Sahi joins us. He is a Hindi poet and professor at Allahabad University. He's accompanied by a translator, an Armenian from Moscow. Sahi is a handsome, dignified man. At my request, he jots down the term for "occasional poetry" from the Indian poetic tradition: *arthamatra*. He believes in the Soviet Union.

He maintains that such an order would be the most suitable for his country. I don't try to dissuade him. I wonder how much our visits cost this country. Where else do they host writers in such a way, when the people remain so poor?

Back in Yerevan, we've become friends with Metakse. She introduces us to her husband, a "graduate student of technical sciences," who is studying Sergei Eisenstein. He has the romantic name of Hamlet. He is younger than Metakse, who is somewhat jealous. They're in love. They have a modest apartment of ninety square feet. Hamlet laments the fact that the people in power here are incompetent and arrogant, crass in the Caucasian manner, irascible and obstinate. "They're all corrupt," he says. The Party is filled with common thieves and criminals. The president of the Armenian Writers' Union, whom we met, is not even a writer. He writes "pamphlets, political brochures." The apparatchiks have big apartments; they build themselves dachas, purchase foreign goods. The Georgians buy places in medical school for their children here: each one costs ten thousand rubles, three years' worth of a university professor's salary.

Hamlet works at the journal *Science and Technology*. He is constantly harassed by the editor-in-chief, who studied at the Faculty of Letters without graduating, and "doesn't have the faintest idea about technology." Metakse says that they deceived me at the Writers' Union by bragging about large print runs and royalties. She's been waiting five years for an "approved" book of hers to come out. She doesn't know how long she'll have to wait for the Russian translation because she has no connections "high up," where they make decisions, where they pay. Kolya nods in agreement. I listen without speaking. I don't know what to say.

They give me a record on which Komitas, after the massacre, is reciting and singing his works (without hazarding a judgment, though certainly it is a variety of poetry). I visit various churches. There are numerous worshipers, young and old. Priests were not persecuted here as they were elsewhere in the Soviet Union. The Katolikos has a special standing among the people. The Armeno-Gregorian Church has played an enormous role in the nation's history. Émigré Armenians support it generously.

"I came to this country as an ordinary traveler. I leave it as a friend," I write, or something to that effect; in the album of the Writers' Union on November 18, 1973, when it is presented to me upon my departure.

Tbilisi, November 19, 1973

The flight to Tbilisi was three and a half hours late because of strong winds. All that time I had to put up with a big shot from the Writers' Union, who waited with us at the Yerevan Airport "for reasons of protocol." A typical literary bureaucrat. They had "ordered" (*zakazali*) a novel on some Armenian hero, and that was what he was working on. A member of the Central Committee of the Armenian Communist Party. When will this country free itself of such people? Can it do without them at all? They certainly can't do without it.

At last we take off in a small, uncomfortable JAK 40. We roll and dip over Lake Sevan. Now it seems rather violet. The airport building in Tbilisi is bigger than the one in Yerevan. We find lodgings in the Hotel Iveria, better looking than any we've been in thus far. There are relatively more cars in town than in Moscow. The drivers ignore the pedestrians. The pedestrians spit on the street. It's just like the Balkans.

All around are small, picturesque restaurants. They drink beer, eat kebab, *shashlyk*, *hinkali*. There aren't long lines as elsewhere. Our guide, Amiran Gabiskiria, is director of the *Litfond*. He's a thickset, fifty-five year old. He speaks Russian with a heavy accent and lots of mistakes. He fought in the war and barely recovered from his wounds. He hates Nikita Khrushchev, calls him a "genuine idiot" (*nastoiashchii durak*). We can't, naturally, avoid a discussion of Stalin. He admits that Yosif Dzhugashvili was too harsh and made mistakes. "But with him we won the war, rebuilt the country from ruins and ashes, carried out the five-year plans." History would show how valuable he was. He was pleased to hear me say I wanted to see Gori, Stalin's birthplace, where they've preserved the Generalissimo's childhood home and built a museum. He did not hear why I wanted to see it.

Gori, November 22, 1973

The town of Gori is some eighty-five kilometers distant from Tbilisi. We take the old Georgian military road. The area is well off, the landscape unusual. The first snow covers the meadows. The Intourist driver tells us about how well the peasants live here. "They rest all winter, hunt, make *shashlyk*, drink wine. That's what Soviet power gave them." I ask whether Stalin contributed to it. "He did a lot for the people. They love him." Khrushchev ordered his museum to be closed and the house where he was born destroyed, but "the people did not permit it." Everyone hates Khrushchev here. There is a large statue of Stalin in the central square. They say it is the last one in the USSR. The only others are in China and Albania.

The little house where Yosif Dzhugashvili was born contains only one room. The entire family lived there. I look at the photographs of Gori from the beginning of the century: cart tracks, wooden fences, mud, poverty. The museum director, a young Georgian woman who speaks good Russian, points proudly to the photographs, bad portraits in which Yosif Vissarionovich looks off to the horizon, foreseeing the future, large historical compositions of dubious quality, a facsimile reproduction of the letter in which Lenin mentioned "the prodigious Georgian." Absent, of course, is the deathbed letter in which he warns that the "crass" secretary has accumulated "excessive power." Also on display are gifts to the "father of the nation," many received on the occasion of his seventieth birthday. The visitors look at everything in detail, listen to the commentary, awestruck. One young "science student" with a wide face, straight black hair, and a large moustache, is writing a dissertation on Stalin's relations with Soviet writers and artists. He shows me a collection of "documents" and "materials," declarations and articles composed on the occasion of Stalin's fiftieth birthday in 1935. I ask him to let me copy out two or three brief quotations and he is pleased to do so. I jot them down for Kiš's collection. It seems they forced even Fyodor Gladkov and Babel to write on the "language" and "literary style" of Stalin. Gladkov: "The simplicity and extraordinary force of the words, characteristic of Stalin, are a lesson to us writers" (*Pravda*, December 12, 1935). Babel: "Witness how Stalin fashions his style. We must work to perfect our language, as Stalin has" (*Pravda*, January 1, 1935). Perhaps others wrote for them and they merely assented and signed. That didn't save Babel. Or Gladkov.

I did not know of these texts, although I wasn't surprised by the fact that they were printed. Đilas wrote similar panegyrics when he was in power, without being coerced. There are two poems dedicated to Stalin by Mandelshtam circulating Moscow: one about the "Kremlin mountaineer," which led to the poet's death, another about Stalin's visions, with which he tried unsuccessfully to save himself. Unfortunately, the second is better than the first from an artistic standpoint. Such is literature. So many and sundry signatures against "enemies of the people" clipped from the newspapers, forced not only from Maxim Gorky and Mikhail Sholokhov (the latter without the need of force), but from Pasternak and Zoshchenko, Shostakovich and Eisenstein. We read them in surprise, but those were different times. I wonder what I would have done, what we would have done, dear Danilo, in their place.

Some of Stalin's gestures are difficult to explain. On the eve of the war he called the Leningrad section of the Writers' Union and asked, "Why are Anna Akhmatova's works not being published?" The call helped get her evacuated to Tashkent, along with Nadezhda Mandelshtam. He telephoned Bulgakov and Pasternak personally, as if he wanted to hear their opinions. The monster had taste. I asked the director of the museum to find me a translation of the poetry that Sosa (his first pseudonym) wrote in his youth, during his seminary studies. She gave me two poems. They are not original, at least in their Russian translation, but the novice was not completely untalented.

I returned from Gori depressed by what I'd seen and heard. One of the five secretaries of the Georgian Writers' Union speaks ill of Stalin to me. "The people are more attached to his myth than to him." Just the people? "A large portion of the intelligentsia does not consider Stalin someone we should be proud of." And the museum? "A toy for simple people." Only them? "Absolutely, the simplest." I wish it were so.

It's hard to get to know a country whose language is utterly foreign. From ancient Georgian literature I've read only Rustaveli's epic, from modern only several poems translated by Pasternak. Yet not even he knew the Georgian language. The Congress of Georgian Composers is being held here, and their works are being performed. I spend the evenings in an interestingly built concert hall with good acoustics. Fortunately, the language of music is more accessible, though I came with great preconceptions, expecting what Igor Stravinsky called Russian and Soviet "musical ethnography," with titles he ironically cited as "Shakh-Senem, Gulsara, Daissi, Abesalom and Eteri, Atchurek, Adzhal-Orduna, Altine-Kiz, Taras Bulba." I was mistaken. They perform modern, experimental music devoid of naive folklorism or forced construction. The musicians are highly cultivated, the audience attentive. I listen to the Second Symphony of David Topadze, which features a women's chorus fancifully coordinated with the orchestra. The excellent violinist Marina Yashvili performs an interesting violin concerto by Nassidze. I hear several other worthy pieces well performed. Just as in Moscow, I see different faces here, composed behavior, and several dignified, beautiful women. The elite?

Before leaving Georgia, something happens that is important for the subsequent course of this journey and for the epistolary that follows. In the evening, after strolling through town, I get back to the hotel rather late and look for a place in the restaurant, but it's completely full. Two Georgians invite me to their table and offer me a drink. They're already slightly drunk. They order another two bottles of Tsindalia, a Georgian white, and toast my health. (The person making the toast here is called *tomado*; they do it with theatricality). After a bit one of them suddenly surprises me by saying, "Sell me your sweater. Your shirt too." I try to get out of it. It's cold here. I'll be in the USSR another two weeks. I'm heading north. He offers me three hundred rubles, a professor's monthly salary. I thank him but decline, getting up and heading for my room. One of them follows me with the unfinished bottle. He looks around to be sure no one is watching and tosses a banknote to the hall monitor as he enters my room. He's a photographer, he says. People here like to have their picture taken. Peasants take all sorts of food on the plane with them to Moscow, meat, fruit and vegetables, everything. "They come back with their bags full of rubles." They organize big weddings. "Everybody wants his picture taken at a wedding." He makes loads of money, but what can he do with it? Clothing here isn't worth anything. Shirts are no good. There aren't any sweaters. He pronounces the word *sherst* (wool) several times and places a pile of bills drawn from his pocket on the table next to the bottle. When he leaves he has the sweater and shirt both. I'm on my way to Odessa, where I know Tusya Mikhailovna and the aging Olga Ivanovna live. The money so easily earned by this photographer will help them survive.

In the end I took it without a second thought.

Odessa, November 25, 1973

We were supposed to land at Simferopol, but due to fog we continued straight on to Odessa. It is ten degrees Celsius in the Crimea. In Moscow it's seven below zero. The clouds are breaking up in places. We fly above the Black Sea. Below the dark clouds, today it really is black. Travelers of various nationalities speak Russian on the plane. I see nothing wrong with this. Russification? Perhaps, but how does one communicate otherwise? Elsewhere it is through the language of Shakespeare or Molière, while here it's through that of Tolstoy and Dostoevsky. Small peoples are afraid of this, I know. Is it possible to rationalize such fear? The Russians use the adjective "Russian" too often. I listen to the radio during this voyage, hear songs in which one is told of the Russian sea, the Russian fields, the Russian steppe, the Russian forests, and so on. If I translated that into Croatian woods, Croatian fields, Croatian rivers, and so on, it would be construed as unpardonable nationalism. The very word "Russian" has long had its own cult in Russia. The Russian people seem to me too exhausted and denationalized to really be capable of "smothering" other nationalities. One must not attribute to them the expansive character of Soviet politics and ideology, which are the very things that contributed most to exhausting and denationalizing them.

Russian nationalism is hard to define. Was it ever really nationalism in the strict sense of the word, or more a feature of Russianness? For Solovyov, the Russian national idea was characterized by self-abnegation. "Nationalism in Russia has always looked liked something un-Russian," writes Berdyaev. This, of course, does not exclude bull-in-a-china-shop behavior, the unreasonableness of the large toward the small, or the hypersensitivity of the small before everything done by those who have more than they. But in this case the bull would be the people, the *narod*, not the nation. Has the Russian nation dissolved inside the "Soviet people"? To a certain degree perhaps it has, more than any others, so much so that Russian and Soviet, seen from the outside, are frequently identified as one. Contemporary Russian nationalism appears dispersed, sporadic, and incoherent. It is not a social movement and hardly a spiritual state. It is motivated by the sense that much has been lost, that Russians have suffered more than others. Is speech about loss and suffering the same as nationalism? Perhaps. Especially if it becomes obsessive and imposing in relations with others. Others have lost and suffered from both the Soviet Union and the Russians themselves.

I imagine this country's future as the squaring of a circle. The nationalism that creates the nation on the one hand, the nationalism that creates nationalism on the other—neither is typical of Russia, which seems to lie outside such schemes. "Russia cannot be understood through reason, only believed in," wrote Tyutchev. With regard to the relations of Russia and Ukraine, I fail to see how the two could completely separate from each other. They have Kievan *Rus* as their common origin. A portion of the population has a regional rather than a national character: if you come from the south you're a *khokhol*, if from the north a *katsap*. The western and eastern parts of Ukraine do not look on these divisions in the same way. Will the reawakening of pan-Islamicism in the world influence the Asiatic peoples of the Soviet Union? For the moment the government is keeping a lid on everything. The pot's water has not yet come to a boil. But it may at any moment. What would happen if the lid were lifted? On their own, the authorities would never allow it to happen. But for how long will they be able to keep it down? No one knows.

With such thoughts on my mind, I land in Odessa. Because we did not stop off in Simferopol, we are an hour and a half early. No one is there to meet us. We take a "private" taxi. It's Saturday, a day off, and there is considerable traffic. "Weddings are on Saturdays," says the driver. "The kolkhoz workers have money and they celebrate. People who go to Siberia put money away; then they spend it. And Odessa is a port, so there's smuggling." He drops us off at an old hotel, the Odessa, which overlooks the harbor. The director of the local Writers' Union chapter, whom I met the year before, arrives at last. He's a young man who runs in a thousand directions at once. I have no idea when he finds time to write. It's how I imagine the *nepmen* (small entrepreneurs) of the 1920s: a little coarse, something of a drinker, ambitious, probably a womanizer. The authorities help him in all this. He is faithful to them.

He introduces me to Tihomir Aćimović, a Yugoslav political émigré who remained in the Soviet Union after the conflict of 1948. With him is Nikola Grujić, who has shared the same fate. As partisan officers, they departed for "military training" in the USSR after the war and upheld the Cominform resolution against Tito's betrayal. The Soviet apparatus exerted pressure on them to "sign" and they did. They were forced to condemn their homeland. Times have changed since. Now Aćimović spends summers with his wife (a Russian) and daughter on the Adriatic coast. Grujić is not allowed to return. He said something in Bosnia in 1968, during the Prague occupation, for which the Yugoslavs first imprisoned and then expelled him. Aćimović suffers from tuberculosis. He has a dacha near the sea in the Arcadia of Odessa. He writes books about the war. He invited us to his home. He was born in Serbia, in Kosmaj. He talks about himself and about his novel *The Kosmajan*. He joined the partisans at a young age, knowing nothing about communism. If he hadn't seen the Chetniks with the Germans, he says, he would have joined them. He was once leading an attack against them when he looked around and saw that he was all alone. His comrades shouted at him to come back, he'd get himself killed. At the end of the war, he was nominated for candidacy in the Yugoslav Communist Youth (SKOJ). "The first time I heard that word," he says, "I thought it was some kind of occupation organization." He was wounded in Bosnia. The Thirteenth Dalmatian Brigade took him in; he was cared for by a Croatian nurse named Katica. He fell in love. She later lost a leg in battle. He would have married her all the same, but she wouldn't let him, impaired as she was. He remained with the Croats until the end of the war. All this is related in his *Kosmajan*. His characters bear Croatian names, Štefek, Ivo, Vlado, those of his companions from the war. He joined the Russians in the liberation of Belgrade and was wounded in the stomach during the battle for Slavonia. Because he was hungry, his intestines empty, he remained alive. They rewarded him by sending him to study in the USSR. He proposed his novel to a Serbian publisher, who turned it down: "To listen to you, all the partisans were Croats." In Zagreb they turned it down because the author was a Serb. I examine his tall, slightly bent figure with its still young, slightly naive face. This is the sort of people our side labeled "hostile elements of the Cominform."

Grujić too has a story. He was born near Drvar, in the portion of Bosnia where the Serbs suffered most under the Ustashe. At thirteen he was "on the run." By the end of the war, at the age of eighteen, he'd become a partisan lieutenant. All around him people shot and died. He saw everything. He had no childhood or adolescence, perhaps no youth at all. As a reward they sent him to a Soviet military school. He was happy to be going to "Mother Russia." He speaks with fervor of how he loved the Russians. There were four Russian soldiers in his brigade, fugitives from German prisons who had joined the partisans. Among them was Vasily, Vasya, a machine gunner: Near the town of Bosanski Novi the SS are bearing down, the partisan division is weak, starving, everyone will die. Vasya, "who otherwise was as kind as an angel," lets the enemy approach to within thirty feet and then "opens a hail of fire." After he'd finished, he was just like before, "a child." He saved the whole division.

I heard a similar story from the Croatian poet Jure Kaštelan. They were being pursued, from Dalmatia toward Herzegovina, by SS and Ustashe units. They would have all died: the partisans did not allow themselves to be taken prisoner. In the company is a Russian, Alyosha, he too a refugee from a German prison. Beside a ravine with a narrow passage he salutes his comrades, *"Proshchaite"* (farewell): he will stay to detain the enemy. He fought them off long enough for the others to escape and then fell. "Ever since that I have never said anything when others criticized the Russians. I always saw Alyosha before me, atoning for our sins."

Such stories, unfortunately, leave out an important detail. POWs who survived and returned to the USSR faced interrogation and punishment. "Why did you surrender?" "How did you escape?" "What did you see there?" And in the end, Siberia, the gulag, from which it was harder to escape than it had been from a German prison.

We struck up a conversation about the Yugoslav conflict with Stalin. Grujić: "Stalin won the war." Wasn't it the unhappy Russian people who won it? "Yes, with Stalin as their leader." Not despite him? On the eve of the war hadn't he executed his best generals, Tukhachevsky, Yakir, Blucher, and all the others? "He himself was a general, Generalissimo."

I think of my relatives who perished and of those nearby whom I want to see again and help. How am I to contact them? I confess everything to Kolya, where I'm from, why I'm here, what I experienced the year before. I trust him. He will help. They allow me to "stroll" through Odessa. They know, of course, what it's all about. Danilo Kiš warned me: "They know everything."

I went first of all to Olga Antonovich. She did not recognize me at first, which wasn't surprising: she is very old and tired. She was still looking after the child of her communal apartment neighbor, a beautiful baby reminiscent of a Russian fairy tale: healthy, plump, blond. In a Socialist Realist story it would serve as a metaphor—an old woman belonging to the past and a youth before whom the "beautiful future" opens wide. An educational Russian fairy tale.

Olga Ivanovna told me again about our family, adding various new details, especially about Grandpa Nikolai. Uncle Vladimir's considerable library had remained intact. "They" had combed through everything, searching for prohibited works, and taken away a few volumes. But Grandfather had managed to save the bulk of the books, hiding them in a ditch. He kept them there in anticipation of Volodya's return. "He would need them." Later, when he'd lost hope that his oldest son was still alive, he started selling them off, one by one, crying. "Poverty forced him." He had nothing left after the camp.

Olga Ivanovna had no children. Her parents had had nine. Three had died of tuberculosis at an early age, while she had cared for and watched over her remaining brothers and sisters. I could see that the good woman did not have long to live, that I'd arrived at the last minute to hear her and note down her memories. As I said goodbye, she gave me several sheets of music notation, a score Grandfather had worked on, and a flask of old perfume, already evaporated, which she had long kept safe. She wrapped it all in wrinkled crepe paper, difficult to come by here. It was very likely that I would never see her again.

I arrive at Mikoyan Street in search of aunt Tusya, filled with anxiety. She recognizes me. She's been waiting. The winter before, she was seriously ill. She's not yet fully recovered. The little packages we sent her helped. She gave the chocolate, shoes, and soap to the doctors and nurses. "Cinnamon and pepper are especially in demand here." She traded them for medicine, selling some, and "managed to pull through." For weeks she lived on fish from the "state-run store" (*iz gosudarstvennoi*), a symbol of the most abject poverty. (In one store I smelled the stench of that fish—salty, acrid, rotten.) Dust-covered boxes are tossed all around Tusya, one on top of another. Her bathroom consists of wooden boards with a hole through the middle. What a contrast between her childhood and her old age! The former camp prisoner tells me how her father, a doctor, became a Red Army general during the Revolution. In the Kiev oblast he had spent days and nights treating soldiers and civilians suffering from the epidemics. He was infected and died. They brought him to Odessa on a special train car, while in a separate car were gifts and food for his family, "eggs, meat, potatoes, all the things we didn't have." Better that he died at his medical post than be carried away as an enemy later.

A neighbor who is a nurse helps Tusya. "I give her some of the things you and Vsevolod Nikolaevich send me. She's going to take you to Pyotr. You have to see him. He'll tell you about the camps. He spent more than twenty years there. He knew your Uncle Volodya. They took them away together. Pyotr isn't his real name, but we call him that because of the others, so they don't do anything more to him."

The neighbor takes me to Pyotr. "He lives far away. You shouldn't go there alone." We walked for a long time together, into Odessa's outskirts. I thought I was going to meet someone who, after so many years of forced labor, wanted to be "as far from others as possible," like Aleksandr Petrovich Goryanchikov from Dostoevsky's *Notes from the House of the*

Dead. I searched through my memory for names and portraits from Russian history and literature: the *starets* (venerable monk) Zosima, Makar the pilgrim, the vagabond (*brodiaga*), Lebyadkin the holy fool (*iurodivyi*), Pushkin's "hermit in a cell," the God-seeker (*bogoiskatel*), the "eccentric" (*chudak*), the *providets* (prophet), *koldun* (sorcerer), *bosiak* (tramp), and so on. Pyotr has something of all that. He's near seventy, but with a youthful expression, bright, profound. He's dressed in normal town garb. He still has his teeth and hair, and a sparse white beard. He speaks clearly, in short, disjointed sentences. His voice is hoarse, calm. (Part of the sense of his words and gestures is inevitably lost in writing.) He traveled for a long time with Uncle Volodya. They lay in the straw next to each other on the floor of the train car. They didn't know where they were being taken. "We told each other everything. It was a long way, which helped. Then each of us went his own way, though we didn't choose it." They walked a little together at a station stop before separating. He closes his eyes as he remembers. "Our real steps stayed back where we'd come from. You walk differently when you come back. If you don't know why you went, neither do you know why you return. You can be proud of your Uncle Vladimir in that he didn't return."

I can't recall the order of his phrases and don't dare place some of them in quotation marks. About the people he had little to say. "The people deserve peace." They created tsardom in the people's name and then destroyed the tsar. "The body of the people takes a long time to heal. The knowledge we gained there does not help here." There are those who are silent out of pride. They don't want others to know what was done to them. "One mustn't seek repentance from anyone." This time may last, or it may end unexpectedly. "It's happened before."

I calmed myself at last, thanked the old man, and offered him some modest assistance. He wouldn't take anything. "They told me you write. Write me a few lines about bread. I'd appreciate that. I've been thinking about bread for some time. I've written a little about it too." I promised him to write and enclose what I'd written in a letter to Nataliya Mikhailovna. "Your guide has gone. It's not safe to leave here in the dark alone. My son will take you."

It was a meeting I had not been prepared for. Again I cried, returning to Tusya. It took me a long time to come to myself.

Kiev, November 23, 1973

There was poor weather above the Kiev Airport as well. Again our departure was delayed. Everything is late in this country. One easily gets used to it. Life lived in waiting.

During the flight I saw the Dniepr for the first time. It wasn't as I'd imagined it. Ice had already taken hold of its banks, though not yet its center. The river was narrow with a white frame.

Kiev struck me as more harmonious than Moscow. It seemed to have fewer of those ugly Soviet buildings, at least in the center of town. I received a good-natured guide from the Ukrainian Writers' Union, Igor Kazimirov. A bibliophile who also collects writers' signatures. He drove Sartre, he says, around Kiev. He's heard that I know him and asks me to talk about him. When we're alone he tells me that his father committed suicide in 1937. "He couldn't stand waiting," he says. Waiting? "For them to take him away." One writer was taken away by accident, instead of somebody else. "They took him and that was that. Never came back." Had he spoken to Sartre about that? He had not. It wasn't possible then. "He would have talked about it somewhere. I'm sure that you won't. You know how it is for us."

Kolya, Metakse, Ivan—if these people could be guides for foreign writers, even if only from time to time, it meant that things in this country could be, must be, finally, changing. I wanted it to be true but didn't know if it really was. Perhaps they were tricking us in this too: it could all be a fraud.

The Kiev-Pechersky monastery surpassed my expectations. Hundreds of small monastic cells in sand deep beneath the earth, some of them walled on every side, door-less, with an opening through which only food and waste could pass. Here a man could barely extend himself. I could not have imagined such utter self-denial and mortification. Someone asked me what I thought of it all. I said that now I understood Dostoevsky better and would read him differently.

Nearby, on the Dniepr, the pagan Slav nation was baptized: Kievan *Rus* in the heart of Ukraine. Russians and Ukrainians speak of it in different ways, even though it was one and the same place. Something that could serve to unite people most becomes the basis of argument as soon as it is expressed in terms of possession, when *whose it is* becomes more important that *what it is*.

The Ukrainian Writers' Union is housed in a splendid villa that once belonged to a wealthy Kievan merchant. President Oleš Gončar welcomes me. They have sixteen branch offices throughout Ukraine, their own *Litfond*, summer residences, medical clinics, book series. He speaks to me, once again, about print runs and royalties. I reply by noting the completely opposite situation of Yugoslavia, where the Writers' Union represents no one and means nothing, where royalties are pitiful and print runs minimal. I know poets who are starving. Almost all our writers who are worth anything laugh at and mock Writers' Union directives. Gončar is not fazed: Ukraine has eight hundred fifty-seven writers, of whom some two hundred live from writing alone. The Ukrainian Writers' Union publishes six journals and the newspaper *Literary Ukraine* in both Russian and Ukrainian. I ask him in which language they publish more. What is happening with the proposals to resume publication of several Jewish publications in Yiddish? We recently read about Shestov's replacement as head of the Ukrainian Communist Party. What were his relations with the Writers' Union? "Comrade Shestov was replaced because he committed political errors." What kind? "Various." How many of your writers are in the Party? "Around seventy percent." Is there nationalism? "There are sick people everywhere." The Ukrainian writers who've been following the conversation encourage me with their eyes. "Is Matvejević a Yugoslav name, Croatian?" asks the President as we say goodbye. No. It's originally Ukrainian, only Russified.

I gave a talk at Taras Shevchenko University. I said the same things as I had in Moscow. One student asked me what the "Zhdanovism" was that I had mentioned several times. "Was it a literary movement?" No, an entire epoch, I joke in response.

I wanted to visit the Shevchenko Museum and asked a passerby where it was located. He refused to answer in Russian, mumbling something in Ukrainian instead. He must have judged from my accent that I was some *katsap* from Moscow.

Moscow, December 1, 1973

Back in Moscow, once more at the Hotel Rossiya. I watch the television coverage of Brezhnev's return from India. He makes a statement at Vnukovo Airport. He speaks the words heavily; his tongue gets tangled as if he's been drinking. He kisses the waiting *verkhushka* (upper crust) on the lips. Yes, on the lips. They say it's an old folk custom. They sometimes hire an actor to read the declarations of the Party General Secretary on television. Political language has degenerated here to such an extent and become so unconvincing that it must be saved by special effects: a young actor, a handsome voice, attractive diction.

I'm working once again in the Lenin Library. I am treated as one of their academicians thanks to my Sorbonne doctorate. Soviet hierarchy. I have a large, separate table and am aided by the bibliographer of Special Reading Room No. 1. I look through journals from the period just before and immediately following the Revolution. I'm interested in how the nineteenth-century nationalist concept of *tendentsia* (political orientation) was translated into communist *partiinost'* (party-mindedness). I look at the yearly collection of the monthly *Krasnaia nov'* (Red Virgin Soil), which was founded by Vronsky in 1921. The contributors are Bukharin, Pilnyak, Ivanov, Babel, Trotsky, Lenin in the first year, Seifulina, Lunacharsky, Yesenin, Mayakovsky. The gray tedium of contemporary Soviet journals is nothing in comparison. I follow the polemic of 1925, "On the Roots of Trotskyism." Responding to attacks was still possible then.

On day three, I note, a typical incident. I hand some texts over to the photocopy center. Until now this has gone smoothly and quickly. Among the texts is a Bukharin article. "This one, no," says the librarian. I insist but it doesn't help. I ask to see the departmental head. In his will Lenin spoke of Bukharin as "the Party's favorite." Here in the Lenin Library you are ignoring Vladimir Ilyich's own words (though I just say "Ilyich's," the way that they do.) "We have our rules, Comrade Matvejević." I take out the first issue of *Krasnaia nov*, in which Lenin writes that Bukharin is "an extraordinarily well-educated Marxist economist" (June 1921). The answer: "Bukharin has not been rehabilitated." Next I want the Petrograd *Novaia zhizn'* issues from May 1917 to July 1918, in which Maxim Gorky criticizes the Bolsheviks. It's the same story, even though no "rehabilitation" is in question. "That issue is at the bindery." I could not even get the 1905 *Vekhy* with Bryusov's article against Leninist *partiinost'* in literature (the author's "complete" collected works were published without the article in question).

I hear several uninteresting concerts and attend a performance of Shchedrin's ballet *Konek Gorbunok* at the Bolshoi, avoiding the opera. The productions of contemporary music on the radio open my eyes to the other side of Russian musical life. Shostakovich is naturally beyond all this. He demonstrates the difference between what ought to be and what is. Stravinsky diagnosed the problem: "The Russians are probably one of the most musically gifted peoples," but musical creation requires "meditation and analysis, education and intellectual constancy, and of this Russia has never been more deprived than it is now." In the Kremlin's concert hall I was surprised by an extraordinary ballet exhibition of young ballerinas from the Zhdanov choreography school (nothing in common but the famous surname with the notorious commissar). They danced with imagination, in a manner both free and disciplined at the same time. Their movements united with the music without being limited to mere illustration. Once again I had occasion to be consoled.

How often have Vasily Rozanov's words been cited, that "Russia lost its color in three days, if not two." I leave Moscow with the impression that all has not been lost, although the loss was immense. Perhaps I've led myself to such a conclusion from the empty desire that it should be so. I've been looking for the places where some portion of what was valuable remains, where, despite everything, something has been conserved. There are few such places and we usually don't know where they are. Who knows? When will Russia succeed in defeating Russia? The question has been pondered since the country's very existence.

I found barely enough time, the day before my departure, to write a letter to Pyotr, the "few lines about bread" that he'd asked of me in Odessa. I tried to harmonize them with his manner of speech, different from mine, from ours. From ours who had not been "down there."

I have not traveled the earth much and know little of bread, said the pilgrim. Bread is the earth.
Don't cut it, break it with your hands, said the monk from Rostov-on-the-Don. We have sailed the river. Your prayers will be answered.
Only bread and salt will be left to welcome them. The old woman waited still. Her sons were gone, her house empty.
Bread and water. Heavy water does not run to the sea. The words of my Suzdal' companion. We measure our steps and have no measure. Years on end of failing crops. The grain spikes have bowed down. We had to nourish the army. Bread and love, Vasilisa, to share in our autumn.

We recall the loaves prepared by southern brides. Preserve the crumbs in our kerchiefs for Fast and Sacrament. The snows conserve the healthy kernels in the earth.
The exile advanced into the steppe beyond the Yenisei. The bread is distributed one day at a time there. The flour has been scattered. Who will reunite us as a happy people? Bread and wine.
The messenger's voice was heard as well. He called as loudly as he could so that not a syllable would be lost. Bread and kvas, brothers. We've waded through the mud. There are still pure springs here.
We sing softly on this side, barely hearing ourselves: a crust of earth and a husk of bread. Russia is flat, I wrote, at the end of a letter to you.

I sent the letter to Odessa, to the address of Nataliya Mikhailovna, Tusya, with a request that she forwards it to Pyotr. I left Moscow on December 5, 1973. The plane departing from Sheremetyevo was delayed by fog. Snow covered the runway.

Russian winter.

The Gulag Archipelago

If Solzhenitsyn's The Gulag Archipelago *were translated in Yugoslavia, its distribution throughout Eastern Europe would proceed more rapidly. I was working on achieving this goal when the book came out in Paris in 1973. I wrote an introduction to the work and sent it to the Zagreb newspapers* Vjestnik *and* Vječernji list: *the first rejected it with an excuse, the second without a word. I tested fate elsewhere in the country, where such texts sometimes passed the censor more easily. Some parts finally came out in Montenegro and Dalmatia. I put them together and published them in the book* Toward a New Form of Cultural Creation. *But this was still not enough to get the* Archipelago *published.*

I attracted the attention of the publishing house Naprijed *and put together a précis for the editors, attempting to make the work as acceptable as possible. A day or two later, the publisher was visited by the Soviet General Consul in Zagreb and asked not to allow the publication of "anti-Soviet propaganda." How had he discovered what we were planning? The Central Committee had sent out a warning. The proposal for publishing the* Archipelago *was refused several more times. In the meantime, Solzhenitsyn was exiled from the* USSR *(in February 1974). Others of his works appeared abroad:* The Oak and the Calf, Letter to the Leaders of the Soviet Union. *I added to my text, taking these latest works into account, and handed it to the smaller, less conspicuous press August Cesarec, where I had friends, but not even there could the* Archipelago *appear.*

From this history the following letter remains.

Zagreb, Spring 1974

The reactions that have accompanied the publication of Solzhenitsyn's works are no measure of their value. Neither the 1970 Nobel Prize, which the author was not allowed to accept in Stockholm or Moscow, nor the expulsion of the writer from his homeland, nor even the publication of his works abroad constitutes adequate reason for preventing the publication of *The Gulag Archipelago*. The positions taken by Solzhenitsyn in his journalism do not lessen the value of the work in question: Solzhenitsyn cannot be reduced to his articles. *The Gulag Archipelago* is something else altogether.

Many people did not believe in the existence of the Soviet labor camps and do not like to be reminded of that fact. *The Gulag Archipelago* precludes any alibi. While arguments over dissidents most often result in petitions, Solzhenitsyn's dissidence became action. The majority of dissidents have no original ideas about how to transform Soviet society (Andrei Sakharov is an exception in this regard): Solzhenitsyn converts his ideas into deeds. His views are not without contradictions, which he himself appears disinclined to conceal. He has made it possible to separate Sovietophobia from Russophobia, to cease blaming the Russian people for the actions of the Soviet regime. But the very manner in which he has expressed his national sentiment has appeared to many as nationalistic.

The experience of the Soviet Union's socialist totalitarianism has induced Solzhenitsyn to identify any socialism as totalitarian. He exalts the Russian people on the one hand, but labels it unready for true freedom on the other. His grasp of democracy is close to the kind of populism (*narodnichestvo*) preached by the precursors of Bolshevism, except that where the Stalinists cynically manipulated the myth of the people, Solzhenitsyn believes in it. He praises Stolypin and his land reform (*zemstvo*), all while ignoring the fact that this tsarist statesman is seen as having been an oppressor by non-Russians, by the Ukrainians for instance. He is against all revolutions and utopias and sees them as a source of evil and violence. He maintains that Christianity will carry man and society onto the right path, that Russia can be saved only by the Orthodox faith, "the seven-century Orthodoxy of Sergei of Radonezh and Nil Sorsky, not shaken by the reforms of Nikon, not bureaucratized by Peter the Great." He condemns the Bolsheviks for the Red Terror and considers Lenin the founder of the gulag, but makes no mention of the White Terror or of the violence committed by the units of Vrangel and Denikin, the gangs of Yudenich and Petlyura. The believer has no Christian mercy for the communists who ended up in the gulag and speaks of them without compassion or understanding for their faith in truth and equality. In Part Three of the *Archipelago* he writes of the death of the Trotskyites who had conducted a hunger strike in 1937 in the Central Asian camps, and of the sadly notorious "Kashketin executions" at the train station of the old brick works, south of Vorkuta: "There in the old brick works, in filthy frozen shelters, in poor stoves that put out no heat, the cruel fervor and vain desires of twenty years of revolutionary restructuring ceased to burn." The one-time Komsomol member refuses to forgive Gorky, Mayakovsky, or Ilya Ehrenburg for a single line written in favor of revolution. Gorky was murdered by the Stalinists. Mayakovsky took his own life. Ehrenburg wrote his *Thaw*. Not enough for Solzhenitsyn.

Despite all this, the *Archipelago* cannot be bypassed. The moral conscience of our time cannot ignore it. Socialism, in the best sense of the word (if such a sense still exists) must face up to it. Even having known what happened in the Soviet and Stalinist camps, this work is a revelation: a sacrifice of illusions, a "*j'accuse*" for our time, a tragic monument of history. The author designates it as "an attempt at literary research." The work is only partly literature. The calling of the author, the pledge of the man, and the vow of the witness are all combined in it. From the resulting precious alloy, politics is the slag, ideology the dregs. Few of Solzhenitsyn's literary writings rise to the top of Russian literature (*A Day in the Life of Ivan Denisovich*, "Matryona's Home," and some of the short stories). This work is more important than literature. It stands above everything else that Solzhenitsyn has written to date. It is difficult to believe he might write something more important. It is entirely possible that our time, in the divisions to be placed upon it by the future, will be seen as that which proceeded and that which followed *The Gulag Archipelago*.

To summarize such a work is impossible: it is itself a summary of life and fate, insult and humiliation, crime and punishment, privation and suffering inflicted on individuals and entire peoples. The gulag is the space in which totalitarianism realized absolute power, subjugating human will and human difference to its end. One after another, "waves" pounded the archipelago's shores: waves of constantly flowing "social preventive measures," fierce "waves of traitors to the motherland," "*nepmen*" and "ringleaders of famine," individuals who "concealed their social origins and previous social status," long waves of those who, in any manner whatsoever, were linked with "the Whites," "enemies of the revolution," "Trotskyites," "saboteurs," occasional "waves of rumormongers and provocateurs," the "Kirov waves," the "special waves of women" (family members), especially those "who had refused to renounce their own husbands," waves of "priests and nuns," "kulaks," "sub-kulaks," those who merely "did not carry out the mandatory grain requisitions," national waves "of Volga Germans and colonists of the Northern Caucasus," of Estonians, Ukrainians, Lithuanians, and other "secessionists," of Chechens, Kalmyks, Ingush.

Friends and colleagues helped the writer collect the material for this enormous indictment, "providing him with their stories, memories, and letters: the list of contributors runs to 227 names" (naturally the author must conceal the list for the time being). Of greatest help, he notes in the Prologue, were Varlam Shalamov's *Kolyma Tales*, the testimonials of Dmitry Vitkovsky, the memoirs of Evgenia Ginzburg and Olga Adamova Slezberg: "One man could not have created this book alone."

Only Solzhenitsyn—after overcoming so much, even the most serious of illnesses—could find the strength to write such a work. His loud, strong voice accorded with the linguistic and written form best suited to such an undertaking. The tendency toward epic in Russian culture is well known: Solzhenitsyn's is an epic undertaking. One might say that such a colossus could rise up only in that Russia which is inclined to excess, which has excessively suffered.

Solzhenitsyn's political culture is humble and almost exclusively Russian. Perhaps it is precisely this that has given him the strength to carry out what others could not. His national and religious views, his ideas and ideology, constitute a challenge to many of us, perhaps most of all to those of us who have attempted to critique Stalinism from the point of view of "socialism with a human face." But the effect of his work has been much greater than ours. I sense how weak and inadequate are my reservations toward the ideologue (and in some measure toward the writer, especially the novelist) when faced with the staggering accomplishment of the *Archipelago*.

This work must be published not for the love of Russia, neither for the old love that no longer exists, nor for the newfound love that will not exist for some time to come, but for the truth and for all of us who have a fundamental need for it.

POSTSCRIPT – The Gulag Archipelago *was published in Belgrade only in 1988, fourteen years after this letter was written. It was the first translation into a Slavic language. After the fracture of 1989–90, it appeared in Prague, Bratislava, Warsaw, Sofia, and then, at last, in Russia.*

Book Two
STELES

Soviet Itineraries
– Continued –

USSR, September 23, 1976

The Congress of African and Asian Writers is being held in Uzbekistan, in Tashkent and Bukhara. On the recommendation of a friend from the Magreb, I attend as an "observer." My new guide from the Soviet Writers' Union, Leonid Semyonovich, "Lyonya," drops me off at the Hotel Yunost, where numerous African and Asian delegates are arriving.

I request permission from Ivan Akimovich Kharitonov, who has been burdened with the organization of my stay, to visit Bukharin's widow, Anya Larina, and her son Yury. He's embarrassed. He doesn't decide such things. "We'll see." I ask him to get me a ticket for the Taganka Theater, which played *Ten Days that Shook the World* in Zagreb during a recent tour. In Belgrade I saw *Hamlet* under Lyubimov's direction, the best production I had ever seen. I had occasion then to meet Vladimir Vysotsky, the extraordinary actor, poet, and singer. We got plastered in a Belgrade tavern and confessed all our secrets to each other. He played the guitar and sang protest songs in a raucous voice. The Taganka actors speak differently from those of the Moscow Art Theater or of the Vakhtangov School. Nor do they move in the same manner. On stage they are looser, not "typical" as the reigning theory recommends. Vysotsky is unfortunately not in Moscow at the moment.
(POSTSCRIPT – *I believe it was at that time that his great love affair with Marina Vlady, the French actress of Russian descent, had begun. They were together constantly, he visiting her in Paris, she him in Moscow.*)

I meet the same old types at the Writers' Union. Bureaucrats, secretaries, a few writers. I call Bulat Okudzhava, whom I met at Lake Ohrid in Macedonia the summer before, when he attended the Struga poetry readings. For ten years they had not let him leave the country, after he'd signed the petition to free Sinyavsky and Daniel. For "signing" (which is what petitions are called here) one can be severely punished. Bulat's wife answers. He's in Moldavia and won't return for a few days yet. Perhaps I'll catch him when I'm back from Tashkent.

The head of the International Department, Yury Surovtsev, whom

I met some two years before at the Zagreb Literary Colloquium, takes Kharitonov and me in an official car to the outskirts of Moscow. We have lunch in a wooden house that resembles an old peasant hut, or *izba*. "A river view, deer, the kind of countryside described by Turgenev, Leskov." I notice for the hundredth time that the regions of Russia are *familiar* to me; I've seen them before, in the descriptions of Russian literature. I see the country through literature. (In the USA I recognized what I had previously seen in film.) The literary view can be misleading—I am aware of the danger—especially when what lies before us is not a landscape but a society, not sights but events.

Two officers sit at the next table. At the other end of the room is some sort of a delegation. My hosts talk about print runs and royalties, noting that "in Yugoslavia Russian works are not translated much." I try to explain how we parted ways when the battle against Zhdanovism began in Yugoslavia. Surovtsev expresses surprise at the word: "Zhdanov helped writers." In 1939 he argued that the "law" be respected and that the unjustly accused be released from prison. I object to this presentation of the facts. It was a two-faced Stalinist game: first condemn the innocent, then pretend to defend them. Zhdanov took part in the game, sometimes led it. His condemnation of Anna Akhmatova in 1946 as a "whore" and a "nun," his attacks on Shostakovich, Sergei Prokofiev, Zoshchenko, and so on, nothing could forgive all that. Kharitonov looks off to the side in silence. I repeat how great a shame it is, and not just for literature, that the work undertaken by the Twentieth Party Congress has been halted. The Soviet Union is losing the trust of many members of West European communist parties. Surovtsev has an altogether pragmatic response: "We're creating great things here now. Why should one burden oneself with what used to be? What end does stirring up (*volnovat'*) the people of this huge country serve?"

I tell them with what difficulty we managed to publish several of Trotsky's works in Yugoslavia. The Soviet diplomats filed protest after protest in an attempt to convince the Yugoslav authorities to prevent it. My hosts have never read anything by Lev Davidovich. I recommend *Literature and Revolution*. Surovtsev maintains that Trotsky's ideas are similar to those of the Chinese "Cultural Revolution." I ask him which ones. He's writing a doctoral dissertation in which he'll be working out that very question. The discussion goes no further. He gives me a pamphlet he has written, "People of Art and Science in the Contemporary Novel," and signs the cover.

September 25, 1976

A portion of the route to the Arkhangel'sk Palace follows the Moscow River. I examine the landscape once more: woods along the bank, willows, dunes, a few pines. I won't describe them. It's been done by others. Near Yusupov Castle stands a small church to which the Tretyakov Gallery consigned some of its icons from the seventeenth and eighteenth centuries (from the Ushakov school). A restorer who looks like a young priest is inside. "Our leaders and the Party have made possible the restoration of many monuments in our great land, even of the church you are about to visit." So it begins. Our guide, who comes from territory that previously belonged to Poland, smiles good-naturedly.

We return by way of Zhukovka, where the most highly placed leaders' dachas are found. As a rule they don't bring foreigners here, but for me, says my driver, they'll make an exception. "Comrade Stalin had two dachas, one here in Zhukovka, the other in a Moscow suburb." We stop near some specialty stores, where one can purchase imported goods. I ask them to keep going. Poor Kharitonov is embarrassed. I console him by saying that Comrade Tito too spends the summer with his cohorts in luxurious villas on Brioni Island. "Real socialism."

A "special" evening performance at the Obraztsov Puppet Theater, a synthesis of brilliant imagination and good taste. In a scene entitled "A Choral Choir," small paper singers cry out "Vitamins, vitamins!", opening and closing their mouths in unison, waving their arms and crunching their teeth. They are parodying collectivist art. A slogan is painted on the wall: "The Writers' Union Seeks the Classics." I return to the hotel, once again consoled. I keep repeating the word but find none better. Being consoled here substitutes for being happy.

They won't let me into the hotel. Young people in a throng at the entrance are trying to push their way in. The porters shove them back. I can't tell what's going on. There's music in the main hall and dancing. The city has few entertainment spots. They let me in only when I show the pass that I must carry in place of my passport. "Papers!"

The *Pravda* editorial of September 25 is devoted to the theater. It bears no resemblance whatsoever to what I saw last night: "The new season begins; the workers of Soviet theater orient themselves to the historic resolutions of the Twenty-fifth Party Congress. The high evaluation given in the report of Comrade Leonid Brezhnev regarding the efforts of the artistic intelligentsia and its role in the construction of communism gives wings (*okryliaet*) to the masters of the stage, to those who dedicate themselves to the heroic achievements of the Party's and the people's revolutionary history... Cultural organs, the Writers' Union of the USSR, regional theatrical organizations, and Party organizations of creative collectivities are all encouraged to maintain a constant awareness of this." And so on and so forth, all delivered in the same party-militaristic idiom. This was the mode of expression of Andrei Zhdanov, whom members of the Writers' Union continue to defend. To be sure, it is no longer necessary to heed such directives as it once was. Measures taken against the inattentive are less severe.

Moscow, September 26, 1976

We walked to the Tretyakov Gallery because there were no available cars at the Writers' Union due to the number of delegations visiting Moscow. Near the station I encounter a large number of people rushing toward a kind of fair (*iarmarka*). Tens of thousands, perhaps more, push forward and hurry, meet and disperse, form lines, call out to husbands, wives. It's an indescribable throng. They've improvised stands under the eaves; people have come from all over to sell all kinds of things, books among them. I buy an issue of *Lef* from 1923, which costs thirty rubles, almost an entire month's pay for Aunt Tusya. An old (uncensored) edition of Dostoevsky costs three hundred. I try to make out individuals amidst the crowd. Our eyes meet: they turn away as if in embarrassment. Is it because I'm seeing them in this kind of place?

I have constantly come across people carrying empty bags in Moscow. I ask my guide what they are for. "To buy something, just in case." There isn't enough of anything. If something's available today, you can't be sure it will be tomorrow. The same kind of daily life (*byt*) that was so thoroughly discussed during the Revolution, and to which was attributed a marked social and moral value then, is now offensive and humiliating. Poverty on the one hand, pressing demand on the other. A wretchedness in which the noble remnants of modesty disappear. The authorities have exhausted the people with their ambition; people could not care less about "historical tasks." The truth of life has been sacrificed to the notion of progress, while those in power have attempted to fill the void left in both by recourse to rhetoric without content. They have allowed neither economy nor culture an existence independent of ideology and politics. They have left to the "working people" the consolation of being able to work little. And on their own the people have acquired the right to steal. Work has been deprived of value. Quantity has taken precedence over quality, just as the collective has taken precedence over the individual. Among the Russian people, since antiquity, belonging to a community was more marked than belonging to society. Bolshevik theory and praxis imposed itself on this basis, subordinating a communitarian to an overdrawn social foundation of life. The faces I see lead me to such thoughts.

The throng that rushes toward the fair does not ask for much. Many console themselves with the simple fact that today it is better than before. They recall "how it was" in the war years and just after. Everyone compares with his past without seeing what is contemporary for the rest of the world. "Idolatry of the future is the product of a bad past," wrote a certain Russian religious philosopher. It has been some time since the people believed in the "sunny future" promised to them by the authorities. And the authorities themselves, do they believe? The notion of how the "virtues of the Russian people have been freed of earthly interests" is unconvincing. Time and the realities of life have destroyed these so-called virtues.

Does something that might be called "public opinion" exist among this people? Those who *know* what is happening are few and far between, cloistered in their private worlds. Many *sense* that there is "something out of place," that they are as if standing in a line, waiting. They honestly don't know either why they are standing or what they are waiting for. Among the individual communities that constitute the people as a whole, a consciousness of loss has spread to some degree. The authorities are maintaining surveillance over this consciousness, not letting it become public opinion.

Even at the Tretyakov there is a long line. We go in without waiting, as our guide has pronounced the word "delegation." I'm beginning to be embarrassed, not because they open doors for us everywhere, but because I'm getting used to it.

At last I see paintings I've known only from reproductions. Some are so different in the original that I have the impression I was tricked. Some are better, others worse: from Rublev to Realism, the antique icons to Repin, the "Cossak Franz Hals," Malyavin's "Russian Jordaens." Like Russian history, Russian painting developed slowly and with difficulty.

The breaks are most notable: there has not always been history here. Modern art is kept elsewhere. A considerable portion is hidden away in museum and gallery basements. Recently a bulldozer cleared "decadent paintings of the modernists" from a sidewalk. Bulldozer as art critic. Not even Zhdanov thought of that! Still it's better than the gulag.

Contemporary portraits take the place of modern art in the Tretyakov: General Secretary Brezhnev in a field marshal's uniform with several rows of colorful braids and layered medals, the work of the "meritorious artist" Popov. There is one still worse, the work of the "meritorious" Nalbandyan. I don't hide the smile on my face from the guide. He says nothing.

We set out toward the old Arbat and encounter a line. Watermelons for sale. Lyonya Simonovich approaches the salesperson: "Delegation." We obtain our watermelon without waiting. I don't even taste it. I've seen the way the women in the line look at us.

In the evening I attend a performance of Miroslav Krleža's *The Glembais* at the Vakhtanov Theater. I promised the author I would see whether there were spectators and how the play, which the Russians put on in Zagreb, was received here. The audience is large, the impression favorable. I'll cheer up the old man, an incurable Russophile.

I sent a telegram to Nikolai Kiselev, asking to meet. He came to pick me up at the hotel and took me to a suburb called Kazanets krasny. He lives far away so we took a local train. The streets are muddy and, in the dark, dangerous. A friend is visiting the Kiselevs, Aleksander Alekseyevich Vekhov, an engineer who is studying astrophysics, a handsome, intelligent young man. Kolya is more distracted than his usual kind, slow self. "Aleksander has joined our Christian group. He's been baptized and was married in church. He prays with us." For the time being he's had to remain in the Party. "Freeing yourself from the Party is not so easy here." Kolya has a spiritual guide, Father Vladimir (it seems to me he said Smirnov), who is close to Solzhenitsyn. He's in Tashkent now. They suggest I should visit him when I go to Uzbekistan. They want to hear my thoughts about Solzhenitsyn. I tell them about my continued efforts to induce the authorities to allow the *Archipelago* to be translated in Yugoslavia. "It will be difficult. The Soviet Embassy is making every effort to prevent its publication. It is a grand work, although I don't agree with the author's political ideas. I think completely different reforms are needed in the USSR."

They tell me that Russian Christians of today condemn nationalism and, especially, anti-Semitism. Priests now tell their parishioners that Christ was crucified by the Romans, not, as used to be taught in Russia, by the Jews. They no longer hide Christ's Jewish origins. "Only spiritual transformation can renew Russia." They recall Christians among dissidents, a friend of theirs reduced to eighty pounds in a *psikhushka* (psychiatric ward) who, in that state, "confessed" to having smuggled a Bukovsky manuscript out of a camp. He denied it at the trial, but his confession during interrogation was judged admissible. The authorities are merciless towards such people. "An anti-dissident campaign is underway by the KGB." I notice that my companions avoid naming names. I understand and don't ask for particulars.

(POSTSCRIPT – *I recorded this portion of our conversation only after my return to Zagreb. It was clear someone had once again rummaged through my notes at the hotel and had probably photographed some pages.*)

We are all filled with admiration for the small group that protested on Red Square after the occupation of Prague. My friends repeat, "We deserved to be hated by the world. We will atone for it." Those people who risked their lives by appearing on Red Square on August 25, 1968 were trying to do that. We must not forget them. They are not widely known. I list their names here: Pavel Litvinov, Konstantin Babitsky, Nataliya Gorbanevskaya, Larisa Bogoraz, Viktor Fainberg, Vadim Deloné, Vladimir Drmljuga. "Hands off Chechoslovakia!" and "For Our Freedom and Yours!" read their slogans. Thanks to these little known individuals, "Russia will be forgiven."

Aleksandr Vekhov accompanied me to the hotel. We waited a long time for a taxi. In the taxi we were silent. The driver examined us mistrustfully. Moscow is silent at night, with only policemen and drunks on the streets. We passed the Kremlin, the guards alert. I arrived at Hotel Yunost late, past one-thirty. Tomorrow, that is, today, I leave for Tashkent. It is my first trip to Asia.

Tashkent, September 27, 1976

At Domodedovo Airport, "delegates" are arriving from nearly all the countries of Africa and Asia, some from Europe as well. I recognize the Italian writer Edoardo Sanguineti, whom I met once before with Vasko Popa in Vršac. I've read his *Capriccio italiano*, as well as his articles and poetry. We approach each other spontaneously and quickly become friends. Edoardo is pale and anxious. Neofascists beat up his seventeen year-old son in Genoa. He's a sensitive boy. "He's still being treated for shock." I think of my interlocutors from the night before, of the humiliation they have undergone here, and of the Left to which Sanguineti and his son belong there. Here and there—two different measures.

We fly over the Volga, the Urals, the Aral Sea. For most of our flight, the sky below is covered in fog, but then the clouds suddenly disperse and unusual sights come into view. I've begun to recognize Russia from the air, having passed above it several times. I find myself above Asia for the first time and know too little to recognize it.

A bus takes us to the Hotel Uzbekistan in the heart of Tashkent. As a rule, each major Soviet city has one such hotel that displays distinctive national traits. As in Moscow, there is a monitor on every floor. I walk through the city, at first alone, then with Sanguineti. During the war Anna Akhmatova and Nadezhda Mandelshtam both lived here for a time after being evacuated from Leningrad. Together they "destroyed" the poetry that, in the hope of saving himself, Osip had dedicated to the construction of the Belomor Canal. I wonder where they lived, what streets they used to pass.

The city has changed since the recent earthquake. It's been renovated, though ruins are still visible. Sanguineti tells me about his son, a member of the Communist Youth organization. He asked his father to buy him a small Lenin or Stalin bust while in the USSR. Edoardo is not a member of the Italian Communist Party but he's followed their line since 1968. He is a candidate on the "Party list" for the elections. He can "do more for the Party" that way than as an ordinary member.

In Sanguineti I see the writer who continues to associate the avant-garde in art with the avant-garde in politics. Communism, meanwhile, is no longer the political avant-garde. I don't hide from him the impressions gleaned from my two previous visits to the Soviet Union, though I do refrain from telling him everything I think: I don't want to offend him, especially not in his present state, after what happened to his son. He listens to me but makes it clear he does not agree. We both see the differences in our positions, which become clear during our exchange. We come to a stop in front of an immense, badly executed portrait of Brezhnev, some sixty feet high. The large letters beneath him spell out: "The Soviet People know that where lies the Party, there lies success, victory." I translate the text for Sanguineti and add, "If the Soviets already know it, why drill it into them like this?" He's not put off. He admits the portrait is not very good. "Propaganda doesn't serve the same function today as it did in the time of Lenin and Stalin. But would a Coca Cola ad be better?" I don't accept such a comparison. I want neither Coca-Cola ads nor propaganda. As for Stalin, I see him as one of the darkest figures in history.

Edoardo sees things differently. In his opinion Stalin belongs to the strong personalities—both positive and negative—of a certain epoch: Mussolini, Hitler, Churchill, de Gaulle, Franco, Tito, Mao, Stalin. Each time has its own needs, even its own fixed necessities (we're speaking Italian, though I use some French words to make things clear). The historical processes of our century were articulated in such a way, they favored such personalities. In any case, we'll find no answers by ruminating about "what would have been had this or that not been the case," or "had someone else been in his place." If it had been Trotsky, the relation to culture and individual freedom would perhaps have been different, but we don't know "whether things as a whole would have taken a different course."

Such ideas strike me as too deterministic: necessity exists but so does freedom. Sanguineti recalls an Italian communist friend of his, an old professor who, when he was told that Stalin was dead and that there would no longer be a cult of personality, responded that there are no longer any personalities who deserved their own cult. Does anyone deserve a cult? It becomes clear to us that we see dialectics differently too. I use such phrases as "dialectical relations" or "processes" with great reserve. Sanguineti says he is nearly a "fanatic of dialectics."
(POSTSCRIPT – *He would later repeat this claim in the verses quoted at the end of this section*).

We go our separate ways, each with his own thoughts. Despite my insomnia, I was overcome by sleepiness. I dreamed extraordinary things, which I immediately noted down in order not to forget. Monks with long beards pulling an enormous boat. At first it seems to be on the Dniepr, but then I realize it's the Volga. The *burlaki* (barge haulers) pull thick ropes along the edge of the bank, trudging through mud, barely moving. They wear clothes that make it clear they are monks. They are all dressed the same, symmetrically arranged as in an Eisenstein film. They strain, fall into the slime. I want to run and help them but cannot. I call out to them but can't say it in Russian. I recognize details from Repin's paintings, which I saw during my Tretyakov visit not long before. Two armies threaten each other, facing off. They haven't yet begun to fight but they will. The *burlaki*-monks continue to strain. Somewhere nearby is my grandfather. I wait for him to come near but he doesn't. Pyotr from Odessa and Pavel from Leningrad pass by without looking at me. They are like the apostles Peter and Paul. Did I really meet them or only dream them? Out of breath, sweating, I wake up all at once. The first thing that comes to mind: I dreamed about people who had spent years in the gulag. I recall the story of Karlo Štajner's dreams, after seven thousand days in Siberia.

I am again overcome by fear, just as I had been a few minutes before, while dreaming. I am far from any refuge here. Anything could happen to me. They can prevent me from going home. I recall Krleža's boyhood friends who came full of hope to this country and disappeared here without a trace. The Cvijić brothers, Djuka and Štef, Kamilo Horvatin, the three Vujović brothers from Montenegro, Gorkić, who led the Yugoslav Communist Party before Tito, my Uncle Vladimir, Boris Davidovich, the Jewish cosmopolitan and internationalist from Danilo Kiš's *A Tomb for Boris Davidovich*. For some time I cannot master this fear. The painful dream from which I have just emerged and the wakefulness that I force myself to accept are intermingled, between literature and reality. I stand and walk around the room. It is night. Will someone knock? I wait for the dawn. The fear begins to subside. What was I afraid of?

Tashkent, September 28, 1976

With Sanguineti once more. I am tired and sleepy. We continue to demonstrate how differently we see things, though without feeling the need to persuade each other. I like Edoardo. He is utterly devoid of authorial conceit, which I cannot stand. I understand his political stance. I would have probably positioned myself in a similar way if it were not for the Russian influence in my life and the Yugoslav conflict with the Soviet Union, if I had spent my youth in Italy or elsewhere in Western Europe, if I did not know all that I know. Sanguineti is surprised when I say that I consider myself left of center and that in Zagreb, even more in Russia, friends "lament" my being left of center. "You are honest," he says, "but not on the left." (These are his exact words.) History has, besides all the rest, confused the notions of left and right in the East, in the other Europe. Western political concepts do not have the same significance here.

The official program begins with ceremonies: a bouquet of flowers placed on the tomb of the Unknown Soldier, visits to institutions, speeches. Is all this necessary for a literary meeting? But this meeting is not just literary.

The climate in Tashkent is dry. The steppe surrounds it. The day was warm. I got away from the crowd and took a taxi through town. I looked for the remains of the ancient quarters, traces of Anna and Nadezhda that no one had taken note of, not even they themselves. I saw the dugouts where people still lived, tiny paths down which barefoot children ran, dilapidated, wretched houses. I didn't meet a single beggar. I compared this with what I'd seen the previous spring in Egypt. Despite everything, the USSR brought more progress to its Asiatic than to its European portion. Its greatest success. Perhaps its only one.

A propaganda film is screened "for the guests" in the *Dom Kultury* (House of Culture). Uzbekistan is known as "the country of white gold": on the screen I see countless fields of cotton; I can't recall how many millions of tons are produced here each year. A plane descends on Tashkent Airport. Comrade Brezhnev emerges from inside. The camera lingers on some red poppies next to the runway. The secretary of the Uzbek Communist Party, a comrade Rashidov (who, I am told, is also a poet) approaches Leonid Ilyich. They kiss on the lips. Together they award decorations to various people. Then again we see other cotton plantations: white gold, red poppies. Bulldozers make canals, water runs through the dry earth, the fields grow fertile. Hydroelectric plants have been built on the Amu-Darya and Syr-Darya rivers. Most of the guests from Africa and Asia react enthusiastically to the film. When one compares it with the situation in Pakistan or the Congo, the difference is truly enormous. The difference is indeed impressive but not the film.

At last the Congress proper begins. First several introductory speeches and salutations, then Chingiz Aitmatov, as the best-known Asian writer of the Soviet Union, speaks about bilingualism as a new form of culture. An interesting speech. Afanasy Veseletsky, a likeable, utterly unbureaucratic intellectual from the Writers' Union, translates everything for Sanguineti. With us is Antoniya (Tonya) Viktorovna Lomakina, a specialist on Mongolian literature, a subtle young woman, discrete and timid. I have the impression that she, like Kolya Kiselev, is a Christian. I am pleased at not being surrounded by bureaucrats alone. Edoardo and I have a long dispute about the relationship of cosmopolitanism, which I defend, and internationalism, whose side he takes. Unfortunately, Stalin turned cosmopolitanism into a scarecrow: here they say *bezrodnyi kozmopolitizm* (rootless cosmopolitanism). What were the *philosophers* of the eighteenth century if not cosmopolitans? Sanguineti responds that internationalism is to the working class and the proletariat what cosmopolitanism was to the bourgeoisie. Such a division seems too categorical to me. Wasn't Apollinaire, for example, a true cosmopolitan, without one considering the bourgeoisie or the proletariat? I incline toward cosmopolitanism in questions of culture. Internationalism is best left to politics. As for literary and artistic creation, international is often the opposite of universal. Here our conversation is interrupted.

We spent one evening at the "Blue Cupola" *salon de thé*, then another in the bar of our hotel. There were more examples of those accursed occasions when Russians arrive with one aim—to get drunk. The poet Rimma Kazakova was with us. I didn't dare interpret her references to Communism and socialism to Sanguineti, or explain the irony of her reactions to anything smacking of ideology or politics. Edoardo didn't give in: "I am a fanatic of the dialectic." "I hate fanatics and love decadence," replied Kazakova, drunk on I don't know how many bottles of Crimean Champagne and white wine from Samarkand that we'd emptied together. We drank like the *nomenklatura*. I was ashamed of it.

In Moscow I had already met Valentin Kotkin, one of the most hated commissars in the Writers' Union of the Soviet Union (this is the organization's official name: the pleonasm does not grate on the ears of its members). He's here too, following the proceedings, watching over them, wide faced, strong jawed, his body clumsy. He makes one feel uncomfortable. When Danilo Kiš and I used to see such people in Soviet delegations, we'd say to each other, "Here come the fat mugs." Poor Russia. Look who represents her!

Tashkent, September 29, 1976

The Congress continues its "work." I still don't know whether, as an observer, I'll be allowed to speak. They suggest that I write the text of my comments beforehand and give it to the organizers, who will provide it to the simultaneous interpreters, and then we'll see. I refuse. To me this is censorship. I tell them that I haven't come to provoke anyone but wish to speak freely. An agreeable member of the organization, by the name of Miriam Lvovna, smoothes things over. Because of the large number of French speakers from the Magreb, I can speak French and my comments will be translated into Russian: "In this case our guests are more important than our local participants." I know that they can omit from the translation whatever doesn't suit them but agree all the same.

The plenary session is opened by Robert Rozhdestvensky, whom I met several years before in Zagreb. I read his first collections of poetry. We considered him a representative of the Thaw, a writer "with promise." He did not live up to it. He stammers when he's excited but not when he is at the podium. From the Congress podium he delivered one of the most shameful speeches I have ever heard. "I don't like braggarts. I dislike them as a rule. But here, standing before you, I cannot help boasting. I shall praise the homeland that saved the world from fascism, the youth of its Revolution, whose flags bore that sonorous word from the very start: internationalism! We have provided aid, provide it still, and shall continue to provide it to all peoples fighting for freedom... I am proud of our readers, of our full museums, of the quantities of books we print... Poetry collections in fifty, one hundred, even two hundred thousand copies no longer surprise anyone here. Readers ask for still more. Reading is more widespread in our country than in any other. Here literature is written in seventy-six languages." These are quotations from the conference proceedings. Those present gave him a long ovation.

I decided to respond but had to wait until my turn came. I began with a quotation from Isaak Babel: "Banality is counterrevolutionary." I deliberately quoted a writer who had disappeared in the Purges. I thanked them for their hospitality and continued: "The worst speech one can make to writers from countries in which life is hard, from continents on which children are dying of starvation, where peoples and tribes are killing one another, is a self-congratulatory speech. You know it yourselves. It was the speech of colonialism. We would do better to present before you the difficulties through which we have passed on our own path so that yours might be easier, to tell you what we have lived through—frauds, cults, crimes—so that you might not have to live through the same, and describe our worst experiences so that you might avoid them."

I was nervous. I wondered whether it had gone through, whether it had been translated for those who didn't understand French. The likeable young interpreter, Pavel (Pasha) Pozner, assured me that everything was "all right." I met Valentin Kotkin later. He looked at me with disdain. I understood it had indeed gone through. I was suddenly seized by the fear of the night before, but I repulsed it more easily this time. After all, I had been invited by the organization of Afro-Asian writers. Soviet officialdom would have been compromised if anything had happened to me. I wasn't that important to them anyway.

I met a number of interesting people. Baba Jighida, a writer and journalist from Sierra Leone, told me about the experiences of a black woman fighting against racism. She danced one evening with great character and distinction. I wrote down other names in my notepad: Bonaventura da Silva Carozo from Angola, Djigui Camara from Guinea, Mouloud Achour from Algeria, Dan Izewbaye from Nigeria. Dear friends from a suffering world. I recall each of their honest, innocent faces.

I made friends with the young Uzbek writer Omon (also written as Aman) Mukhtabarov. He spent his childhood in Bukhara, where he met old Islamic theologians and scholars. It pains him to have behaved badly towards them when he was in the Young Communist League. "There are valuable aspects to our antique culture. People with a crude understanding have disregarded it and forced us to do so as well." He would like his daughters Tatyana and Yulduz (Star) to learn what he was unable to. His wife is half-Russian. Omon is no nationalist but nor is he devoid of national sentiment. He has interesting things to say about borders. National boundaries did not exist here as they did elsewhere. For a long time there weren't even any real nations. The steppe is flat. It does not divide well. If you drive in a border stake, the wind rips it out. "Another stake, more wind." Conquerors moved the border as far as they advanced. When they retreated, the border went with them. Others came and put down no stakes. They understood that they themselves were the border. In the steppe, if everyone looked for his own place, no one would find anything. Here everything is always mixed and mixing. "We live as we live, in friendship." I know that "friendship among peoples" is one of the official slogans of Soviet propagandists, but—while I listen to Mukhtabarov—I see no better slogan than "friendship." Every alternative looks worse, more dangerous.

Omon talks about the writers who do everything possible to enter the good graces of those in Moscow who decide what gets published. "I like the fact that my work was translated into Russian and that you can read it, but I wouldn't do what the leaders of the Uzbek Writers' Union do for that." He gave me a copy of his book *Yillar Shamoli* (The Wind of Time) and signed it. On literary history he spoke well, on politics tritely. He talked about how, under Stalin, the Tatars were transported here. At first the local population was afraid of them, but then they got used to them. "They got used to us too. They live with us. In friendship." I had seen blond Tatar children, of Crimean heritage but born in Uzbekistan. I wondered if their fathers wanted to return to the Crimea and the Black Sea, if they had planted the same desire in their children, if they spoke in private of the sea they had been forced to abandon.

A portion of my speech was printed in the Congress program (no. VI). It was reduced to commonplaces: "aspects of our experience," "the difficulties of development in Europe and the Third World." They have a great deal of experience in falsifications of this type. It made my face burn. I met the man in charge of this. He had excellent French, refined manners, was about sixty, graying, with a handsome, slim face. I asked him where he had learned French so well. "I was an émigré before the war." It was all clear. One of those who'd been blackmailed for what he had been before. It's this or the camps. I don't know how I would have acted in his place. I don't judge him. I won't mention his name.

I'm interested in the general, shared traits of Soviet intellectuals, the so-called *deiateli kul'tury* (cultural workers). The majority writes and speaks with the help of references. Probably it's how they think as well. They cite "the classics of Marxism and Leninism," then the "progressive thinkers" who have cited those classics in the past and dispute with those whom the classics refuted. They repeat themselves. The repetition is seen not as a shortcoming but as an expressive procedure. Cosmopolitan culture is alien and mostly unknown to them. They draw from Russian culture only what is accessible, from popular culture usually folklore.

The generic and banal quality of their written and spoken statements and commentary is sometimes comic, other times tragic. They remind me of the "idiotic" phrases parodied by the young Nabokov on the eve of his departure from the Crimea. "During the hot evenings, Vladimir Vladimirovich would say, 'The evening is hot.' Usually he would first light a cigarette and then smoke it afterward." Apparatchiks speak in a similar manner about "objective reality" and "dialectical relations." Statements of devotion to the regime and leadership, exaltation of the resolutions of the latest Party congress and the words of the *gensek* (General Secretary), are at times so ingratiating that I am certain many Party members are simply ashamed, though few admit it.

The Yugoslav journalist Sveto Masleša recently gave me an excerpt from a text by Solzhenitsyn currently circulating in Moscow in *samizdat*, in which the author writes of the "imprint" that has been placed on the thought and behavior not only of Party members. "We have been silent for decades. Our thoughts have dispersed in seventy-seven directions; we have not been able to call on one another, to know one another, to dispute amongst ourselves. An imprint of forced thought has been placed upon us, which is not even thought but ready-made phrases churned out by the radio, multiplied in millions of journal copies, as similar to one another as twins, regurgitated in political instruction circles. And we have all been so disfigured by this that there is practically not a single mind that has not suffered. And when, at last, the strongest and bravest among us attempt to lift themselves up and shed their worn-out rags, not even they are able to rid themselves of the ugly traces of the imprint placed upon us in our youthful immaturity."

Samarkand, September 30, 1976

The departure for Samarkand cheered me up. We traveled there by bus and returned by plane. The sights surpassed my expectations: the Registan, the Sher-Dor Madrassah, the tomb of Timur Gur-Emir, the Mausoleum of Rukhabab, the frescoes of Afrosiab. The tomb of the fierce Asian tyrant Timur or Tamerlane, is covered by an enormous slab of agate. I was told that *temour* means iron, just as *stal* means steel. Stalin likely knew the connection when he chose his name: the political culture of Dzhugashvili.

Halfway to Samarkand we stopped in the village of Giulistan, "City of Roses." A reception was held in our honor with celebratory speeches (and quotations from Brezhnev's latest speech). We were served lunch in a model kolkhoz. The kolkhozniks have their own hospital, electricity, a public bath, an elementary school. They are also building a technical school. Compared with what was here before the Revolution, this is certainly progress. But not all the collective farms are like this one, which is for show. I ask a woman who is part of the farm's administration whether the men have changed in their behavior towards women here. She responds in the language of the five-year plan: "One hundred percent." There are also Tatars working in the kolkhoz. Some of them still live in dugouts. I asked for permission to visit the *kolkhoz* living accomodations. They are all identical with nearly the same things inside. I saw no distinctive, personal objects. I read a similar statement in André Gide's *Return from the USSR*. Even then it was like this.

They arranged a banquet for two hundred fifty guests on our last evening. There was too much food and drink. Many got drunk. Edoardo observed that under Stalin nothing of the sort would have occurred. I interpreted for him and we made a call to Italy. The news was not good. He worried.

The end of our stay in Uzbekistan. Colleagues from Moscow have made various purchases and are carrying them back in plastic sacks and cardboard boxes. The foreigners either don't notice or don't understand. They have no idea of the scarcity of this country, especially in Russia. Those Russians who have not lost their sense of self-worth hide it. They are ashamed. Afanasy Veseletsky is falling down drunk. We hold him up. He's forgotten his suitcase at the hotel. Kotkin fixes him with a menacing stare.

The Russians have always drunk but probably never like this. They drink anything, whatever they find. They spend days on end in sobriety and falsehood and then, all of a sudden, they can't take it anymore and get drunk like animals. As if they wanted to annihilate themselves. Edoardo has a different explanation, more literary: "Scratch a Russian, find a character from Dostoevsky." We agreed to write a kind of recommendation for Veseletsky to the Writers' Union, explaining how happy we were with his work, how helpful he'd been, how grateful we were, and so on. This we did, to protect him. Amen.

I formed some comparisons of Soviet leaders with characters from Dostoevsky's *Demons*. In Stavrogin, the younger Verkhovensky, or Shigalyov there is, despite everything else, a kind of savage dignity, while with these leaders only the savagery remains. The cynicism of Dostoevsky's characters is not without a kind of crass style. These others are too boorish to be cynical, too primitive to have a style.

Upon our departure we were given some propaganda, among which was the latest issue of *Voprosy literatury* (Questions of Literature), with a text by Ozerov entitled "The Twenty-fifth Congress of the CPSU and the Problems of Literature," which begins with sweeping quotations from Comrade Brezhnev and ends with the moral, "To work with Party spirit (*partiinost*)—that is what Soviet literature teaches its readers." It would be difficult to be more self-ingratiating, more servile to the party in power, than that. I did not translate for Sanguineti.

Moscow, October 1, 1976

Back in Moscow, we call Sanguineti's family in Genoa in the evening. He hasn't been able to get a ticket from Moscow to Milan. He'll have to return with me through Zagreb. We call my wife from the Writers' Union office so that she can reserve him a place on the Zagreb–Milan flight. Buying gifts, I find a record with Lenin's voice for Edoardo's son.

At the Writers' Union I meet Ivan Kharitonov. He is sorry he hasn't been able to invite me to his home. His wife isn't well. He doesn't feel well either. It's not the real reason. I know he lives in a tiny, one-room apartment that he's ashamed to let me see. He's a good person, a philologist by profession. He's still bothered by the wounds he suffered in World War II. Such "officials" are often like state executors. Many are poor.

I call Bulat Okudzhava again. He's back from his Moldavia trip but not feeling well. He invites me to his place. My guide, Leonid Semyonovich, wants to accompany me to the house but I ask to be left alone with Okudzhava. My request is granted.

The taxi ride is long, the streets muddy. The rain falls stronger and stronger. Most people have no umbrellas. I ask why not and the cabbie says there aren't enough umbrellas for sale (*ne khvataet*). We look for the suburban address, *Leningradskoe shosse, korpus 2, kvartira 72, etazh 9*. Soviet addresses have something military about them. We aren't able to let Bulat know we're late because I forgot his phone number in my hotel room. Moscow has no telephone directories. There was one of some kind, I'm told, several years before, but it's no longer available. As we separate, Leonid Semyonovich says, "I envy your being able to visit Okudzhava. It's a great honor. He's the idol of our young people. We know all his songs by heart."

A little boy opens the door, Bulat's son. His wife is out of town. He hardly moves from his place on the bed. A telephone, notebook, and teapot are on a little table within arm's reach. The apartment is crowded. A piano is shoved against the wall of the little room. It looks larger than it really is in this space. We move into the kitchen, where my host has put out everything he could find: a piece of Soviet sausage, two tomatoes, a fat pepper, a bottle of Yugoslav *rakija*.

Bulat is straightforward and sincere. It was a long trip and he's tired out. The phone rings, a call from Vladivostok. They invite him to give a concert there, they'll pay well. He turns them down. He's sick; he won't travel by plane, only by car. Vladivostok is too far. He says he can't live from his writing alone. He must give concerts, but his voice grows weaker all the time. I tell him about Tashkent, the congress, Rozhdesvtensky's speech. He's not surprised. "If I gave those kinds of speeches, I'd have an apartment in the center of town. I wouldn't be in this dump." He knows Valentin Kotkin well. "When I meet him at the Writers' Union, if he's smiling, I know everything's fine. If he's sullen, it means I've done something he didn't like and who knows what they're preparing for me." At the moment they're putting together an attack on his last novel, which was published in *Literaturnaia gazeta*. "Don't have any illusions about them. They're fascists. Yes, this regime is a kind of fascism."

I look at him, surprised, and recall the words of my guide: "the idol of our young people." And here the idol thinks he's living in "a kind of fascism." He was recently expelled from the Party, but then they let him back in. "Actually, they suspended me for a year. Then they removed the suspension. They only pardoned me because they have problems with Solzhenitsyn now and they don't want to create another one. If they expel you from the Party here, you lose everything. No more publishing, you're finished. And if you leave it on your own, they could kill you for it. It's a gang. You leave the gang, you're dead." Bulat is feverish. He speaks more sharply than usual. I listen to him and think of Edoardo, who's on the Party election list in Italy. Not the same party. Nor is the Yugoslav Communist Union the same.

He speaks of Solzhenitsyn unwillingly. He doesn't like "believers with machine guns." He was friends with Maksimov, who's now in Paris editing the literary review *Kontinent*. He was disappointed by him. He shows me a photograph of the two of them together, from their childhood. Heinrich Böll wrote him about how Maksimov supports people like

Springer, with whom progressive German writers are in conflict. But Solzhenitsyn is something else. A great publicist but not a novelist. He has a great deal of energy that is not esthetic. Pasternak was wrong to think that *Doctor Zhivago* was his best book. I add, discretely, that poets rarely write good prose. (I believe Okudzhava's poetry, too, is better than his prose.) On a little table nearby I catch sight of a translation of Proust from 1973. I didn't know it had been reprinted. Lunacharsky undertook the publication of at least a portion of the *Remembrance of Things Past* before falling into disfavor. He even wrote the preface, one of his last works. Karl Radek attacked Proust savagely at the 1934 Writers' Congress, and here they were again, reprinting him. "Tomorrow they might attack him again, and then publish him again," says Bulat. "They're like that."

He gives me an album of his music. On the cover are notes by Yevtushenko. Couldn't he find anyone else? "Yes, well, all things considered, Yevtushenko is a useful person." I tell him Brodsky doesn't think so. People like Yevtushenko are useful to the people in power. They create the impression that there's more freedom than there actually is. He says, "You can't forget that he protested against the occupation of Prague, the expulsion of Solzhenitsyn from the Party, and in other cases as well. That's not easy here!"

I try to explain to him why intellectuals in the West tend to belong to the Left. He understands more than other interlocutors I've had, but he can't stand it when Western visitors come here, are treated like kings, and then go home singing the praises of this regime. "Sometimes worse things happen because of the people who actually understand this regime well. A Yugoslav once came to visit me, Mihajlo Mihajlov. I liked him. I spoke openly with him, some of my friends too. After he went back to Yugoslavia and published *Moscow Summer*, the police called me in, interrogated me. They wanted a public denunciation of what he'd written." I tell him Mihajlov is a good person; he was young then, inexperienced. Soon afterward he himself was arrested.

(POSTSCRIPT – *Some of these letters will come out only after the situation in Russia changes, if it ever does.*)

Okudzhava speaks about himself. He was a Komsomol member. He had believed in communism. Even after he'd lost his mother and father in the camps he had believed. His parents were Georgians, though he doesn't know Georgian well and writes only in Russian. He was seventeen when the war started. On the wall of his room, next to Lenin and Stalin, he'd hung portraits of Dolores Ibarruri, Telemann, "that son-of-a-bitch Rakoczy." He volunteered but was too young. They didn't take him at first. In the war he understood that the Party had "degenerated," that communism was a "chimera," that Stalin was "a criminal."

I relate my experience at Moscow University. "Moscow University is reactionary." And the professors? "Almost all Stalinists." And the embassy people? "Even worse." After we met the last time in Struga, he stayed on a couple of days in Belgrade and Ambassador Stepanov invited him to his home. "Have you seen," Stepanov asked, "the Yugoslav apartment houses? When Brezhnev passed through here, he let out a gasp (*on akhnul*). When he got back to Moscow, he called together architects and engineers to consult about how to make something like that. But nothing came of it." Dear Bulat, we think of our apartment blocks as rather ugly and the newer buildings as completely scandalous.

What would he advise me to read from the latest Russian works? Yury Trifonov's *House on the Embankment*, Yury Dombrovsky's *Keeper of Antiquities*, Anatoly Rybakov's *Children of the Arbat*. I ask him whether the books are written well, which is more important to me than what they're "about." What is Valentin Rasputin's work like? "He's writing some kind of new village prose. There are more and more of such things. It's successful. People read it." Miroslav Krleža wrote in his diary about people who write about the village life: "And what about the flies?" Do they remember the flies in Russian "village prose"? In recent years Western readers have been rediscovering Leonid Andreev and Vasily Rozanov, along with works by Vsevolod Ivanov and Andrei Platonov that hadn't been published in the USSR. No one says anything about them here. I have the impression that they are relatively unknown. They all seem more important to me than any of those that Bulat has mentioned.

We say goodbye. From the ninth-floor balcony my host shows me how to get to the "Red M" subway station. The rain has stopped. There are huge puddles in the middle of the sidewalks. I pass in front of the apartment buildings with a sense of discomfort. Soviet architecture. Two taxi drivers turn me down. I take the metro. There are other passengers. Some are reading books.

I return to the hotel depressed and go to Sanguineti's room to let him know that his Zagreb–Milan ticket will be waiting for him. He has a guest, the son of the Russian formalist Boris Tomashevsky. They're communicating with the help of an interpreter. After a short conversation, the guest leaves. I have the impression he wanted to buy something, foreign currency or some article of clothing, a shirt maybe, or a sweater. Edoardo is the last person who would understand such a thing. Or maybe I'm making things up.

I relate a part of my conversation with Okudzhava (not the comparison of the Soviet regime with fascism). Sanguineti objects. They overvalue the West here. When they come to see us, they're taken care of, charmed. "We get a lot of money here. They get even more there." He was at a reception that a certain baron gave in Italy for Yevtushenko. They coddled him, fondled him every way they could. 'What kind of wine would you like? We have all the best Italian wines.' He doesn't want wine, he wants champagne, French champagne. It's better than Italian. A hundred or so guests have champagne with him. That's what intellectuals from the East base their judgments about the West on. They have no idea how much people suffer to get somewhere. I published my first book with the help of friends who bought up part of the print run." He was living in an attic then, with one room for him, his wife, and their child. What he earned was barely enough to feed them. Now he makes more, but he works ten hours a day.

The stories of Sanguineti and Okudzhava are in a certain way similar. I am struck by the paradoxes of the "idol of young people" who speaks of fascism, and the Soviet poet who likes champagne. One often expects from Russia, from the members of its intelligentsia especially, something special, perhaps a bit eccentric, grandiose, slightly crazy, sacred, and, in part, demonic, all in accord with the myth of Russia or at least the European image of such a myth. Those Russians who possess a good education understand the image and accept, sometimes with elegance, the role they've been assigned. Some of the radical intelligentsia, and some of the Bolsheviks (Bukharin and Lunacharsky among the Soviets, Katov and Borodin in the novels of the young Malraux) were aware of this and made use of it. The great majority of today's Soviet "leaders" haven't the faintest idea.

Moscow, October 6, 1976

On the eve of our departure, we're invited to do a radio interview. There is a queue on the eighth floor. About twenty people are waiting. I approach. They're buying apples. The poor-quality fruit is being sold at a discount to radio personnel. How much does it cost this country to have highly educated people, during their work day, line up for wilting apples?! Sanguineti doesn't seem to notice. Perhaps he doesn't want to.

We'll be passing through Kiev on our return flight. Leonid Semyonovich and Afanasy Veseletsky accompany us to the airport. Afanasy is nervous. Kotkin will surely call him to account for his drunkenness in Tashkent. We try to console him by saying we've written to the Writers' Union. Just before our departure two unexpected things happen. Edoardo has about twenty rubles left, which he plans to declare in customs. I give my remaining rubles to Leonid and ask him to send them to my aunt in Odessa. My carry-on bag, in which I've placed about ten books, turns out to be over the weight limit. They want forty-seven rubles. I argue but it's useless. I run back to Leonid and get back the money. Then, at the passport control, we're told that Edoardo's visa expired the day before. He cannot leave. Again I run back and find Afanasy, who is luckily still there, and he intervenes. Our hosts know very well that such things happen often, so they wait until the plane takes off. They promise to call ahead to the passport control in Kiev as well.

Tired and on edge, we suddenly break into relieved laughter. I learned from Afanasy why there are always two passport controllers: they check each other by turns. One looks at the passport holder, the other at the passport. One looks at the first name, the other at the last. It's why the lines are so long and slow. We're laughing ourselves silly at every phrase, even if there's nothing particularly funny. I indicate the receipts that they've created for us, all in five or six copies, for retrieving baggage, left over foreign currency, reclaiming rubles. "Who reads the fifth copy, or the sixth?" The sixth goes in the archives without a doubt. "For future generations." Moths are well fed here. The production of carbon paper has been "increased by one hundred percent." Maybe even more, but you can't get any anywhere. "Well, you can, but you have to get in line." We shake with waves of laughter. People turn to look, but we don't stop.

Edoardo tells the story of a "repair" job. He knew the Soviet correspondent for the Italian paper *Unità*. The water heater in his Moscow apartment broke. The first technician gets there and says he doesn't do that kind of job. Another comes and says he's not authorized to carry out that kind of repair. The third and fourth also say it's not within their expertise. This goes on for several days. Luckily there's some kind of general service called *remont* (Repair) that comes in only when everything's fallen apart. The correspondent takes a hammer and breaks the basin, the faucet, everything he can. *Remont* gets there finally and puts everything in from scratch. This isn't a Zoshchenko story; it's the story of a West European journalist's experience in Moscow, narrated by a Communist Party deputy, not a Soviet dissident.

Why had we broken into such insane laughter? It's difficult to explain even to myself. Perhaps because we'd been constrained for so long. What was it that had so constrained us? Bureaucracy? Edoardo recalls Lenin's "criticism of the bureaucracy." But certainly it was not only that.

In Kiev. After the phone call from the Writers' Union, we pass through customs much less dramatically and comically. "Moscow called," they say. Everything's in order. We go outside. It's a beautiful day. Once more from the plane I look down on Ukraine, flat, fertile, poor.

In Zagreb the weather is mild. My wife is waiting with Edoardo's ticket. For a moment he is calm and cheerful. Then once more he becomes preoccupied, worried. We embrace. He promises to send me his texts, especially those about our journey.

He kept his promise. We met again later in Genoa and Zagreb. I was always happy to see him.

POSTSCRIPT – *Soon afterward I received Sanguineti's first articles, then a short book of poems entitled* Postkarten *(1972–77). At the end of the collection he mentions our stay in Tashkent.*

> *"...a nightclub ... supporting blue cupolas ... which is a ciaicanà (and actually a tea house) where I discussed with Predrag the cosmopolitan-nationalist-imperialist chain (and its internationalist alternative)...*
> *the mongologism in the upstairs bar of Uzbekistan: (downstairs Ms. Kazakova had just paid homage to decadence, and I had just told her I was a fanatic, and we spoke of dialectics, and she had just told me she detested fanatics, and I had just said I was a fanatic of dialectics still:*
> *because after a hailstorm of Crimean champagne, she gave me a crass kiss right on the mouth:*
> *(amazement all around, applause, etc., and the honest Yugoslav,*

entertained and hurt, calling out to me don't you see that she loves you)...
I must pass through Zagreb; and many things creak here:
... there's an organization called Remont, *which the Moscow correspondent for* Unità *explained to me ...*
(To live through a remont, he assured me, is a frightening experience.)"

These are passages from Sanguineti's book, and, at the same time, the connection between his Postkarten *and my* Epistolary.

On Letters, Open and Closed

Belgrade, October 1976

On the subject of letters, open and closed, public and private, I once spoke with the author of *Zoo, or Letters Not About Love*. I met Viktor Borisovich Shklovsky on two occasions, one in Moscow, the other in Belgrade. I had imagined him as thickset and powerful. He was short and frail. He came to Belgrade with his wife in 1976 to participate in the "October meetings" and stayed with us for several days. He was already over eighty. For years the Soviet authorities had not allowed him to travel, though he had been invited often. This would most likely be his last trip abroad.

The conference organizers arranged a group meeting with him. Someone asked him how he had "survived" when so many others had not. He broke into tears. I found myself alone with him later at the Hotel Moscow and asked his pardon: journalists here do a poor imitation of the sensationalism of their Western colleagues. I recounted to him how Krleža had responded when a similar question was put to Leonov at the 1960 PEN conference held at Lake Bled. "Is a man guilty for having survived?" Krleža, too, had been criticized for sitting out the war in Zagreb.

Here I relate parts of our conversation, the subject of which was letters. When he wrote *Zoo*, Shklovsky was aware that the traditional means of novel writing were exhausted. It seemed to him that "only the epistolary novel could save the novel." He read with passionate interest *Letters of a Portuguese Nun, Dangerous Liaisons, Persian Letters, La Nouvelle Héloïse, Pamela, The Sorrows of Young Werther* and *Ortis*, Dostoevsky's *Poor Folks*, Ovid's *Heroides*, along with the *Epistles* of the New Testament. He paid no attention to distinctions of genre. What interested him was the "literary material." The letter is a special material: "Poetry without rhyme or rhythm."

Viktor Borisovich took refuge in Berlin at the beginning of the 1920s, when the Bolsheviks were imprisoning and executing Mensheviks and Social Revolutionaries. He was then part of an SR group. "The Cheka executed my brother. Gorky helped me by intervening with Sverdlov. They let me leave." Roman Jakobson, Chagall, Andrei Belyi, and Pasternak were all in Berlin at the time. So was Elsa Triolet, for whom the *Letters Not About Love* were written. We didn't talk about that.

Once he had returned to the Soviet Union, Shklovsky wanted to write letters "that were not of the same color as the flag flying above the city's fortress." He was looking for "a certain freedom of writing." He recounted once more the story of how he had written the key word of Russian formalism—*ostranenie* (defamiliarization)—with one "n" instead of two, and how "that word had started running around the world like a three-legged dog." He stopped for a minute to catch his breath. "The work we began had to be suspended. But once something has been written down it can't be erased or destroyed." They demanded a "self-criticism" of the formal method, and he wrote "Monument to a Scientific Error" in 1930. He added: "Still, it was a monument."

Again there are tears in his eyes, and we turn to another topic. "That's all over with," he says. I tell him how much Russian formalism meant to my generation. He says, "It was possible because it had before it, in its own language, a literature like Russia's."

Letters have characterized not just the literature of Russia but its entire culture. Shklovsky recalls Fonvizin's epistle "To My Servants," the "Philosophical Letter" for which Chaadaev was labeled "insane"—a serious warning to Russia. Karamzin's *Letters of a Russian Traveler* helped form the literary language." On one side, Herzen's *Letters to an Old Friend*, which attacked the traditional order, on the other, Gogol's *Selected Passages from a Correspondence with Friends*, which defended it. The letter in which Belinsky subsequently attacked Gogol was "a turning point." Viktor Borisovich's memory serves him well. He enumerates letters and exchanges from twentieth-century Russia: the *Correspondence from Two Corners*, "exchanged by Vyacheslav Ivanov and Mikhail Gershenzon from two sides of the same hospital room" in 1920 Moscow. The letters of Kuprin to Lunacharsky ("Lunacharsky could not satisfy Kuprin's demands; not even his own were satisfied."). Gorky's letter to Anatole France during the anti-SR proceedings in 1922: "I don't know whether that letter has survived." The letters of Mikhail Bulgakov and Yevgeny Zamyatin asking Stalin's permission to leave the country, those of Boris Pilnyak, Bely, Akhmatova, Zoshchenko, Libedinsky, Lili Brik, and so many others, asking his permission to stay. Pasternak's letter to Khrushchev, which, "despite everything, was published in *Pravda.*"

I add: the death-bed letter of Lenin, which he did not dare publish or even read before the other Party members, Bukharin's "letter to future generations," which Anya Larina memorized before destroying, the fourteen letters of *The Philosophy of Equality,* in which Nicholas Berdyaev settled accounts with the ideals of the Revolution; the letters of Marina Tsvetaeva, which never reached Russia; her daughter Ariadna's letters to Pasternak from Siberia...

"So many letters in bottles tossed into the sea," says Shklovsky. Some of them are still riding the waves. The intelligentsia's habit of writing letters for public opinion, the desire that letters written to friends or enemies should one day, sooner or later, appear in print, is not easy to explain. Without epistolary writing it is impossible to imagine literature as a whole, Russian or any other.

POSTSCRIPT – *Before, and especially after this conversation, I reflected on letters from our time and on the consequences to their authors. The letters "to the Leaders of the Soviet Union" written by Solzhenitsyn, Sakharov, Medvedev, and others. The letters written from prison by Sinyavsky, Michnik, Havel, and many, many more. Letters from the gulag that rarely made it to their addressees. The numerous letter-denunciations that, once made accessible, will testify to the tragedy of human nature. Letter-petitions, written out of courage or naiveté, that defended the victims of injustice. Personal or group letters that have proclaimed major events and shifts of history. The "Memorandum" of Hungarian writers sent to the Party's Central Committee on November 2, 1955, in anticipation of the Budapest uprising. The "2000 Words" on the eve of the Prague Spring. The protest letter of Jacek Kuron and Karol Modzelewski to Warsaw in 1965. The "Declaration" of Slovene intellectuals in 1966. The "Declaration on the Croatian Literary Language" in Zagreb, and the "Proposal for Consideration" in Belgrade in 1967, which marked the beginning of Yugoslavia's disintegration. The 1988 "Open Letter of Polish Intellectuals to the Representatives of Soviet Scholarship and Culture," which upheld glasnost and called for the recognition of the crimes committed at Katyn. The "Charter '77" on the eve of "Real Socialism's" fall. The émigré letter to Gorbachev at the beginning of perestroika. All these were "open letters."*

While certainly suffering like the young and enamored Shklovsky, writers of "letters not about love" are more fortunate than those who address the powerful. Postkarten *or open letters might be the "material" Shklovsky had in mind for poetry or travel books, memoirs or novels. One of Okudzhava's poems ends with the lines, "Why do we write in blood on the sand? Nature has no need of our letters." We write them nevertheless.*

After my conversation with Shklovsky, it occurred to me that the old epistolary form might still be of use. I thought about the pieces of correspondence that form a whole, about the reading of letters from the New Testament, which, in the monasteries of the Mediterranean, are called, precisely, epistolary. Some of these letters were written as appeals, some as prayers. The breviary and the epistolary are related forms: my Mediterranean *and this* Eastern Epistolary *were written in parallel.*

Kolyma

The region of Kolyma, which is nicknamed "the fantastic planet," lies in the North-East of Asia. There a "special camp" is located, the most terrible of them all. It was referred to as "Auschwitz without the ovens."

Kolyma is "the largest, most famous island," writes Solzhenitsyn at the beginning of The Gulag Archipelago, "the pole of greatest cruelty in the wondrous world known as the gulag. While geography formed it into an archipelago, psychology has rendered it an entire continent. It is a nearly invisible land, nearly impalpable. It is populated by prisoners."

Rich gold deposits are found here, and mines excavated by the detainees. How many never returned is unknown. It is believed that the poet Osip Mandelshtam disappeared here. Varlam Shalamov, the author of Kolyma Tales, spent fifteen years in this place "too horrifying to be true." The writer feared that no one who had never been in the camp would understand his stories. What of the prisoners survived? "Human refuse," "carcasses," "carrion." The inmates were distinguished from one another as "regular," "political," "criminal," "semi-free," condemned according to various paragraphs, 1, 101, 1,001, 10,001. They were watched over by "guides," "custodians," "guards," "supervisors," "investigators," and others, dogs and bedbugs among them.

On its landward side Kolyma is closed in by mountains, ice, and taiga. Winter lasts more than eight months; the temperature dips below minus seventy-five degrees Fahrenheit. During the brief summer, swarms of mosquitoes chew at the inmates faces: summer is worse than winter. One cannot run away from Kolyma in any season. The Siberian ice protects the cadavers from decay for centuries. The Kolyma Tales preserve their memory.

Shalamov survived Kolyma and returned home but remained "poisoned by the Far North." He promised himself to forget nothing: he strove to overcome the human capacity for forgetting. In this way he conquered himself and the Kolyma he carried inside.

Several times over the years following his return, he made trips back to

Magadan, the capital of Kolyma. He wanted to convince himself that what he remembered had really happened. He asked himself the same question again and again, and responded in the same way. Were those who survived heroes? No, not heroes, he answered. They were martyrs.

The author of Kolyma Tales was "rehabilitated" but lost his hearing and sight. To the rare friends who visited him in the home for the elderly, whom he recognized by touching their palms, he narrated pieces of his stories. They wrote them down and preserved them.

I was not able to meet him during any of my stays in the USSR. They tossed him into a psychiatric clinic, where he soon died. He was buried in a Moscow cemetery, without ceremony, in the heart of winter 1982. His stories were already circulating the country in manuscript and being translated in the outside world. With the help of friends, I was able to read a portion of Shalamov's notes, in one of which he wrote: "I don't believe in literature. I don't believe in its power to make a person better. The experience of Russian humanistic literature led, before my very eyes, to the bloodiest oppressions of the twentieth century."

Thus spoke Varlam Shalamov.

To Varlam Shalomov

Zagreb, July 20, 1976

Dear Varlam Tikhonovich,

I hope to have the opportunity of meeting you next autumn in Moscow. I have asked my friends to give you this letter beforehand. I am afraid that my emotions might get the better of me and prevent me from saying all I would like.

It is hard to convey just how much your *Kolyma Tales* have meant to us, especially to those of us who lost loved ones in Siberia. No one before you has written about it so convincingly, with such literary effectiveness. Numerous testimonials have shown us the material (please excuse this convenient word) you present. We have read *The Gulag Archipelago*, a great and instructive book. Several years ago another exceptional work appeared, *Seven Thousand Days in Siberia*, by the Austro-Yugoslav Karlo Štajner, an interwar communist activist. It seemed to us that after these and many other testimonials, we knew all there was to know. Suddenly your stories showed us what we could not even imagine before.

Štajner (who, like you, was convicted of "Trotskyism") told us many times, after his return from Siberia to Moscow and from Moscow to Yugoslavia, that literature was absolutely powerless before what the gulag's prisoners had experienced. And mostly it is. But you have proven that it doesn't necessarily have to be.

Here I would like to tell you several things, and not only with regard to literature and its powerlessness.

The question of how we discovered the truth about the Stalinist camps and of the influence this truth had on various persons in Europe, particularly among the Left, has not been sufficiently investigated. This portion of history has not yet been written, and one must believe that it will not be anytime soon. There were those here in Yugoslavia, as elsewhere, who did not want this truth known, who were afraid that such knowledge would undermine faith in socialism in general (not just the one that called itself "real socialism," with which it had not been difficult to part ways).

Others, by contrast, precisely in the name of socialism (the one *with a human face*), wanted to make the whole truth known without concessions of any kind. Some of these even sought the punishment of those responsible for committing crimes and for collaboration with those who committed them. This last was my position, though I did not accept it all at once.

I was hindered not only by the attitude of those who wished to conceal or diminish the significance of what had happened but also by the orientation of individuals who, facing their own national past, seemed to take a kind of pleasure in what had befallen them. We suddenly needed to modify many things and contest some of the most established ideas in order to remain faithful to the values that we wanted, despite everything, to maintain. Those who held fast to those values were not in an easy situation, especially when they rejected conformism for its own sake. Those I felt closest to were aided by their experiences in the resistance to fascism: we knew the spirited efforts that sustained it, the courageous beings who took part in it. Conflicts among the old ideologies, exacerbated by national and religious intolerance, had left trails of blood and traumatic memories among us. My youth was characterized by the hope that never again would we have to live through that. And that hope was inseparable from a certain idea of socialism, the socialism that was presented to us as absolutely unified.

This was how we began, I and so many others.

The truth about the gulag has quickly spread, in spite of everything that was done to conceal it, in spite of all the resistance to it, inside us and out. The Twentieth Congress of the Soviet Communist Party revealed little to us in this regard. Since 1948 we had already heard much. *The Gulag Archipelago* offered much more, but to a select group of intellectuals, for in fact it was not published in Yugoslavia, even though all Solzhenitsyn's other books were. I tried various ways of inducing individual editors to undertake its publication, but such decisions are not made by editors alone. In Solzhenitsyn I appreciated the witness much more than the ideologue. Only a few of his fiction texts appealed to me. His political thought remained largely foreign to me, although I held in great esteem the courage he demonstrated in expressing it. His "opposition to all revolutions in general" seems rather naive to me. His exaltation of "the ancient Orthodoxy of Sergius of Radonezh and Nil Sorsky, not yet shaken by Nikon or nationalized by Peter the Great" seems to resemble the very utopias against which he fought. One cannot create a new Russia by means of that which killed the old.

We were waiting for a book like yours, devoid of any partiality beyond that for the truth and the human being. We had asked ourselves many times how everything that happened was possible, how it had succeeded. You gave us the answer: "The unpunished crime of annihilating millions of people was possible only because the victims were innocent."

Reading *Kolyma Tales* we asked ourselves whether what remains of a man in the circumstances you describe is really a man anymore, or, if not, whether the definition of man itself must be altered. These are questions that only authentic, noble works like yours, Varlam Tikhonovich, prompt one to ask.

For this I thank you.

Russian Letters
– Continued –

Moscow–Leningrad, December 12–21, 1977

I expected nothing from yet another trip to the Soviet Union. The Leningrad journal *Neva* was organizing a conference with the banal title *The Writer in Society*, where all the writers who really had anything to say on the topic either would not be invited or would not be allowed to speak. But given that my first stay in Leningrad had been cut short by my departure for Odessa, I decided at the last minute to visit once more what Dostoevsky once called, I believe in *Notes from Underground*, "the most abstract and intentional city in the world."

I shall not describe the "City on the Neva" this time either. Others who knew it better than I have already done so. Many have written about the siege of Leningrad during World War II: the nine hundred days, the one hundred twenty-five grams of daily bread, the hunger and cold, the dead, frozen bodies, the verses with which Olga Bergolts rallied the survivors and the dying.

I walked, penitent, through the Piskarevskoe Cemetery amidst somber music, without listening to the guide.

(POSTSCRIPT – *I later heard Vladimir Vysotsky sing about the "brotherhood of graves," accompanying himself on the guitar: "Here there are no personal fates, / All fates run in a single stream." Banished from his native city, Joseph Brodsky confessed, "It is hard to contradict the inscriptions of funereal monuments. I believe the survivors came to accept the name Leningrad at precisely that moment."*)

I walked along Nevsky Prospect, entered a side street, and got lost. I asked a policeman how to get back to the Hotel Yevropeiskaya. He said he would show me, he was going the same direction. He was a tall, blond young man, from Ukraine. He's lived here a long time and considers himself a native. As we're passing an old church, I ask how it is that there are so many worshipers inside. "There are more and more active churches now, Orthodox, Catholic, even the synagogue. A lot of young people have started going to church because it's fashionable." I consider his words: "active church" means one that is no longer closed; so in the phrase "even the synagogue," what does "even" mean?

At the Maxim Gorky Theater I saw a production of *Summer Folk*, a light piece that Gorky wrote under the influence of Chekhov. The director, Tovstonogov, is perhaps the best in the USSR. This was not his best production but was nevertheless extraordinary. Here the actors can study their parts for months, something inconceivable in Western Europe. This is state theater. In other countries theaters dream of receiving help from the government. Here the government helps more than the theaters could ever want...

The meetings begin. The Leningrad writers appear happy that anything at all is happening in their rather provincial city. A number of Yugoslav writers have come, among others Sveta Lukić, who studies contemporary Russian literature in an interesting manner, the poet Miroslav Antić, the esthete Georgy Stardelov. The conference organizer, Anton Fyodorovich Popov, has the manners of a Russian *intelligent* from the previous century. He is well intentioned, slightly worried. He grows uncomfortable the moment a conversation heats up.

I shall summarize my comments and try to avoid issues that might appear inflammatory. This is not the place for polemics.

The myth of the writer as demiurge, one who creates the world or profoundly influences it, has lost the significance that it may have once had. We have seen how limited is the power of literature, how little we can do to change the world. Writers have not managed to prevent the wars we have lived through or the senseless occupations carried out at times in our name (I look at Anton Fyodorovich, who is afraid I am going to pronounce the word "Prague"; I do not). Nor have writers rendered impossible the "cult of personality" or the concentration camps in various parts of the world (I do not pronounce the word "gulag"). This realization leaves us with a bitter sense of resignation.

In various parts of the world we have been living through our epoch as through a meantime: a moment between backwardness and progress, the past and the present, country and city life, manual and industrial production, the old society and the new, amongst diverse tasks and plans, decisions and reforms. In such situations, ever temporary and ambiguous, one thing can always be disputed or justified by means of another: the ends by the means, failures by promises, everyday banality by a "bright future," the beginning by its end, or vice versa. What was seen yesterday as necessary and useful, tomorrow becomes superfluous and harmful. In such a state of affairs, the writer poses himself the question: how can one be a non-conformist? Can he if he says "yes" to his environment, if he accepts what is being constructed in the country in which he lives?

My Soviet colleagues do not accept such notions as the impotence of literature or the resignation of the writer. Ida Markovna, who has come to the conference from Moscow in the capacity of a specialist on Yugoslav literature, takes the podium: "The writer must contribute to building a better society." Contribute how? Boris Andreeich Nikolsky remarks more modestly that "the writer can comment on what is happening." I agree, but the choice of how to comment must be left to the writer. Andrei Yezuitov, a theorist from one of the local literary institutes, and the critic Boris Bursov, find explanations for everything in the catechism of "Socialist Realism." The Lithuanian Algimantas Bulchis looks at me with understanding but says nothing. (Later he gave me a text on Krleža so that it might be published in Yugoslavia, which he sees as a country of hope.) In the end Yury Andreev takes the podium, a prose writer and one of the directors of the Leningrad Writers' Union. His voice is strong and decisive, as if he considers it his duty to correct the mistaken views of his "Yugoslav comrades": "I am not ashamed of being taken for a conformist when I say that I stand for peace. In our country, one man in six returned from the war." He reminds me that writers have known when to say "no" when it was necessary during wartime. He cites the example of Korneichuk's drama *The Front*, which was published in *Pravda* in 1942, where even Soviet generals were attacked, "those who understood war only in an old-fashioned manner (*po starinke*)."

I responded that Korneichuk's drama merely pointed out to the generals that if they were not obedient, they would suffer the same fate as their great predecessors, Yakir, Tukhachevsky, Blucher, and others, whom Stalin executed on the eve of the war. It was for this reason that the war's beginning was so catastrophic for the Soviet Union and that hundreds of thousands of men died for nothing. I did not mention Aleksandr Nekrich's *July 22, 1941* or Ivan Stadnyuk's *War*, which came out two or three years earlier as part of a campaign to rehabilitate Stalin's "genius." Doing so would have provoked a polemic I wished to avoid.

Andreev did not anticipate such a response. He was silent a moment, then quickly continued, his voice louder than before: "Our humanism is socialist," and so on.

At the end of the table sits Aleksei Ilyich Pavlovsky, graying and small, with thick glasses and a weak voice, a survivor of the siege of Leningrad. He suggests humbly to those present that we should "liberate ourselves from the idea of the writer as prophet." After the shouting of his predecessor, Pavlovsky's words seem so quiet that they are barely audible, as in one of Chekhov's stories: "You feel like as though people are not understanding and you must speak louder, scream. But screaming is unpleasant. You speak softer and softer. Soon perhaps you'll be altogether silent." Russian literature contains the proper words for everything.

Our conversation ended and we had tea.

In the afternoon we took a stroll. We dined in the Writers' Union restaurant, drinking moderately. Everyone spoke more quietly, even Andreev.

The Second World War left profound and tragic traces here. The victims are counted in the millions, certainly more than twenty, perhaps more than thirty. Nearly everyone lost someone close. After the Jews, it was the Slavs that Hitler wanted to annihilate most. Stalin paid no attention to how many would suffer: victory at all costs was what was needed. At every step, in every place, from those who benefited from the regime to those who opposed it, from Party workers to dissidents, I encountered people marked by the consequences of the war's tragedy, with scars on their bodies and wounds in their souls.

Such experiences create solidarity. Politics here seek to associate them with the idea of victory, with praise for the regime that made victory possible, and, until very recently, with the man who led that regime. The propaganda used by those in power—in schools, film, television, a certain brand of "literature"—has not sought to express anti-fascist solidarity, for that could have turned against the authorities themselves. Instead it has fed a sense of common suffering, claiming for itself the role of savior. But despite everything, even in those circles, that one might call anti-Stalinist, one finds little resentment.

A tall man approached me, an actor by profession, with a narrow face and a sharp but pleasant voice. He took me to one side and said in a low voice that he was a practicing Christian. We struck up a conversation. He told me about how his parents had suffered. I told him about my father's four years in a forced labor camp in northern Germany during the war. I didn't recognize him in the photo he sent us at the end of 1942: he had lost nearly eighty pounds. One year, at Christmas, while he and some of the other prisoners were cutting trees and loading the trunks in the frigid cold, a Protestant pastor had invited them to his home. They warmed themselves and rested. The pastor offered them food and drink, a place to wash: "He treated us as men even though we had begun to resemble animals." As a sign of his gratitude, Vsevolod Nikolaevich, his fingers practically frozen, had tried to play part of a liturgy by Tchaikovsky on the harmonium. From that day he had stopped identifying fascism with the German people.

When I was a little boy, just after the war, I took a part of what little food we were given to two Germans, prisoners of the partisan troops in Mostar. They were doing heavy work next to our house, just barely managing to survive. I recall taking them spring cherries. The story of that Protestant pastor's behavior had relieved me from any sense of resentment once and for all.

There are tears in the eyes of my interlocutor, who says he lived through the Leningrad siege. He describes several of his memories with such extraordinary gentleness that my eyes well up too. "We too shall redeem ourselves for what the Russians were forced to do in the Soviet Union. In the war with Germany we defended ourselves. We suffered a great deal. We lost both before and after. An enormous loss." I have not ceased to think about that loss, about all that it has meant. I don't know how else to think about Russia, about all the people whose fates have been linked to it.

I sit down at the piano and play a portion of Scriabin's *Poem of Ecstasy*. One person, or perhaps two at most, recognizes it. I stop, then continue with some improvisations on old Russian romances. They all know these. Alla Borisova, a young, pretty woman from the Writers' Union, whom I mentioned in an earlier letter, sings in a tender voice. The comfortable atmosphere accords with the Russian tendency toward confessions. I ask Aleksandr Popov not to edit too much out of our discussion when he prints it in *Neva*. He answers me with a gesture that seems to say, what can one do?

(POSTSCRIPT – *The review of our meeting was printed in the November issue of 1978. It contains my words on the "impotence of the writer" and Andreev's praise of Korneichuk's* The Front, *but there are no references to Yakir or Tukhachevsky, Stalin or the Cult of Personality.*)

Another walk through Leningrad, this time with Ida Radvolina and Georgy Stardelov. The Macedonian esthete has interesting things to say about the attitudes of the futurists to the architecture of Leningrad. He quotes Mayakovsky: "Rastrelli should be riddled through" (*nado rastreliat' Rastrelli*). Radvolina was married to a Yugoslav officer who, in 1948, accepted the resolution of the Cominform and probably ended up on Goli Otok. She was among the Soviet citizens who were then expelled from Yugoslavia in anticipation of a Red Army attack. As a young Komsomol member, she worked for the Comintern in Moscow in the 1930s, where she made the acquaintance of the Croatian writer August Cesarec.

Cesarec was meeting with Meyerhold, who was quite radical just then. "He provoked the radicalism of those who destroyed him." I didn't expect to hear such words from Ida Markovna. She recalls Cesarec's meetings with Julius Fučík and Sergei Tretyakov, just before the war. Tretyakov was then a defender of the theory of the "literary fact" and held that in such historical periods as theirs, history itself was what contained the greatest fantasy. Fučík was writing little at that time; he had other interests. Cesarec complained that he had written all his books hastily and wondered whether he would ever have the opportunity of devoting himself exclusively to literature. Ida Markovna read Krleža's attack on Cesarec, in which he claimed that in 1941, just before the Ustashe had him shot, Cesarec confessed and took communion. "Unthinkable," she says. On the whole, she doesn't like Krleža.

A tall, lanky young man approaches. He asks whether we want to change money or sell anything. Ida Markovna gets angry and starts shouting: "Aren't you ashamed of yourself!?" We calm her down and tell her we see such things every day and have such people in our country, too. She tries to justify the incident by saying, "Our country is enormous. It has a little of everything."

Back at the hotel, Ida Markovna and I are alone in the sitting room. She comes from a Ukrainian Jewish family. While pogroms once pushed her parents to associate themselves with the Left, the continued presence of anti-Semitism has introduced a note of caution in her devotion to the Party. We take up the thread of our previous conversation, from before the moment when the lanky youth had interrupted. I tell her about my impression that young Soviets know very little about the history of their own country, about Bukharin, for instance, or Trotsky. I deliberately mention Trotsky, a favorite target of anti-Semites. What do today's young people know about the denunciations of the Thirties?

"How do you define 'denunciations'? We defended our country. The Soviet Union was surrounded on all sides. We saved the Revolution." The process of de-Stalinization has unfortunately been interrupted. I see that the word "de-Stalinization" bothers her as well. I want to show her how this country is losing friends left and right. At the Belgrade Airport we saw the secretary of the Spanish Communist Party, Carillo. He too has gone over to the "Yugoslav revisionists." The Soviet papers don't even dare publish Palmiro Togliatti's "pro memoria." This can't go on much longer. Nothing's changing. No reforms are being undertaken.

"What sort of reforms would you undertake?"

I smile. I don't know what can be "reformed" in the Soviet Union. I am no reformer. When she insists, I say that I can only make some observations and ask her to forgive me if she's already heard or read as much. Some things can be changed immediately, but many more only over a long period of time and only provided that one begins now and does not let up.

"What do you have in mind concretely?"

The simplest everyday things. First of all, reduce the pressure of ideology and politics on public and private life. Set gradual limits on the sphere of activity of the state and the Party, separating social and political functions. Substitute government procedures with organizational ones. Decentralize administrative bodies, planning commissions, and so on. Define the norms of a state of law and (I put emphasis on this) augment in citizens the consciousness of their own rights, revise the penal system, eliminate the labor camps. Before all, separate political from criminal prisoners in the gulags, revisit their cases and immediately free those convicted merely for "thinking differently."

Ida Markovna does not respond.

Anyone with even a little knowledge of the Soviet Union will understand that the first thing that must be reformed there is work itself. The demagogic slogans about the worker and the working class must be demystified, and criteria must be set for valuing production and profit. The distribution of profit must be re-examined, while measures are taken to prevent corruption. The privileges of the Party bureaucracy, the means by which "they" provide themselves with special food and merchandise, must be abolished (a reform which should have been placed at the beginning, this order is improvised). At the same time, certain political and social ceremonies, which sometimes seem to be comic caricatures, should be eliminated. Religious beliefs should be given greater freedom, while greater critical expression should be allowed to the media. The esthetic and ideological "orientation sessions" in art and philosophy should be terminated forever: questions of creation and reflection should be left to the artists and philosophers themselves.

I know many of these observations have been made before but repeat them anyway. Some of them are more theoretical than practical, but when the model of the society in question is derived from theory, then it must be judged according to theoretical categories. It is important not to leave to the authorities the right to be the sole judges of them. All these factors influence one another, and it is difficult to separate what is sometimes cause, sometimes effect, sometimes cause and effect simultaneously. In the end, I am not sure that the whole can be "reformed" without changing the nature of the society itself, its mode of being and functioning.

Ida Markovna listens but does not accept my observations. She has an absolute faith in communism. "On a path that no one has taken before, mistakes are inevitable." But they can be corrected. The role of her generation and the one that preceded it was enormous and decisive: "All of that must not be left to collapse and disintegrate." I bring our conversation to a close with the words of a thinker (Lev Shestov) whom she certainly has not read and whose name I do not mention: "The sin lies not in our seeking the absolute but in the fact that once we see that we haven't found it, we proclaim as absolute any kind of science, state, morality, or religion whatsoever."

The next day I fly back to Moscow, as usual looking at the ground and its colors through the window. I recall images that evoke the immense spaces of Russia, from the Baltic to the Caspian, from the Black Sea to the White. Writing in the late nineteenth century, the historian Sergei Solovyov remarked that the traveler who crosses the Russian plain grows accustomed to its monotony and, seeing no points of relief ceases to notice any differences at all. Victor Hugo imagined Napoleon's great retreat across snow-covered fields thus: "After the white plain, another white plain."

The plains are so similar to one another that knowing where one ends and another begins, or which is wider or longer, is impossible. The very notions of width and length are lost. The horizon is the same in one direction and another. I reconstruct in my mind several phrases of Nikolai Leskov: "You cannot know how far your gaze reaches, beyond that space without limits, infinite to the point where suddenly nostalgia takes hold of you... All at once a monastery or temple emerges from who knows where, and you remember that blessed land and break into tears." Somewhere in the distance could be the invisible city of Kitezh from Russian fairy tales. You catch sight of it but can never draw near: perhaps for that reason utopia, too, took on such dimensions here. Chekhov writes of how the person in Western Europe is so constrained that he suffocates, while in Russia it is precisely the great expanses that torment him. He confesses, "Space, in a certain sense, overcomes time. Time slows to a halt." Might not such phenomena influence people's behavior, the formation of their character?

One must guard against such romantic generalizations.

Many have described the slowness and inertia of Russia, the "Russian soul." In order to generate movement in such a spatial-temporal environment, powerful planning and stimuli are needed. Perhaps this lies at the origin of the excesses of temperament, the lack of restraint in Russian actions and emotions on the plains of history, morality, and the individual. Perhaps the sense of property is weaker amidst such expanses. In any case, the cultivation of the land is more often extensive than intensive here. One's energy is dispersed or remains in large measure unutilized. Work remains forever incomplete. The sense of never being able to finish what has been undertaken seems to color the very orientation to work. It is doubtless this factor that has given rise to sudden, unexpected, uncertain moments, which then fed on all those reserves of unused energy. Numerous examples, literary and otherwise, come to mind. I try to rid my mind of them.

The clouds make way here and there, enabling me to glimpse the land below. It is difficult to define its color, a jumble of close colors. The North? Metaphors linked to the land in Russian poetry: a metaphysical, pagan orientation that has nothing to do with the "ideology of the earth"; an understanding of the earth as collective possession, divine gift, of the *zemstvo* as the original "Russian idea," of the folk rather than the nation.

In poetry the earth is heavy, flat, gentle. In the literature devoted to the last war it is plowed by shells, cloven by trenches, sown with graves, wounded but indestructible. It is more of a principle than a simple love of the homeland (in the sense of *Heimat*). In the depths of the very best works a telluric drama plays itself out inexplicably.

I consider my own travels through this country. I look at my traveling companions, observing their faces, their hands.

Moscow, December 18, 1977

I wanted to see Varlam Shalamov but have been unable. They tell me he does not want to meet people with whom he isn't acquainted. He is sick and mistrustful. I've tried to find a man by the name of Motorin, who was supposedly in a camp with Mandelshtam and defended him against criminal prisoners at a moment when the poet was losing his mind, at the tiny station of Vtoraya rechka, near Vladivostok. But that attempt, too, has been unsuccessful.

Sveto Masleša, who has lived in Moscow for some time as a Yugoslav newspaper correspondent, has helped me a great deal. He contacts me each time he returns to Yugoslavia, bringing me new *samizdat* works and other things I've asked him to find. Generous and frank, he loves Russia and has genuine friends here. There is more sadness than pride in his Slavicism. His wife is a Muslim from Herzegovina. Yugoslav nationalisms are foreign to him. He detests Stalinists. Thanks to him I have met many people, developed contacts with the families of camp victims, read some of their inaccessible testimonials. Without his help I would not have been able to write a good portion of these letters.

We meet and he takes me to the studio of the sculptor Vadim Sidur on Komsomolsky prospekt. It is an enormous basement of a Stalin-era apartment building. Here Sidur's *grob-art* (funereal art) was born. The sculptor's face is scarred from the war. There are traces of the grenade that broke his jaw in two. His hands are strong. His wife is kind, attentive. Sveto keeps him supplied with whisky, him, Vysotsky, and a handful of other friends. As a foreign correspondent he can buy it in the "special stores" with his foreign currency. Sidur lives from private commissions. "At the moment of their death, as a sign of repentance for their own hypocrisy" (these are his words), the academicians want somebody to put up a statue on their graves. A large sculpture of his, dedicated to the victims of the war, was recently sold in Germany. A book on his work has also appeared. At the recent exhibition of dissident works in Venice several of his sculptures were displayed. Not even he knows how the collectors managed to get them there.

We talk about dissidents. Sidur divides them into three categories. In the first are those who once had an important social or material position and have given it up and placed themselves in opposition to the authorities. For example: Sakharov, an academician, General Grigorenko, who enjoyed a large Red Army pension, the singer Aleksandr Galich, who earned a great deal from his movies.

In the second are the usual cheats (Sidur calls them *zhuliki*, "petty thieves"), who want to get themselves talked about at all costs, even if they're not worth it. He names the journalists Solovyov and Kleptikov, who previously wrote articles to order for the authorities, the most official kind one can imagine. Then one day they called a press conference, started denouncing the regime, and moved to America. Of this type, too, according to Sidur, is the writer who, in emigration, runs the journal *Kontinent*. When he found out that Sidur's monument to the victims of the war was to be erected in Konstanz, this man declared that he would contribute five thousand marks. But he cheated the German foundation that was counting on the sum. "He got himself some publicity."

The third group comprises the most desperate people, those "with nothing to lose." They are the least spared by the authorities, the least helped from abroad. "It's hard to imagine how they live."

While Vadim Alekseevich is speaking, his wife looks around as if she's afraid someone might be listening. I recognize such behavior. "Still, people are not as afraid as they used to be," Masleša tells me. "From time to time the authorities tighten measures against the dissidents, arrest some, kick them out of the country or send them to a camp, but then they loosen the reins a little and everything goes back to how it was." These days they don't give credence to just any denunciation.

The very fact that Jews have begun leaving the country for Israel has brought a change in the relationship of the authorities to those who "think differently" (*inakomysliashchie*). The Party reaches conclusions but only slowly. It is "filled with old cadres." Demichov, the Minister of Culture, recently replaced the secretary of the Moscow Central Committee, Yagotkin, who had attacked the "disobedient intelligentsia" à la Zhdanov. "They've got as many Yagotkins as they like," says Sidur. On saying goodbye, he gives me a *grob-art* engraving from 1973. I promise to try and organize an exhibition of his works abroad and leave his house once again with a feeling of consolation, a substitute for joy.

The next day, Sveto and I visit the "exhibit of shame," as it is called unofficially in Moscow: *On the Path of Lenin: Sixty Years of Soviet Art*. It is being held not far from the Mausoleum, next to the Kremlin walls, on Manezhnaya Square. The writer who is guiding us does not hesitate to use the word *govno* (shit): a portrait of Brezhnev in blue tones, a kind of kitsch it is impossible to imagine. Then another Leonid Ilyich on a gaudy red placard, then a third on an enormous panel together with Kosygin. They deserve as much!

At the Hotel Rossiya I watch a television program on Mikhail Sholokhov. The critic Lukin is striving to demonstrate that the author of *The Quiet Don* showed "great talent" even at the very beginning of his career. Actors read selections from *Tales of the Don*, accompanied by clips from films based on his works. The broadcast is certainly an attempt, though no one says it outright, to refute Solzhenitsyn's claim that *The Quiet Don* was plagiarized. Masleša has learned that in the year Sholokhov was awarded the Nobel Prize, the USSR ordered several large ships from Swedish shipbuilders. Who knows whether the two incidents were related? I have never much admired the taste of the Nobel committee.

Three specialists on Yugoslavia—Nataliya Vagapova, Galya Ilyina, and Nataliya Yakovleva—have invited me to lunch. It is a great expense on their meager salaries and they divide it three ways. Galya Ilyina's family perished in the camps because her relative Bety Glan was married to Milan Gorkić, Tito's predecessor at the head of the Yugoslav Communist Party, who disappeared in 1937. Each of the women had a similarly harsh experience. The very fact that they were scholars of Yugoslavia and did not attack the country as they'd been instructed made problems for them. When they travel to Belgrade and Zagreb, many of my colleagues consider them spies for the KGB. How many such misunderstandings there are! Too few understand the life of people in this country.

On the advice of Nataliya Agapova, who is studying the theater, I go with Sveta Lukić and his wife to see an "experimental performance" by a group of young actors (*Molodyozhnyi Teatr na Krasnoi Presne*): a collage of scenes set to music dedicated to Stenka Razin, a kind of historical parody with a number of allusions to contemporary situations. The room is small, confined. It holds barely sixty or seventy people. The audience is completely different from what one sees in the large, official theaters. "With a dozen theaters like this one, theater life in Moscow would be reborn," says Lukić. We attend a meeting of Yugoslavists at Lomonosov University. Likeable young people. They look upon Yugoslavia as a place of dreams without a suspicion of what smolders there. As a "delegation" we toured the portion of the Kremlin once occupied by Lenin: bedrooms, household furniture, a worktable, a writing desk, everything modest. "He received a salary of five hundred rubles. He objected when they tried to raise it," says the guide. Hagiography? Most interesting in Lenin's texts is the relationship between writing and action: writing without metaphor, concentrated on the action alone, with nothing left over. "Only Russia could have sacrificed itself for such a utopia," says the poet Miroslav Antić, accompanied on this occasion by his wife, younger and even more beautiful than her three predecessors.

Moscow, December 19, 1977

With some difficulty I manage to obtain Nikolai Kiselev's new phone number. Today is the feast of Saint Nicholas, Kolya's name day. He invites me to dinner; there will be "interesting people." He recalls that I like Russian choirs. "Go to the Church of Ilya the Prophet, next to the Kropotkinsky metro, tomorrow morning at about ten. The best choir in Moscow sings there." I follow his advice.

The church is full. Most of the worshipers are elderly. There are more women than men. They write on little bits of paper, handing them from one to another, collecting offerings. They cross themselves. Then they begin singing an old liturgy, perhaps of Bortnyansky, I've never heard it before. How much believers have suffered in this country. I look at their faces, which bear signs of intense faith born of suffering. "The church of the catacombs?" It is capable of kindling not just religious but specifically Christian faith. Western Christianity has developed theology more than faith, stressing piety more than prayer. Today, perhaps what it lacks most is the spiritual experience that has brought maturity to believers here. If the Eastern and Western branches of Christianity were ever to grow closer, the representatives of renewal would have to take serious consideration of the wounds inflicted on the "offended and humiliated" here. The man who draws near me, singing, probably does not think of such things.

The harmony of the choral singing and *sobornost* (communality): I compare one with the other. Only agnostic resignation prevents me from joining in.

Is the Russian national idea "a kind of theodicy"? To what degree might Bolshevism be considered that very theodicy "turned on its head"? What has been preserved in Russian Christianity, which of its constituent elements? The ascetic, monastic yearning that cherished the beauty of faith? The cosmocentrism and theocratism that esteemed the divine energy? The historical and eschatological aspect, which sought to locate the place of man within the world and the universe? Today it is difficult to make out the traces of these remnants. The persecution lasted too long. The rift is deep. It seems that a fixed spiritual order would be needed to attain *sobornost* of faith, but in this country such an order is nonexistent. With such thoughts on my mind, I join in the song without praying. Russian music lacks a great requiem, the kind that might have been written by a Modest Mussorgsky, a requiem for the Russian people and its past.

I arrive at the Kiselevs' in the evening. Fifteen or so of his friends have gathered, all of whom have recently become Christians. Several are co-workers of the art historian Lazarev. Also present is Father Gennady, assistant to Father Vladimir, "Solzhenitsyn's spiritual father." Everyone has been influenced by the writer. They refuse "to live in falsehood." One tells me of the hypocrisy that is difficult to bear. "We elderly people have learned to hide our thoughts. But we did not accustom our children to that. In kindergarten, at school, at the university, they don't hide what they have heard at home, what they know. They reveal us and themselves." He recommends to me a book by Sergei Sergeevich Averintsev, devoted to the question of "hypocrisy" as a Byzantine tradition.

(POSTSCRIPT – *I had heard of Sergei Averintsev at the time but did not meet him until December of 1990, in Palermo, not far from the cloister of San Giovanni degli Eremiti. He recited to me his verses about "the fingers of Doubting Thomas," the places where those fingers "touched," and gave me a copy of the Italian translation of his book.*)

They show me Solzhenitsyn's *Iz pod glyb* (From under the Rubble) as if it were a religious relic. Friends smuggled it to them from Paris. They recommend that I read Father Sergei Dudko's *Conversations with Believers*, which has come out in a Russian edition in France. They tell me about how difficult it is to live as solitary dissidents. The Solzhenitsyn fund from the Nobel Prize winnings is completely empty. Of Sakharov's only a small amount remains. The state requires that foreign currency be converted at the official rate, which it sets as it chooses. "Despite everything, we are able to put something together. People do without what they don't need." I ask myself where, in this place, is the boundary between what one needs and what one doesn't. "People who have more than we do help those who are poorer than us." Even Natasha Kiselev's father, a Soviet admiral and military attaché to Cuba, has given aid to the Christians, though he is not a believer. Her mother has returned to the faith.

Father Gennady stands and everyone follows suit. They recite "The Lord's Prayer." I stand up as well, waiting in silence while they pray. A colleague from Professor Lazarev's institute, whose name I don't know, is standing next to Father Gennady. He reads a congratulatory note for Nikolai's name day. It is written in an ornate, slightly archaic style, with quotations from the Scriptures. Several icons hang on the walls. The guests look up at them. Some drink a glass of wine in toast, others nothing at all.

The conversation continues, sometimes in groups, sometimes one on one. Will the Russian Church renounce any of the practices that had damaged it in the past? "We have nothing to renounce. So much has been lost." The priesthood was at the service of the Tsar. Solzhenitsyn wrote an open letter to Patriarch Pimen, reprimanding him for serving the Soviet regime. "That is not the most important thing in the history of the Church. Only faith can renew it. The Church must serve Christ." Is there any conceivable reconciliation, I ask, between Christian thought in Russia—Solovyov, Leontev, Berdyaev, and others—and Russian social thought, from Herzen and Chernyshevsky to Plekhanov and Lenin? "The social thought you speak of has brought us to this point. It has shown its true nature." Not only the Left intelligentsia of Russia was inclined toward utopian thinking. I quote the lines from Chekhov's *Three Sisters*: "In two hundred, three hundred years life will be marvelously beautiful and pleasant. We live and suffer for that new life." My interlocutor does not consider that terribly important.

What about Tolstoy? "Tolstoy was not interested in the Church." Is dissidence an expression of Christianity? "The greater part of the dissident movement is not Christian. Sakharov goes so far as to attack us. Even with Solzhenitsyn we don't always agree about everything." Is it possible to see a connection between Christianity and socialism in Russia? I remind my interlocutor of Solovyov's claim that "one must recognize the truth of socialism in order to prevail over it." Naturally by socialism I don't mean the current Soviet regime. "We seek the universal Christian truth. The Gospel is above tsars and regimes." I answer with the words of Berdyaev: "The Gospel does not contain the openness and fullness necessary to allow one to apply its criteria to all life's circumstances."

The experience of these people in matters of faith is greater than my own. I quote from works, they from life. I felt secure discussing literature with writers in Leningrad. Here I hesitate. In the course of these journeys and while writing the letters that followed them, I often asked myself where were the places in which, despite all that had happened, something valuable remained, in which what remained was being cared for. It seems to me that I found one of those places in Moscow in 1977. My journey had not been in vain.

Aleksandr Vekhov and Lyudmila Dashevskaya help me find my way back from Krasny kazanets to the Hotel Rossiya. We talk more in the car. Aleksandr Alekseevich intends to obtain a certificate demonstrating that someone on his mother's or father's side is of Jewish descent, which will enable him to emigrate. Lyudmila Nikolaevna, the daughter of a Pole and a Russian, an ecumenical Christian, tries to dissuade him from having recourse to such a system. But he will go nevertheless. "I can't take it here anymore," he says.

POSTSCRIPT – *A year later I received two letters from Aleksandr Vekhov, the first from Vienna, the second from Rome. He had first been in a transfer camp, waiting for permission to emigrate to America. "They need astrophysicists there," his specialty. He later wrote from California. At the end of 1982, I spent several months in the US and contacted him. He answered my letter immediately and returned the money that I had sent him in Vienna and Rome to help him get settled. He was living near San Francisco and had found work. We spoke on the telephone. When we had the opportunity to meet, he let me know, almost with shame, that he was no longer the same sort of person that he once was. We did not see each other again after that.*

Moscow, December 21, 1977

Today is the first day of winter. It's my first time in Russia during the winter. I tell Sveto Masleša, who has come to say goodbye, that I don't intend to return to this country anymore. He says he knows that state of mind. He's made similar resolutions in the past, but he's come back. "The illness of Russia is contagious. Be careful."

I had several free hours before my departure and went to the Kremlin. Stalin's bust stands next to the wall. I swear to myself that I will not come back while that bust is there. Then I wonder why it is that I must swear to myself. But I find no answer.

POSTSCRIPT – *I received two letters from Nikolai Kiselev. In the first dated November 20, 1974, he wrote: "I consider you a friend who understands me even when I speak in half-sentences, someone before whom I mustn't try to be other than I am." One night he called out of the blue from Belgrade: he'd been allowed to travel to a congress of art historians and he wanted to visit. He stayed in Zagreb only one night. The following morning I showed him the city, the churches of Saint Mark and Saint Catherine, the cathedral, several Croat relics. He stayed with us. His face beamed.*

On the other occasion, he wrote in a tone of friendly reprimand: "Your public and scholarly activity fuels the Marxist mill, the darkest and most reactionary, laden with violence and criminal massacres." He had "blushed" with shame while searching the Moscow bookstores for a work on Soviet esthetics for me. He asked me to find him Solzhenitsyn's new books in France, as well as works "of the Russian philosopher Sigismund Frank and a children's version of the Bible in Russian."

When I completed the first draft of this epistolary, I sent the portions in which he is named to his address in Krasny kazanets, *so that he might read and edit them. The package came back with the notation, "Addressee unknown." I later learned from friends in Moscow that Nikolai had entered a monastery.*

Sveto Masleša returned from Russia several years later. In an unexpected "changing of the cadres," which happened from time to time in Yugoslavia, he was named director of Sarajevo Television, which was then under rigid Party administration. He was constantly controlled, reprimanded. He was accused of working on behalf of the Soviet Union. The truth was that he simply loved Russia.

On February 17, 1985, he took his own life.

Hostage to the Truth
To Andrei Sakharov, detained in the town of Gorky, USSR

Milan, April 1984

Dear Andrei Dmitrievich,

I am hopeful that our Italian friends are able to convey this message to you in Gorky through those who are well disposed towards you in your country. Previously I have tried to visit you, in particular during a previous stay in Moscow in September of 1976, before you were exiled. The most recent news of your situation and of the illness of Helena Bonner, of the harshness of your detention in Gorky and your probable expulsion from the USSR, has caused us great anxiety. Anyone who has witnessed your boldness and rectitude and who appreciates the significance of your position, your commitment, would have much to tell you. In a situation such as this, in a letter whose fortune I must entrust to friends, I shall surely not be able to express everything.

The isolation to which you have been subjected, the pressure placed upon you, the sorrows you encounter every day—all this appears before us as soon as we call to mind your present situation. We are fearful of the effects of such a situation on you and your decisions. I would like to tell you how important it seems to us that, in spite of everything, you remain in your homeland. Your presence there is essential: you are a hostage to the truth.

I would need much more space than this to express to you how important your interventions have been, especially for those of us who have not stopped believing that socialism "with a human face" remains, in the end, possible and, perhaps, attainable. Your conception of the contemporary world and of your country within it—a conception unaltered by any ideology, old or new—immediately evoked, upon the publication of *Progress, Coexistence, and Intellectual Freedom*, our most sincere sympathy and trust. We understood also the other ways of seeing things, those that propose a return to the past and to national tradition, but those we could not altogether accept or support: one cannot revive Russia with that which killed the old Russia. You understood and expressed this truth.

He who knows Russian reality better than the multitude of superficial observers and biased witnesses with which we abound might take note of a singular phenomenon: the strongest and most numerous people in this great land, whom the others accuse or reprehend, are the worst off, worse than any of the other peoples within the country or allies outside it. I have been in the Soviet Union on four occasions, in various locations, and each time I have grown more convinced of this. Perhaps no other great power has ever experienced such a fate. The colonial empires with which we are familiar all seized the most for themselves. Russia has remained poor.

In such a situation it is difficult to endure the scorn and rebukes of others. They drive one's sentiments, one's conscience to turn inward in search—sometimes tragically—of one's own identity. But what one finds most often is only a myth. The contours of Russian culture have lost their determinacy. We understand therefore why many people need the *Russianness* of faith, language, and the conception of belonging, in order to save themselves and subsist as a culture, a people, a personality. In the face of this unhappy state of affairs, you have known how to speak in a dispassionate and just manner, demonstrating to all that one can speak in such a manner and, indeed, that it is the only just way to speak: "To preserve what is humane in humanity, what is natural in nature."

Your words and example are needed by the people from which you originate and by all those who love and respect that people. It is very important that you should remain, whatever the price, in your country. You are a hostage to the truth that is so needed there.

Cause for Dimissal*

Danilo Kiš's A Tomb for Boris Davidovich *appeared in 1976. This novel, composed of "seven chapters of one and the same history," was the first work of Yugoslav literature to recall the victims of the gulag. Yugoslav political leaders did not want it discussed. The leaders of the Writers' Union supported them. Mediocre writers listened to them. Among other things, they were envious of the author who had written such a brilliant book.*

The gulag victims that Kiš wrote about were Jews of Central Europe. Anti-Semites did not like the work. A Tomb for Boris Davidovich *was based upon documents collected from various witnesses (Štajner, Medvedev, Kravchenko) and incorporated extra-literary elements in the manner of modernist and postmodernist fiction. For this the writer was accused of plagiarism.*

To such an absurd accusation both he and I responded with harsh words, he as the book's author, I as its reviewer, each of us ridiculing in turn the extremely tendentious attacks launched against the book, which were likely written in collusion between the Soviet ambassador and the illustrated "magazine" Duga.

The editor of Duga *brought a suit against Kiš in Belgrade and me in Zagreb, seeking to have us "removed from public life," which is to say, put in prison for a certain number of years ("approximately ten"). Students came to our defense in the courtrooms of Belgrade and Zagreb. It was one of the most violent literary-ideological polemics of the post-Zhdanov thaw.*

A lively polemic with the president of a literary organization unfolded, prompting the triumph of Kiš's The Anatomy Lesson. *From the various texts I published for the occasion, in journals and in the collection* Those

---

* *The following pages, up to and including "Confession," do not appear in the 1994 Croatian edition of the* Epistolary. *This translation is based on the French edition of 1995 and the Italian edition of 1998.* [– Translator's note.]

Windmills, *I created an open letter with the title "Cause for Dismissal." It was dedicated to the author of* The Master and Margarita, *whose characters, through an act of black magic, played a role in our dispute*:

> To Mr. President, Editor-in-Chief, General Secretary,
> Critic of Literature, and Master of Philosophy,
> Officer of the Literary and Philosophical Association,
> Professor Doctor Emeritus Of Letters and the Arts,
> Omnipresent and omnipotent
> IN MEMORY OF MIKHAIL AFANASEVICH BULGAKOV

> Zagreb, October 7, 1984

It seemed impossible to dismiss a man who performed so many functions in such a manner: writer and president of an organization of writers, philosopher and member of the presidential committee of an association of philosophers, critic and editor-in-chief of critical journals and reviews, scholar of esthetics and professor of esthetics at the university, candidate of the Academy and academic author, *i prochaia, prochaia, prochaia.**
For years he had consolidated his power and extended his influence, passing from one responsibility to another, or rather assuming various responsibilities simultaneously. "It's like a natural disaster," said his friends and colleagues on the street. We grow accustomed to disasters at the moment when they begin to seem "natural." Such was Dragan Jeremić.

It had long been anticipated that the thaumaturgical Woland of *The Master and Margarita* would arrange things so that the "director of Massolit"** would slip, as in the famous novel, on a spot of grease, sending him under a tram: the funeral would have been solemn and the farewell speeches eloquent.

But our director avoided trams.

Also helpful to Jeremić was the fact that he really looked like a cri-

---

* Enumeration of the tsar's various titles ended with this old Russian formula, which can be rendered as, "and so on and so forth." [– Translator's note.]

** An abbreviation of the Russian for "mass literature," employed by Bulgakov. [– Translator's note.]

tic. Nadezhda Mandelshtam describes a bearded man with glasses, who had an uncanny resemblance to Anton Chekhov: his very appearance was enough to produce a noteworthy impression on bystanders, while the authorities obtained through him whatever they wanted. Our president, it's true, with his stocky figure and filthy beard, looked more like Rasputin than Chekhov, but there was something in his manner—the way he carried himself, his gestures, his speech—something that corresponded to the image that popular writers and advisors to cultural committees have of the critic. It seemed truly impossible that anyone should ever dismiss him.

From the very first, Jeremić proceeded with firm, confident steps. His first book bore the important title *Contemporary Philosophy of the West* (Belgrade, 1952). From the moment that the first breeze of the Thaw began to be felt in Yugoslav culture and the battle against Stalinism was underway, this author was "firm as a rock," and urged prudence. He continued to denounce the dangerous influence of occidental philosophy, real (objective) and possible (subjective). He railed against "the philosophy of Bergson as the philosophy of French imperialism," against "the reactionary finality and hostility of Heidegger towards society and the masses," against "the solipsistic fortress and anarchic individualism" of Sartre, and against existentialism as a whole, which "personifies powerful hostile forces." He mercilessly branded the famous "Vienna Circle," which, under materialistic guise, spread the worst kind of "spiritualist theses," reproached Bertrand Russell for directing "his keen pen against the philosophy of the proletariat and socialist society," in particular against the Soviet Union, attacked a certain Vladimir Jankelević, who attempted to defend bourgeois "decadence," and loathed Russian émigrés like the Christian Berdyaev and the mystic Shestov. We learned from Jeremić that "businessmen and bankers are not without philosophy" and therefore that Western philosophers are lying to us when they complain of receiving little support from the commercial and banking world. The break with Stalin's Cominform and the gradual abandonment of Zhdanovism in Yugoslavia were somewhat mitigated by the coherence and radicalism of the first Jeremić (one might say the "early Jeremić," as one says the "early Marx"), who now turned his interests from philosophy to literature. His lively voice resounded during the decisive polemics of the fifties, making his brisk presence felt.

When the promising and not especially attentive editors of the journal

Mladost began to get mixed up in the rehabilitation of the surrealist heresy, demanding to be "free of all limitation," Jeremić rose up against their "anarchist ideals." "While our people believe profoundly in our successes," he wrote, "the authors of this manifesto are rotten with doubt." His judgments were inspired by an ardent faith and an unshakable certainty. Such was Dragan Jeremić.

He was soon to realize that it was better to adapt his positions to the changing circumstances. In the conflict between the conservative review *Savremenik* and the modern (modernist) review *Delo*, in which those leading the dance were the suspect surrealists (Trotskyites), Jeremić quite naturally sided with *Savremenik*. It was not long before he had become its editor-in-chief. Somewhat later he assumed the editorship of *Književne novine*, after that, the leadership of the Writers' Association, then that of the philosophers. And so on, and so forth.

He consigned his prolific contributions of this period to works with characteristic titles: *The Fingers of Doubting Thomas* (1965), *The Epoque of Anti-Art* (1970). Articles from this last work, rich with learning, have titles such as "Literature, Pedagogy, and Science," and "Lenin and Art." From these one may see how Jeremić's views evolved as he altered certain of his conceptions: "With existentialism, philosophy grew closer to literature than it ever had before. [...] Thanks to existentialism, living philosophy is no longer the privilege of philosophers alone." In such circumstances one must not, in truth, expect too much coherence or consistency, especially from someone who did not have to account for himself to anyone about anything. I lack the courage to summarize his books.

His speeches during various celebrations and jubilees, or at the release of new works by writers richer in influence than talent, deserve attention, but more as an application of literary criticism than as literary criticism per se. His position in the Writers' Association was stable and solid. But, at precisely the moment when he seemed to have risen to the summit, Providence sent... Woland. The latter did not attempt to decapitate him on the rails of a tram, no. He simply abandoned him to the fragile pen of the Master.

The conflict with him and his, surrounding the testimonials about the purges and the gulag in Danilo Kiš's *A Tomb for Boris Davidovich*, was, from an esthetic or critical standpoint, scandalous and shameful, although from a political and ideological point of view it was completely natural and necessary. The more educated portion of the public had read Kiš's

The Anatomy Lesson (1979), where Jeremić, as well as Branimir Šćepanović and their respective acolytes, received due representation. In *Those Windmills* (1977) I analyzed a number of "maxims" that had appeared in a certain work of Jeremić's entitled *Both Sides*. These have contributed to our understanding of the depth of thought and the breadth of opinions displayed by this philosopher, writer, esthete, scholar, president, and, in the end, moralist:

"Honorific recompenses should beautify life and compensate at least somewhat for what has been invested."

"Man is always, most of all, proud of himself, of his profession, of his accomplishments. Woman is prouder of others and of what surrounds her, of her husband, her children, her home."

"In matrimony, an institution which should ensure love (sic!), sometimes love is forgotten."

"From wit to thoughtlessness to frivolity is often just a step."

"Wit can never be sublime."

"Humor is often a method of avoiding a serious approach to problems and their solution."

"Good style is sometimes more a means of concealing the absence of ideas than of rendering them clearer."

A writer without style, a philosopher without ideas, a critic without wit, a dignitary without honor: everything that he lacked he made up for with his titles. When he had lost those he had nothing left. No one wanted anything to do with him anymore, not the Party, not the nationalists, not the Marxists, not the populist writers, not the people themselves, who, it seems, were corrupted through contact with the outside world. The comedians of the satiric theater Cabaret were the only ones to appropriate and present him in their program, along with the novelist Branimir Šćepanović, his protégé and, depending on the circumstances, protector. Woland must have had his say there, his minions having infiltrated Belgrade's cabaret infrastructure.

It is understandable why Jeremić tried so hard to revenge himself on us. Against the author of *The Anatomy Lesson* he wrote an enormous professorial tome entitled *The Faceless Narcissus* (1981), where he attempted to show that Kiš's "modernist prose" did not have the right to use citations drawn from documentary sources (especially from those that treat of the gulag), or that the novelist must, in the manner of a professor, indicate his sources in footnotes at the bottom of each page. He succeeded in making us laugh but also made himself more ridiculous than he could have foreseen.

He devoted a chapter to me, as well in said treatise, a sort of fable in which all the characters were animals. He was not able to resist demonstrating his true nature or concealing his ideology. "Some of the animals considered him [Matvejević] an 'outsider' since they recalled that his grandfather had come from another valley after a cataclysm had befallen it." Translation: "Dirty foreigner!" My grandfather, Nikolai Ivanovich Matveevich, spent his old age in a gulag. His eldest son, my uncle Vladimir, died at Kolyma. At approximately the same time, another of his sons, my father, Vsevolod, was in a Nazi prison camp. There is nothing, Dragan Jeremić, for me to be ashamed of. The shame falls on those who, in this country of differences, demonstrate their own baseness.

People of his ilk would like nothing better than to rid all national cultures of all that, according to them, is not "rooted" in them. It is no accident that in the dispute with Danilo Kiš, he reminds us that the writer "is not descended from our tradition and does not write about our reality. In his rejection of nationalism, Kiš rejects the national character of literature as well. Writing about the Jews, especially in our day, is nothing special at all."

We are not so naive as to miss the significance of this reference to Kiš's origins or to those of my father. Is Jeremić so limited that he himself is not aware of it? He understands, in any case, the practice of denunciation: "Kiš (consciously or unconsciously) forgets to say anything regarding the politico-literary and social orientation of Borges"; Matvejević "mentions Kardelj only once and then only to criticize him." But on this occasion this tactic did not serve him well. His fall was already decided on high.

Woland, Master, Mikhail Afanasievich, I thank you.

POSTSCRIPT – *This letter was written and published well before the death of Dragan Jeremić. Otherwise I would not have made it public. In the meantime, Danilo* Kiš, *too, passed away, in Paris in 1989. If it is true that serious shocks are sometimes at the origin of malignant illnesses, I believe I know what caused my friend's death. It is perhaps my turn now...*[*]

---

[*] At the time the author was writing these pages, he had been diagnosed with cancer. [– Translator's note.]

Yellow Star, White Star
To a friend who
died in the 1980s

These letters could not have gone unpunished. Interventions on behalf of dissidents such as Sakharov, Solzhenitsyn, or Shalamov, Havel and his associates, signatories of the Charter '77 and members of Solidarity, petitions requesting the clemency of the Yugoslav authorities toward the nationalist opposition (*mea culpa*), requests addressed to Soviet and other leaders asking for the rehabilitation of a Bukharin or a Trotsky, a Kropotkin or an Imre Nagy, or of Yugoslav militants who disappeared in the gulag, a letter to Tito asking, discreetly, for his resignation, moderately insulting epistles entitled "Slaps in the face of Guests of State" composed on the occasions of visits by Ceaușescu, Husák, Zhivkov, and others of their ilk—all these writings ended by drawing fire.

My position was perhaps aggravated by the fact that my father carried the mark of being a "white Russian," one who had emigrated with the army of Vrangel. I whispered to Danilo Kiš, "Your star was yellow, mine was white." At times they were equivalent. The constellations were not without effect on our destinies, though perhaps less than it seemed to us, for others suffered too.

In the Yugoslavia of the 1970s and 1980s there was no more gulag. The police were concerned most with nationalists and separatists. Nevertheless, we were not spared unpleasant criticism, often accompanied by threats. The Interior Ministry publicly, in the main Zagreb daily of the time, denounced my "secret intentions" and "connections abroad." The leading Party ideologue, the Minister of Culture, took public issue with my "errors" and "deviations," labeling me a dissident. An official of the Socialist Alliance, a member of the Central Committee of the Communist League and editor-in-chief of a "cultural organ," added to the charges against me a list of qualifying notes that surpassed everything that Zhdanov, Vishinsky, and Dzhugashvili put together could have invented:

"Predrag Matvejević is one of the scourges of our cultural life, responsible for many of our misfortunes in recent years... In reality his efforts are fueled by nationalism. Predrag Matvejević is a nationalist of the social-democratic stamp, an anti-communist in any case, and therefore a moral and political nonentity... He is connected to political crime and terrorism... He is even interested in cannibalism... His theory is no less dangerous than AIDS."

"Matvejević is an epileptic brandishing an axe," a "dictator," an "evil genius," a "sorcerer," a "shaman and a guru," "an animal both pleasant and terrifying," "prepared to give up the blood of others freely," "capable of murdering a corpse twice over and sending its butchered body through the mail." "When he butchers, he does so with a dull knife"; and, he can "rip away the bloody scalp of a living man." I know it seems improbable, but this is what was really written and published.

I was close to suicide. I decided to publish, in the form of a defense, a kind of confession in *Borba*, the official daily paper of the period. Under that title, borrowed from Artur London, I tried to "save myself," though not without a certain irony.

I confessed to everything and more.

Confession

Zagreb, April 10, 1984

Caught in the act and with my back against the wall, I must confess: yes, it is true; I have indeed written texts signed under different names.

I confess to having worked not only for the two foreign intelligence agencies that I have been accused of aiding but also, from time to time, for a third (the French *"Deuxième bureau"*). I require pseudonyms in order to hide my tracks.

I confess to having allowed myself to undertake operations requested of me by Ustashe and Četnik émigré organizations, as well as by various other cosmopolitan groups, who have paid me through the intermediary of the International Monetary Fund.
(POSTSCRIPT – *The IMF was at the time providing Yugoslavia with large sums of money*).

I confess to having spread the false rumor that the New York writers Joseph Brodsky and Susan Sontag, who had read my book *For a Poetics of the Event*, published in France with the aid of foreign intelligence agencies, invited me to the United States. The renegade André Malraux is well acquainted with this affair
(POSTSCRIPT – *I had written an afterword for the Croatian translation of his* Antimémoires).

I confess that, at the 1975 Congress of the Association of Yugoslav Writers, I gave a liberal (that is, "liberalist") speech according to the instructions given to me by the KGB: in truth the agents of the East had become more aware than others of the dangers to our country of a "corrupt liberalism."

I confess to having accepted the special mission of approaching Miroslav Krleža in order to discover the secrets entrusted to him by the highest circles at Brioni.
(POSTSCRIPT – Krleža *used to pass part of the summer with Tito there*). I also wrote my 1980 work *Yugoslavism Today* with the intention of smashing Yugoslav unity and inciting particularistic nationalism. I hypocritically played the man of the Left and even joined the philosophical

school of Korčula because my employers did not have sufficient confidence in individuals such as Herbert Marcuse and Ernst Bloch, due to their Marxist past.

I do not believe I have left anything of importance out of this document but could, if necessary, add all that might be requested of me. For all those who have had relations with me and provided me with their names as pseudonyms I ask mercy. I have neither merited nor do I seek such mercy for myself.

Unmasked and disgraced, I conclude, according to the terms of my accuser, as an "animal carcass," a "rat" atop *the dung heap of history*; or, in the historic expression of Comrade Vishinsky, as a "rabid dog."

POSTSCRIPT – *My Russian friends envied me for being able to respond in such a tone to my accusers. It was inconceivable that someone in the USSR might have published such a response, if not under a false name, in* samizdat, *or abroad. An action of this nature would have landed one in the gulag.*

Book Three
Epitaphs

Rehabilitations

At different times I wrote letters seeking the rehabilitation of people condemned or executed in the Soviet Union, and read them at public forums. I sent the "Proposal for a Statute on Rehabilitation" printed below first to Leonid Brezhnev, then to Mikhail Gorbachev, to the Central Committee of the League of Yugoslav Communists, and to the Supreme Soviet of the USSR. I sent the final version to Boris Yeltsin in 1991.

Zagreb, 1980–1991

It may seem unlikely but it is true: there are no studies, either theoretical or legal, on rehabilitation. I have searched the catalogues of various countries. What I have found has mostly to do with individual cases, not the issue itself. There are therefore no statutes regarding rehabilitation. Rehabilitation is as arbitrary as the sentence that it annuls. It is an eloquent fact that such studies do not exist or, if they do, are not well known. When one considers the enormous quantity of statutes that regulate and determine sanctions, such a dearth points toward the confirmation of a diagnosis: our civilization is much more concerned with punishment than it is with liberation. Rehabilitation nevertheless is an everyday phenomenon. One encounters the concept in medicine, ethics, religion, politics, and law. From the revision of the Calas Process, through the Dreyfus Affair, to the case of Bukharin, history records numerous examples: people are rehabilitated, and so are ideas and doctrines, events, concepts, behaviors.

Rehabilitation may be defined in various ways depending on purpose and application: annulment of a sentence or condemnation; alteration of a decision or judgment; absolution or forgiveness of sins; changes in criteria, procedure, or values. Political rehabilitation demonstrates a new attitude towards sanctions more than a desire to truly render justice unto those who have suffered. It is distinguished according to nature, expression, and degree: in part or in full, temporary or permanent, public or secret. It is also characterized by the hierarchical instances of decision and proclamation. The more legitimate such instances are, the more they express public opinion, and the more effective and complete is the rehabilitation itself.

In practice there are various kinds of rehabilitation: legal, civic, political, Party (the rehabilitation of members, of "fellow travelers," and so on), ideological, institutional, of persons or groups, in name or anonymously, during life or after death. The rehabilitation that history brings is, as a rule, the most secure, but for that one must generally wait the longest.

At the end of the 1950s in the USSR numerous victims of the "cult of personality" were rehabilitated. Such political (and legal) rehabilitations are insufficient because, in attributing all blame to a single subject (the "personality"), they avoid more profound objective faults, those of institutions (for example, the judiciary), of political processes (the Party or its leadership), of the social system and its administration.

Between an imposed sanction and the rehabilitation that annuls it a shorter or longer period of time may pass. This duration reveals the dynamic that is characteristic of the movement, ideology, or institution in question. For example, on November 15, 1979, the Church rehabilitated Galileo—347 years after his condemnation. Pope John Paul II declared, at a solemn ceremony, that the men and institutions of the Church had sinned against Galileo, causing him great suffering. He called for reconciliation between science and faith, between the Church and the world. The three-and-one-half-century interval between the condemnation and the rehabilitation testifies to the slowness with which ecclesiastical doctrine modifies its relations with the world.

Stalinist communism was somewhat more rapid than this, though even in Yugoslavia, despite its opposition to Stalinism, the pace of rehabilitation was not markedly rapid. Serious discussion of the Yugoslav Communist Party leaders who, in the 1930s, had disappeared in Siberian labor camps, did not begin until the 1959 Party Congress in Belgrade, a decade after the break with Stalin, while their official rehabilitation was not undertaken for yet another ten years beyond that. Rehabilitation takes into account effect and exemplarity, usually as a function of the political trend of the moment, which wants to differentiate itself from that of the past. One should distinguish *rehabilitation in itself* from *rehabilitation for oneself*. The first takes the value and merit of the rehabilitated person into greatest consideration; the second uses that value for its own purposes.

The act of rehabilitation often implies a mythic message: human justice is fallible and slow, but there is a superior will (that of Party, state, religion) that complements and corrects it. In cases of complete rehabilitation, not only is the original sanction annulled but those responsible for its imposition are condemned in turn. Essentially, it is on this point that the degree of rehabilitation turns. While some cases have passed in silence, rehabilitation generally takes the form of a proclamation or spectacle. In most cases, the signals oscillate between discourse and ceremony, between metaphor and *mise-en-scène*. The procedural semiotics are more complex than they might appear at first sight. What begins with a simple mention ends with a monument.

Let us take a characteristic example, drawn from a civilization in which communication and writing are based more on signals than in our own. At the end of the 1970s numerous rehabilitations of individuals and groups took place in China. These included Liu Shao-Chi, accused in his time of apostasy. He was a "renegade," an "agent" in the hire of foreign governments, a "traitor of the working class," who had been expelled from the Central Committee of China's Communist Party and subsequently executed in prison in 1960. In 1979 the readers of the journal *Jen Min Jih Pao* were able to discern a characteristic signal: the name of the condemned man's widow was mentioned in print; she had "obtained employment"—the detail itself was unimportant; what was important was the fact of being mentioned at all. The dead man was referred to as "Comrade Liu." Shortly thereafter a statement appeared, according to which "all the accusations against him were false" and his "honor" was restored. Finally, an official proclamation was made in the course of a solemn ceremony (*mise-en-scène*) on February 29, 1980, which rehabilitated the "great Marxist" and "hero of the proletarian revolution" Liu Shao-Chi, and, at the other end of a semiotic chain initiated by an incidental reference, a statue was erected in his native city.

The characteristics of a civilization, the degree of its development, the institutions and customs of a society, the rituals and ceremonies of social life are all reflected in the manner in which rehabilitation takes place.

Communities that are based on religious or totalitarian ideologies impose severe conditions of ransom on the person seeking rehabilitation. The dead are better able to meet such conditions than the living.

The freedom of a society is measured, among other things, by the conditions that must be fulfilled so that rehabilitation can occur. In this regard, after the fall of the Soviet Union, in Russia and the other countries that were under its leaden mantle, much remains to be done.

POSTSCRIPT – *Obtaining the right of rehabilitation was not easy. Earning the right to rehabilitate another is impossible. A person who has for years unjustly worn a "guilty" sign does not accept proof of his innocence from the hands of just anybody. In the Other Europe the question of clean and dirty hands is connected first of all to the question of rehabilitation. It is a question that has more to do with morality than with justice per se.*

Rehabilitation is, in most cases, the expression of shallow politics, and recourse to it generally indicates an untutored political culture. But despite this, the act of rehabilitation has had a significance that is not only moral for those who have been caught up in oppression. This is why we attribute such value to it.

I have before me the correspondence of Boris Pasternak and Ariadna Efron, the daughter of Marina Tsvetaeva, who spent sixteen years in the gulag. "Oh, if I could just be rehabilitated!" complains Ariadna from Siberia, in the autumn of 1954. In spring of the following year she proclaims exultantly from Turuchansk: "My dear Boris, you may congratulate me: I have been rehabilitated… Now I shall be able to get an internal passport and come to Moscow."

But many others, having received the document attesting that they were not guilty or that their crimes had been pardoned, looked at it with despair: this piece of paper, the bumazhka *as Karlo Štajner says, using the Russian word, cannot replace the years—ten, twenty, who knows how many—torn away from a life.*

These are the two faces of rehabilitation.

Nikolai Bukharin

> "Remember, Comrades, that on the red flag you carry on the victorious road toward communism lies a drop of my blood as well."
> BUKHARIN

Zagreb, 1976, 1980, 1988

The question of the rehabilitation of Nikolai Ivanovich Bukharin was under discussion for many years by various individuals in various forms. In 1963 a group of old Bolsheviks who had survived the purges sent an open letter to the Presidium of the Central Committee of the USSR's Communist Party, reminding them once again that in his dying "testament" Lenin had named Bukharin the "Party's favorite." On the occasion of the fortieth anniversary of Bukharin's execution (1938–78), the Russell Tribunal demanded the abrogation of his sentence. Yury Larin, Bukharin's son, addressed the Soviet authorities in the summer of 1977 and received the response (by telephone) that "examination of the documents has not been completed yet and therefore the question of rehabilitation cannot yet be resolved."

In Bukharin's (posthumously disseminated) "Letter to future generations" the following lines are written: "I ask you—young people, new generation of Party leaders—to read my letter to the Party's plenary assembly, clear my name, and reintegrate me into the ranks of the Party. [...] One of your historical tasks will be to conduct the autopsy on the monstrous cloud of crimes that, in these terrible times, is assuming frightening proportions." This desire was never satisfied. At the end of 1962, under Khrushchev, it was officially recognized that Bukharin had been "neither a spy nor a terrorist." And that was all.

The terrible accusations contained in Stalin's *Brief Course on the History of the Communist Party* were never retracted: "Enemy of the people," "anti-Bolshevik," "bedbug of the White Guard," member of a "gang of political hypocrites and thieves," "spy, parasite, and traitor," "renegade," "rightist," "fascist lackey." At the execution pronouncement, Vishinsky added a definition that had perhaps never been uttered in court before, when he called Bukharin a "cross between a wolf and a pig."

The "young people" and "new generation of Party leaders" to whom Bukharin addressed his words did not have the opportunity to read even a part of what he had written to them, but the censures and insults by means of which his work was proscribed, those they could read. Today the books of Bukharin are published in numerous languages but not in Russian. (Émigré publishing houses are also naturally not interested in him.) A decade ago, at the Lenin Library in Moscow, I tried to collect those of his texts that were devoted to cultural and literary questions for an international edition. I was not even given permission to see them.

Specialists have written nearly everything essential on the works of Bukharin. Here, given the finality of this open letter, we shall only recall the significance of his ideas yesterday and today and confirm their presence in contemporary history. The rest, in substance, is well known.

"Leninism does not consist of ready recipes."

"We began our revolution without imagining the colossal difficulties that this revolution would bring. This must be said with great clarity."

"After the working class has taken power, the question of culture at a given moment of the revolution becomes the principal question of the revolution."

"We offer incredibly monotonous ideological nutrition."

"Our circulars and paragraphs are written with such annoying monotony that those who are unaccustomed to them very often start to feel nauseous."

In the face of Stalin's relentless thesis concerning the "intensification of class conflict," Bukharin proposed "civic peace," "reciprocal collaboration," and "social unity." His call for respect for legality at any cost ("the time of terror is finished"); his opposition to the "arbitrariness of bureaucracy," to the state as an "instrument of pressure," to "state monopoly," and "planning as a systematic disruption of socially necessary proportions," his orientation towards "gradualism" and "reformism," his support for the New Economic Policy in "transitional form" and the "development of the bases of *market relations*," of a "long-term mixed economy"—the correctness of all these ideas and positions has been verified in the USSR and other countries by time and by the experience gained through it.

Wherever radical economic reforms have been undertaken, the ideas of reformers have, in many respects, been close to those of Bukharin, whether they were traced (or, as more frequently, not traced) to him: Yevgeny Varga, Boris Kidrich, Ota Šik, Liberman, the projects of the Polish and East German economists of the 1950s, the Hungarian initiatives, or those of the Chinese in the 1980s. The future will tell whether this is also true of the radical reforms for the economy announced by Mikhail Gorbachev, which seek greater autonomy from central planning for industries and more spontaneous initiative from producers. The very fact that such "radical reform" is still needed is itself significant.

Bukharin was a man of surprisingly broad culture, a true heir of the Russian liberal tradition, the nineteenth-century intelligentsia. The range of cultural and literary questions treated in his articles and pamphlets is extraordinarily vast: "The Fate of the Russian Intelligentsia," "The Proletarian Revolution and Culture," "Party Politics in Literature," "The Formal Method in Art," "The Tasks of Culture and the Struggle against Bureaucracy," "Ancient Traditions in Building Contemporary Culture." He stood against the vulgar cultural reductionism of Dmitry Pisarev, and, at a time that sought formulas for "proletarian literature" and for a new kind of writer's organization, he pointed to the errors that bring harm to literature and to writers:

"Our proletarian authors should be writing works, not theses."

"Why do you think that the Communist Party ought to prefer one form of writer's organization over another? Let there be a thousand, two thousand different organizations."

"Eliminating free competition among different artistic movements is the best way of destroying the young proletarian literature."

"Remember that cultural problems differ from military ones in that they cannot be resolved by the application of mechanical force."

"No Politburo gave directives to Pushkin about how to write verse. Think this fact through on your own."

Bukharin was one of the main authors of the "Resolution" of 1925, the broadest, most meaningful official text of the 1920s on the relation of the Party to artistic creation, of the Revolution to art. At the First Congress of Soviet Writers in 1934, his presentation "On Poetry, Poetics, and the Tasks of Poetic Creation" was greeted as a promise of hope. But the gray conformism of "party-mindedness" was soon to take hold as Zhdanov replaced Lunacharsky as Commissar of Education.

Bukharin's readiness to help writers in distress has not gone without acknowledgment. In her memoirs, Nadezhda Mandelshtam noted how he tried to help Osip and her as much as he could. He responded to Anna Akhmatova's request by attempting to save the life of Nikolai Gumilyov but was unsuccessful. In his 1926 poem on the destinies of abandoned children and poets, Yesenin cited the names of Pushkin, Lermontov, and Nikolai Nekrasov, and, alongside them, Lenin, Trotsky, and Bukharin. In 1931 Pasternak dedicated his poem *Volny* (Waves) to Bukharin. When in 1936 the inquest on right-wing "counterrevolutionaries" and "spies" was temporarily suspended, he sought out Bukharin's wife and gave her a letter: he had never believed the formal accusations about Nikolai Ivanovich. It appears that this letter has not been preserved. Perhaps it floats in a bottle somewhere on the open seas of history.

Bukharin's faults are not hard to find. It would be difficult for us to defend today his conception of dialectics, his recourse to dialectical materialism. In his testament Lenin offered a partly contradictory judgment: "Bukharin has never completely understood dialectics," but, nevertheless, "he is the Party's most important theoretician." All the while seeing the dangers of bureaucracy, he overestimated the Party's ability to restrain it ("the Party won't allow it"), not seeing the Party's own bureaucratism. His views were overly self-confident. The criticisms he formulated were used by Stalin to destroy Trotsky and settle scores with his opposition. Gramsci, in polemic with Bukharin's positions, critiqued certain details that came to be more and more often presupposed in the Marxism of the Third International. Bukharin howled with the wolves. And the wolves, in the end, tore him to pieces.

In the proceedings against the "anti-Soviet, rightist, Trotskyite bloc," Bukharin's position was tragic: his accuser held his young wife Anya Larina and their newborn son Yury as hostages, using them against the accused. While apparently acknowledging the infamous accusations leveled against him at this monstrous trial, Bukharin was able to find a tone, words, and expressions to discredit his own "confession."

He did not ask for forgiveness.

He was executed between the 14th and 15th of March 1938.

His place of burial is unknown.

As I write these lines, he has not been rehabilitated.

Just before her own incarceration and interment in the gulag, Anya Larina memorized and then destroyed the "Letter to Future Generations," a portion of which I quoted at the beginning of this letter.

Kropotkin
THE DARK PRINCE

Anarchist criticism, perhaps more directly than any other, revealed the mistakes of Bolshevism and the crimes of Stalinism. For this reason it became difficult to publish the works of anarchist authors in Eastern Europe. There were nevertheless good reasons to attempt to do so.

The pages that follow summarize the preface to an edition of selected writings by Pyotr Kropotkin, published in Belgrade in the Orwellian year of 1984. They included Kropotkin's protest letter to Lenin "On the Subject of Hostages: To Lenin and the Soviet Government," written at the end of 1920 and completely unknown to readers in the "socialist countries" of Eastern Europe. We published the letter before the book, in the Belgrade journal Interview, *thus making it available to "the broad masses" under the title "The Dark Prince of Anarchy."*

In 1930 the Soviet journal *Zvezda* published the memoirs of Vladimir Bonch-Bruevich, Lenin's secretary. These describe a meeting, in 1919, between the leader of the October Revolution and Pyotr Kropotkin, who had returned to Russia in the spring of 1918. Kropotkin refused to allow his works to be published in a "state edition" as Lenin was then proposing. Kropotkin died in 1921, a month before the anarchist insurrection of Kronstadt. A hundred thousand people attended his state-sponsored funeral, the last at which the black anarchist flag was flown. The deceased's family and friends only consented to such a ceremony after receiving promises that all imprisoned anarchists would be released. The organ of the Third International published an obituary.

The following year (1922), the Moscow-Petrograd publishing arm of the anarchist trade union *Golos truda* (The Voice of Labor) published the pamphlet *Anarchy* in a special edition. Other texts by Kropotkin appeared subsequently in Russian, but all these were presented in such a way that it would have been better had they not been published at all. There is, however, a Kropotkin Street in Moscow, and, if I'm not mistaken, a subway station: these are all that remains of Lenin's proposition to raise a monument to him. I was not allowed to consult his works in the Lenin Library.

Writers as diverse in their views as Oscar Wilde, Maxim Gorky, Bernard Shaw, André Malraux, George Orwell, and Emmanuel Mounier have cited Kropotkin's works. Bertrand Russell, imprisoned for pacifist activities in his country during the First World War, presented himself as Kropotkin's disciple in his early work *Proposed Roads to Freedom: Socialism, Anarchism, and Syndicalism*. But nothing would be more mistaken than to reduce Kropotkin's opus to the categories of literature or philosophy. Paraphrasing Herzen's judgment about Bakunin ("history did not find use for his heroic nature"), we can maintain that the leaders of the October Revolution, and especially those who succeeded them, did not know how to profit from the warnings of Kropotkin: "All forms of society may petrify and cease to develop." "One must offer the greatest space possible for the development of individual traits." "We seek the free union of interested parties and not the centralization of power." Kropotkin sent out a warning against those "communists" who, "by the methods they employ, end by rendering the very name of communism hateful."

In a nearly forgotten letter, from which I have selected several passages below, Kropotkin took Lenin and the Soviet government to task, emphasizing their first and perhaps most fatal mistakes:

Dmitrov, December 21, 1920

Dear Vladimir Ilyich,

Izvestiia and *Pravda* published the statement indicating the Soviet government's decision to take members of the Social-Revolutionary groups of Savinkov and Chernov hostage, along with the white guards of the national tactical center and the officers of Vrangel. In case of attempted attack against Soviet leaders, they are to be "destroyed without mercy."

Is there then no one among your entourage to warn you, you and your comrades, against such measures, which indicate a return to the darkest times of the Middle Ages and the wars of religion [...]?

Is it possible that no one has explained to you what, in essence, a hostage is?

A hostage is not arrested for having committed a crime, only for the purpose of blackmailing an enemy with the threat of the hostage's death. "If you kill one of ours, we'll kill one of yours." Is this not the same as leading a man to the scaffold every morning, then leading him back and saying, "Wait a little more, not today"?

Might this be the proof that you consider your communist experiment to have failed and that you are no longer defending the system that is so dear to you, only yourself [...]?

Pyotr Kropotkin

POSTSCRIPT – *I placed a wreath of red carnations on his tomb in the depths of Russia. The tomb seems long neglected.*

Maxim Gorky

In the fall of 1980, Oleg Bitov, an editor from Literaturnaia Gazeta, *traveled from Moscow to Zagreb to interview Miroslav Krleža. Someone had given him my book* Conversations with Krleža, *and he asked me to introduce him to "the leading Croatian and Yugoslav writer." Krleža agreed and, having only a passive knowledge of the Russian language, asked me to serve as interpreter. The interview was published in* Literaturnaia Gazeta *on December 3, 1980, with a notation by Bitov at the beginning and end of the piece that we had worked on it together.*

I knew the work of his brother Andrei. We talked about him and about various other matters, touching on the subject of Maxim Gorky. I got the impression that Oleg despised Gorky: like many other Russian intellectuals, he had no way of knowing certain texts that were unavailable in the USSR. For that reason I noted down some "unwelcome thoughts" of Gorky concerning the beginning of the October Revolution, not for the Literaturnaia Gazeta *naturally but for him and his co-workers...*

In the meantime, news of the incredible case of Oleg Bitov had broken: he had fled to London (Soviet sources maintained that he'd been drugged and abducted by the CIA) where he railed against the USSR. Then he had suddenly returned to the USSR and from there railed against the secret intelligence services of the West (while this time it was the other side which maintained that he'd been drugged and abducted by the KGB). It was said that he'd been a double agent.

For several weeks the story was in the papers all over the world. The interview in Literaturnaia Gazeta *gave some local Party parasites proof that I too was involved in foreign espionage for "at least two intelligence organizations." This "proof" appeared in print.*

But besides collaborating on the interview with Krleža, my relations with Oleg Bitov had been limited to the following letter, which I sent to Moscow but which was presumably never received. For a long time I did not want to publish it for fear of hurting the person for whom it was intended.

Zagreb, December 11, 1980

I read the Krleža interview in *Literaturnyia Gazeta* of December 3. It seems good to me, and Krleža is pleased, which doesn't happen often: for years he's been banned from the literary journals of the USSR. For that reason he saw this interview, published on the front page of the official organ of the USSR's Writers Union as a kind of rehabilitation. An eighty-six-year-old man who has been attacked as both a communist and a "renegade against communism," as both a radical and a leftist-backslider, cannot be indifferent to such things.

But in regard to Gorky, whom we spoke about briefly, it must be said that he was not the person they have tried to depict him as in the USSR. At the start of the October Revolution, Gorky opposed the Bolsheviks' cruel methods, criticizing them more severely than even certain Menshevik or Social Revolutionary writers had. During my stays in the USSR, I never encountered anyone who was aware that Gorky had written for *Novaia Zhizn'*, a newspaper published in Petrograd from May 1917 to June 1918 by a group of "internationalist" Social Democrats (Vladimir Bazarov, Vasily Desnitsky, Nikolai Sukhanov, Aleksandr Tikhonov, and others). Little is known about this outside the USSR either, where interest in Gorky has faded.

In our book of conversations, Krleža justly referred to the "devaluation of Gorky, which had a long history. Not even after the victory of the revolution was he spared invective. He was labeled as a denigrator of Bolshevik class consciousness, a degraded member of the émigré lumpenproletariat, the bastard of a vulgar prostitute, a counterrevolutionary scribbler, a mystifier, and so on." Krleža considered the author of *The Artamanov Affair* and *The Lower Depths* a writer of great value, better than Beckett, especially when he wasn't "playing the part of the engaged author."

Here are several of Gorky's thoughts from various articles, which you and your colleagues at the *Gazeta* will find quite surprising. Aleksei Maksimovich described Lenin as a "slave of dogma" who transformed his Party comrades into "slave personnel." To Lenin, "the working class is like metal to the blacksmith": he shapes it how he wants for the necessity of the moment. "Lenin proceeds like a chemist in a laboratory who employs inert materials, the difference being that his material is alive, and he guides the revolution to its ruin" (*Novaia Zhizn'*, November 10,

1917). "Lenin and his accomplices consider it their right to commit all variety of crimes, like the massacre near Petrograd, the brutalities in Moscow, the suppression of freedom, the absurd arrests, and other infamies similar to those committed earlier by Stolypin" (November 7, 1917). "The people's commissars don't hesitate to shoot, imprison, or murder those who think differently from them. They don't shrink from any calumny or falsehood" (June 19, 1918).

"Are you the instigators of massacres?" the author of *Mother* asks the Bolshevik leaders, in *Novaia Zhizn'* of March 17, 1918. And the day before that: "Our revolution has opened the gates to the vilest of bestial instincts, which had accumulated under the iron veil of the monarchy. It has rejected the intellectual potential of democracy, the country's moral energy. [...] They have lit a torch. Sweaty, drunk, and cruel, Russia reeks. And here they are dragging this poor Russia, urging it on to Golgotha to be crucified for the salvation of the world. [...] The Soviet leaders are occupied with the future, having forgotten that the future is created in the present moment."

Such were the thoughts of Gorky during the revolution. These articles are completely absent from any of the myriad so-called complete editions of Gorky's works in the USSR. They were partially published abroad (for example, in Berlin in 1918, under the title *Unwelcome Thoughts*). This does not disturb the editors of Soviet Gorky collections in the least, since the works are intended to educate and provide examples for Soviet readers. The heretical thoughts expressed in *Novaia Zhizn'* don't accord with the official images of the "father of Socialist Realism" and are therefore unnecessary.

About Socialist Realism, too, many necessary pieces of information are unknown in the USSR. Various studies from abroad have shown that this movement appeared before Zhdanov and the Writers' Congress of 1934: it had already been formulated in Capri between 1908 and 1909 by a "school" of Russian revolutionaries: Aleksandr Bogdanov, Mikhail Pokrovsky, Lunacharsky, Gorky, and others. Their ideas are in fact the same kind of utopian schemes that have appeared in various forms from Plato to Proudhon (see the Proudhon volume in the Lenin Library entitled *Du principe de l'art et de sa déstination sociale*, which anticipates all the "Party directives" for the use of literature for "social praxis"). But there is a largesse and hopefulness of spirit in the ideas of the "school of Capri," and one cannot identify its members or their plans with the positions of those who persecuted writers in the name of *partiinost'* (party-mindedness) solely because of the manner in which they wrote. Gorky is not to blame for that.

He paid a high price for his utopia. When he returned to the USSR in 1928, he was fatigued by illness and by life, and troubled by all manner of doubts. He wanted peace and quiet and so in the end returned to his country. Zamyatin, who had by then emigrated, wrote a curious obituary for Gorky in 1936 (which, of course, was not published in the USSR and which is impossible to find in its libraries), in which he spoke of the duality that was Aleksei Maksimovich Peshkov and Maxim Gorky. Zamyatin placed the writer beside the man, who had done everything, worked every job. He'd been an adventurer, a porter, a baker, a tradesman (an "icon merchant"), a barge hauler, a drifter, a barefooted *narodnik* (back to the people) radical, who had walked and seen more than his share: Nizhny Novgorod, his birthplace (now Gorky), the Volga Basin, the Kama river and "the little city on its banks, we don't know ourselves where it is," the Caspian Sea, the Don, Ukraine and Bessarabia, the steppes of Mozdok, the mountains of the Caucasus and the mountains of Zhiguli, Astrakhan, Kazan, the Kuban. Peshkov once confided to Zamyatin: "The Bolsheviks have grand plans, and that justifies everything." Perhaps it was on this point that Gorky had his doubts.

The writer admired the Belomor Canal, which was built by *zeks* (political prisoners) from the gulag. But who knows what the man thought? Mandelshtam, too, visited the canal before being arrested and sent to the gulag. In the presence of Anna Akhmatova, his wife Nadezhda destroyed the poem he had dedicated to the canal with the hope of saving his life. It seems incredible but it is true. It's easy to speak of Shakespearean situations when we are not mixed up in them ourselves. When will Russia at last speak of all this?

Gorky was murdered. This too is not spoken of publicly in the USSR, even though the court transcripts from the trials of the thirties confirm it. I searched and found them in an old private library. Before the tribunal, during the trial against "Bukharin and his accomplices" at which A. Y. Vishinsky served as prosecutor, a defendant by the name of Dr. L. G. Levin (whom Yagoda, the ex-head of the NKVD, had charged with "caring for" Aleksei Maksimovich) made the following declaration:

"In the winter of 1935 Gorky was in the Crimea. We came to an agreement as to what measures would cause him harm. We gave him medicines that would hurt him—camphor, caffeine, Cardiosol, Digelan. [...] The doses were enormous—for example, thirty to forty injections of camphor per day, two injections of Digelan, four of caffeine, two of strychnine."

Vishinsky made a hypocritical attempt to appear scandalized and exclaimed, "How terrible!"

Thus was one of the great twentieth-century writers killed. In the last years of his life he was ill and depressed. At the fleeting encounters with friends who managed to see him, he complained of being tired and alone. He let them know by gestures that he was under surveillance and afraid.

The case of Gorky requires greater understanding. The writer deserves greater respect, the man, rather than disdain or oblivion, deserves a moral and intellectual rehabilitation.

Lev Trotsky
ON THE SEVENTIETH ANNIVERSARY OF
THE OCTOBER REVOLUTION.
TO THE COMMISSION ON REHABILITATION, CENTRAL
COMMITTEE OF THE COMMUNIST PARTY OF THE USSR,
AND GENERAL SECRETARY MIKHAIL GORBACHEV

Zagreb, October 1989

It is at last possible to recall the name Lev Trotsky in the USSR without making accusations against him, or drawing accusations against oneself. For sixty years this was impossible. Nevertheless, the rehabilitation of Trotsky and of the enormous number of those condemned as Trotskyites is not yet the order of the day.

We have waited too long to see the official Stalinist charges at least partially overturned, those charges that made a counterrevolutionary out of one of the leaders of the October Revolution, that transformed the founder of the Red Army into a traitor, and that condemned one of the greatest exponents of Soviet power as a "servant of imperialism." All attempts to evaluate the historical personage of Trotsky according to the categories of history itself have concluded tragically both in the Soviet Union and outside it. Individuals were proclaimed Trotskyite who had nothing to do with Lev Davidovich Bronshtein or his ideas: communists and non-communists, old Bolsheviks and ex-Mensheviks, anarchists, Social Revolutionaries, social democrats and socialists, anyone who opposed the ideology or practices of Stalinism. Finally, in the Soviet Union people have begun to speak in a different manner about the author of *The Revolution Betrayed*. But the "re-examination of the past" has been easier in other cases.

More could have been expected from Mikhail Gorbachev's speech on the occasion of the seventieth anniversary of the October Revolution. In the face of resistance from the Party and the armed forces, from the ideology they have created and maintained, the creator of *perestroika* merely repeated the diagnoses we have heard before: "A petit-bourgeois spirit was predominant among certain 'authoritarian personalities' who conducted a fractionalizing battle. They continued to provoke a schism even when it had become clear that their propositions were mistaken and could lead the country along a false path. This applies most of all to Lev Trotsky, who, after the death of Lenin, showed excessive pretensions to Party leadership. Trotsky and the Trotskyites denied the possibility of building socialism in a position of capitalist encirclement. Externally they insisted on exporting revolution, internally on 'tightening the screws.' Trotskyism is a political orientation whose ideologues hide behind leftist phraseology but act from capitalistic positions (sic!). It was, in essence, an attack against Leninism, and in such a situation it was indispensable to fight Trotskyism openly and unmask its anti-socialist nature. [...] Bukharin, Dzherzinsky, Kirov, Ordzhonikidze, and others played important roles in this ideological battle."

What are these "capitalistic positions"? And before whom did Trotsky capitulate? Wasn't it before Stalin? Which one of them did more harm to Leninism? Wasn't it precisely "Trotskyism" that was used as the most serious of charges against hundreds of thousands of anti-Stalinists? Wasn't Bukharin accused of Trotskyism even though he was opposed to Trotsky's "new course"? These are not empty rhetorical questions. *Perestroika* and *glasnost* have not even attempted to answer them.

The attempts thus far made to rehabilitate Trotsky in his homeland have received no encouragement or support. As of this writing *Literaturnaia Gazeta* continues to affirm that Trotsky "was an advocate of barracks socialism, the militarization of work, forceful repression in the army, a regime of the 'full self-limitation' of the revolution." Certain decisions made under extreme conditions at crucial moments of the revolution thus become Trotsky's "fundamental ideas." *Pravda* has not yet even dared to refute the notice published in its pages after the execution of its founder: "A man whose name is despised and reviled by workers the world over has gone to his grave, a double agent and murderer who resorted to any means whatsoever" (August 24, 1940). The name of the man who sank a pickaxe into Trotsky's cranium at Coyoacàn is not mentioned in the pages of the official organ of the Communist Party of the Soviet Union. Readers were not even informed that Ramón del Río Mercador was decorated for his deeds with the order of Hero of the USSR.

I write this letter after the bitter experience of attempting to contribute to the rehabilitation of Nikolai Bukharin, Alexander Dubček, Artur London, Zvonimir Richtman, Andrija Hebrang, Milan Gorkić, Imre Nagy, and Živojin Pavlović. For a long time we have not been able to present publicly the reasons for the rehabilitation of Trotsky. I have kept the responses from the editorial boards of newspapers that have refused my modest and measured requests year after year. In the 1960s an edition of Trotsky's selected works was prepared (six volumes, selected truly without prejudice). Soviet diplomacy did everything it could to prevent its publication, including resorting to the worst kinds of blackmail. Thanks to the tenacity of men who ended up themselves being accused of Trotskyism, one after another of all six volumes was published. Our endeavor was proclaimed an act of "dissidence."

In 1980 a Belgrade weekly translated and published in installments *Werther Has Already Been Written* by the Soviet novelist Valentin Kataev. It was presented as a work of the "new thaw" which brought to light the "arbitrary killings by the Cheka" in the years immediately after the revolution. The work's principal villain is a Cheka functionary named Naum, "with curly hair and thick lips," who speaks with the accent of the Jews of Odessa. "His god is Trotsky, who proclaimed permanent revolution [...] and who maintains that only for this cause must one inundate the entire world with blood." I managed to publish a protest against such a falsification of history and such anti-Semitism, despite the pressure that Soviet diplomacy exercised in various sectors of Yugoslav public life in the time of Brezhnev.

We translated, not without difficulty, Isaac Deutscher's biography of Trotsky. In a veiled polemic we presented to the public the analysis offered by George Steiner in his "Trotsky and Tragic Imagination":

> The Judaic quality of [Trotsky's] vision and sensibility are difficult to deny. Like Marx, he was Jewish in his instinctive internationalism, in his strategic and personal disregard of national borders and antagonisms. In Stalin's hatred of Trotsky, in his power to isolate Lev Davidovich Bronshtein, and make him seem as alien to the party *cadres*, there ran not only the dark, perennial thread of Russian anti-Semitism (as pronounced in Stalin the Georgian, as in Khrushchev the Ukrainian), but also the insecurity, the sour fear which the chauvinist, the man rooted in his own ground, feels in the presence of the cosmopolitan, of the wanderer at home in the world.

The case of Trotsky cannot be reduced to anti-Semitism or his Jewish origins. The settling of accounts with him had more than merely ideological significance. Those who reject everything connected to the October Revolution are uninterested in its destiny. In the same way, party bureaucrats neglect it when they continue to see in Trotsky what Stalin taught them to see. The rehabilitation of Lev Davidovich should be historical, legal, and moral. Trotsky is not the only person at issue — let me repeat — but all those ever condemned as Trotskyites. They are more important than Trotsky himself today, but the process must start with him.

Only then — should the question be resolved in a definitive manner — will it be possible to move ahead, to publicly explore the Bolsheviks' settling of accounts with the opposition, the measures taken against "class enemies" of the Right and Left. In this, Trotsky, along with Lenin, bears part of the blame. But first he must be cleared of those charges falsely attributed to him. It is the most difficult test of all rehabilitations.

The Soviet Union is now faced with a multitude of problems. A number of these cannot be resolved without the clarification of its own history. The question of Trotsky is one of these. We understand that the position of a reformer is difficult and that it is better not to create still more troubles for him. But the deferment of the task in question is itself troubling. The longer such questions of history and morality are put off, the more *glasnost* and *perestroika* become a banal ideological discourse without credibility or meaning.

Your colleagues have works at their disposal that treat Trotsky in an honest and credible manner (those of Deutscher, Pierre Broué, Pierre Naville, and others) and more extensively than is possible in this letter. I am appending a memorandum, which I published many years ago in an attempt to present the works of Lev Trotsky to the Yugoslav public. I also include with this letter a proposal for a *Rehabilitation Statute* addressed to the Commission on Rehabilitation elected from among the Central Committee of the Soviet Communist Party.

POSTSCRIPT – *The proposal in question comprises the first chapter of Part Three of the present epistolary.*

Goli Otok
Another Gulag*

For many of us, the conflict between the USSR and Yugoslavia of 1948 was like a continuation of World War II or the beginning of a new war. The condemnation pronounced in the "Resolution" of the Cominform against Tito and the "revisionists" seemed at the first instant unbelievable. In the beginning the West did not believe it. The East was surprised. The settling of accounts with those who, in the ranks of the Yugoslav Communist Party, adhered to the "Resolution" was merciless. Sovietophiles were removed from their posts and thrown into prison. In the battle against Stalinism, Yugoslavia had recourse to Stalinist methods. Goli Otok, "Naked Island," in the northern Adriatic Sea, became the Yugoslav gulag: a "defensive camp" but severe nonetheless.

For many years no one dared speak of it except in any but the most general terms. Editors and the critics of officialdom did not consent to the publication of any book about Goli Otok or what had happened there. The two letters that follow are a reaction against that proscription. The first is composed of fragments published or read aloud at literary gatherings in the 1980s; the second was written as a proposal for the publication of the novel The Special Line (Vanredna linija) *by Čedo Vulević, an ex-detainee of Goli Otok.*

Danilo Kiš put me in contact with Vulević, while the latter spared no effort in persuading me to undertake the publication of his book. My proposal and his manuscript circulated in innumerable forms among all the possible editors and editorial committees of Belgrade and Zagreb. The novel came out only at the beginning of the 1990s, when the regime that had prevented its publication had begun to crumble. It was awarded a literary prize in 1991, at the beginning of the Yugoslav war.

---

* The present chapter does not appear in the 1994 Croatian edition. This translation is based upon the 1995 French edition and the Italian edition of 1998. [– Translator's note.]

Zagreb–Belgrade, 1982, 1985, 1987

I.

We can define the works that speak of it, which grow more numerous and courageous each day, as the "literature of Goli Otok." Without closing our eyes to its imperfections, we cannot ignore this literature as if it did not exist, or rely on the old formula of "enemies in our ranks," among writers, the editorial world, the press, or, especially, critics. The problem is much more complex, the issues much more serious than that.

Why are these works appearing so long after the events they depict? What is prompting writers to turn back to 1948 and its consequences? Is this theme an alibi for something else more current? What was Stalinism and what did it lead to, even after our "settling of scores" with it? Who is writing these books and with what intention? Finally, how are they written and what is their literary value? Under normal conditions this question ought to have been placed first.

Who and what stand in opposition to this kind of literature? The response that it is the hard-line Party "cadres" and followers of "Marxism-Leninism" in the cultural sphere will satisfy very few: they are not the only ones who believe it would be better to remain silent about Goli Otok. But those who are ready to identify any form of socialism with Stalinism (including that socialist orientation that opposes Stalinism) promote this very opposition and use it as a justification. The absence of any authentic criticism, and the impossibility that such criticism might express itself, favors the closing of the circle—around both the subject and the literature that addresses it.

After the conflict of 1948, Yugoslavia found its very existence threatened. The country was subjected to an economic and political blockade. Soviet tanks appeared on its border. All this is true. But it cannot justify everything. The definitive isolation of those who supported the Stalinist "Resolution" of the Cominform and who were prepared to seek the "fraternal assistance of the Red Army" was a necessary step but did not have to happen the way it did. After what took place in Budapest in 1956, in Prague in 1968, before and after that in Berlin, Warsaw, or Afghanistan, it would be difficult to deny that the Yugoslav break with the Soviet Union was achieved with great skill and that, despite certain "sticking points" (including those treated by the "literature of Goli Otok"), it was providential for the country as a whole. To doubt such things would be naive and senseless from both a historical and a political standpoint. The very fact that we are able now to speak about such books is a result of the rupture with Stalin. But this is not enough. Such are the paradoxes of history and politics and of literature as well.

A great deal of time has passed since 1948, since the Cominform's "Resolution" and the tragic events of Goli Otok. Literature reclaims its right to speak about these events, as about everything else. Those who expect writers to deal with this subject with moderation and care, attempting to find a way to justify the "particular circumstances" and understand the "necessities of history," have a mistaken idea of the function of literature. The decision what to write and how to write takes place only in the work itself.

Goli Otok existed. Many people have seen it. It was known that horrible things went on there. Literature has helped us to see what. There were various categories of prisoners on the island. The largest group consisted of people who refused to deny their previous beliefs, the ideals they had served. There were also, among the guards and "re-educators," certain depraved individuals who tortured and killed the prisoners, on orders from above or their own initiative. There have been worse places in the world, but that is another question. No one can be justified by such an argument. We have at times behaved worse towards our own people than others have behaved towards us. It was not the first time in our history.

The works about Goli Otok describe various forms of torture. There was, for example, the *špalir* (gauntlet) through which each new arrival had to pass while his co-detainees—especially those who wanted to improve their situation—flogged him, spit on him, punched, or struck him with rocks. Placement "under the lamp" meant having an electric light directed into one's eyes. "Rock splitting" on this rocky island was a true labor of Sisyphus: the pieces were not used for anything, they were tossed into the sea (these are the "millers without mills" of Antonije Isaković's novel *The Instant*). Other torments included the "bunker," a kind of cell inside a tunnel; "boycotting" meant complete solitary confinement; the "bucket" referred to having one's head placed above a receptacle filled with excrement; also noteworthy was the ritual of "testifying," which was termed "criticism and self-criticism" in the jargon of "re-education." And so on.

The literature of Goli Otok seeks answers to numerous questions: the nature of the role between judge and accused (not just in the sense of the mythic connection between executioner and victim); the confrontation between history and the individual, the sacrifices offered to the one and the violence performed against the other. "Violence will dominate the world for as long as we do not understand that any power that doesn't cultivate and stimulate heresy against itself is nothing but another of the many forms of dictatorship," writes the Slovene author Branko Hoffman in his *Night Until Morning*.

In writing on such themes it is difficult to avoid conventional novelistic techniques, journalism, didacticism, and historicism. But this does not justify that criticism which, for fear of having to make riskier judgments, proclaims *a priori* that all such works are weak or insignificant, harmful or useless.

II.

Goli Otok and what happened there has been described in various ways: in an attempt to understand and take into consideration the situation of the time, or without such an attempt; from the point of view of the accused or the accuser; with the desire to create a work of literature or without that desire; by those who have been to the island and those who have not set foot on it.

The author of the short novel *The Special Line* was there. He writes in the form of a testimonial, without the need to explain or judge. *The Special Line* is a work of literature. An ex-medical student from a small coastal town, designated by the initial "P," sketches an incredible story in his notebook. Imprisoned on an island called Nevid (Unseen) he is given the task of coroner on a ship flying no colors and bearing the name "Special Line," which transports cadavers to the Velika Draga inlet where they are thrown into the sea. Nevid is a stone island. The prisoners break enormous blocks into pieces out of which they make gravel. "The rock beneath was whiter, but also harder. It fought against tools, tearing away bits of flesh and steel. By day it was sun scorched, by night as cold as ice. Scorching or frozen, the stone burned the hands and bodies of the men all the same."

The ship's captain is Luka, who performs his work in silence without paying attention to the young medical examiner. The doctor will later care for the elderly captain among the patients of the psychiatric ward of P's hospital. They are each tormented by their memories. The doctor tries to avoid "thoughts that compel him to remember the events of long ago, flees from any occasion that might bring to mind Nevid and the Special Line, the small, almost insignificant human operation of the cursed yawl on which he had traveled for some ten months of nights between the stony island and the depths of Velika Draga." The little town of P begins to resemble Nevid, the first being a place of death, the second a place of agony. Only ghosts remain in the town, where there are two times as many houses as there are inhabitants.

Confession thus mixes with the phantasmagoric—the reality of memory passes into the reality of everyday life, which is sometimes more difficult to bear than the worst reminiscence. It is a work about what happens outside and what remains inside oneself. The doctor is torn between his profession and his nightmare. Captain Luka kills himself to extinguish his memories and liberate himself from obsession. When, at the end, the protagonist returns to prison in 1973, we are not sure whether it is a real prison or some other, more terrible structure whose bars he himself has created. There is nothing left for him but to live as an island, with Goli Otok inside him.

POSTSCRIPT – *I have known many people who were "condemned to the marble," a euphemism for having been sent to the island where Yugoslavia defended itself against the USSR. These detainees idealized "the first socialist country" or loved "Mother Russia," which they had never seen. Their suffering and sacrifice was the price of their dream, their love. I never cease to compare their lot with that of my relatives in Stalin's camps. Our history is full of such paradoxes, tragic and inexplicable in practice.*

Let me repeat that my proposal to publish The Special Line *continued, for a decade, to be turned down by editors and publishing directors, a number of whom became, after the collapse of the Yugoslav regime, "staunch adversaries of communism."*

Book Four
APOLOGIAS

The literary rehabilitation of an author was linked to his or her political rehabilitation. Party politics determined the fate of literature. The following letters were attempts to facilitate the publication of books that had been prohibited. For years it was impossible to publish The Gulag Archipelago *in Eastern Europe, even in "revisionist" Yugoslavia. Nadezhda Mandelshtam's* Hope Against Hope *came out, at the risk of the translator and editor, in an abridged and mutilated form. Milan Kundera's* The Book of Laughter and Forgetting *was heavily censored: those parts that might have been an "offense to the president of a neighboring country" (Husák), a crime punishable by law, were excised by the very editor who had fought to have the book published in the first place. The publication of the anarchist Kropotkin's letter to the Bolsheviks on the taking of hostages caused a scandal. The testimonials of Štajner, Medvedev, and Antonov-Ovseenko waited for years. Danilo Kiš's* A Tomb for Boris Davidovich *occasioned the greatest literary-political uproar in Yugoslavia since the Second World War.*

I wrote prefaces, afterwards, and reviews; I invited speakers and held conferences so that these books might be published or, once published, not banned. In these texts I wrote on the basis of materials accessible at the time. In some I have added no new information; in others I have appended Post scripts.

These letters were written in defense of the right to literature, not to some simple form of literary criticism. Criticism should not have to defend a right, especially the literary one. Texts of this sort belong to a special genre that is known in regimes that practice censorship. I call this form of defense and illustration an apologia. *I have written many. They have helped me justify my actions to myself and to others, in literature and in life.*

Mikhail Bulgakov

With Krleža and Kiš I shared a special love for Mikhail Afanasevich Bulgakov. Being inclined to negation and undervaluation, Krleža discussed few writers with such benevolence and sympathy as he did the author of The Master and Margarita. *He saw in Bulgakov one of the rare heirs of "glorious Russian prose." He spoke about him frequently. In his Diary of 1968 he wrote, "Bulgakov and Russian literature!* Shliapu doloi! *(Hats off!)." On the eve of my first trip to the USSR, he suggested I try to discover how the author had spent his last years. Kiš, by contrast, was especially interested in the exchange of letters between Bulgakov and Stalin, and in a play about the youth of "the shepherd," which we did not want to believe really existed.*

Friends in Moscow (Sveto Masleša in particular) collected several important and little known documents for me: testimonials of the writer's contemporaries, notes from his wife's diary. Soviet institutions and libraries of the time wanted nothing to do with this.

Moscow–Zagreb, September–October, 1978

Mikhail Bulgakov sent a number of letters to the Soviet government and to Stalin personally. No one knows exactly how many. Several of his contemporaries claim that he wrote often and that he sometimes signed his letters with the pseudonym "Tarzan." But this does not seem to be true.

In a letter of 1929, which can be attributed to him with certainty, Bulgakov asked for permission to emigrate with his wife, Lyuba Yevgenevna Belozerskaya. A longer letter, in the form of a five- to six-page essay, circulated through Moscow, which is what Bulgakov supposedly wrote and which begins with the words, "All my works are banned." Lyuba Yevgenevna denies its authenticity and cites another, shorter letter to Stalin, written in 1930, filled with despair and presages of death.

After Mayakovsky's suicide, Stalin preferred to avoid the possibility of a suicide by another great writer, particularly the author of *The Days of the Turbins*, a play noted in positive terms in the eleventh volume of *The Collected Works of Yosif Stalin*. It was quite likely this circumstance that induced him to call Bulgakov on the phone. According to Lyuba Yevgenevna, who was next to her husband, near the telephone, Stalin spoke in the third person: "Stalin has received your letter [...]. Stalin has read it." This is entirely possible. Tvardovsky writes, in his collection *Distance Beyond Distance*, that Stalin had by this time already begun speaking of himself in the third person.

There are three other letters in circulation, which appear to be authentic, from 1931, 1934, and 1938. In the last, Bulgakov defends the playwright Nikolai Robertovich Erdman, who had by then spent many years in Siberia. Bulgakov received no response to these. I include here an instructive and little known passage from the letter of 1931, addressed to the Soviet government and to Stalin.

"Since 1930 I have suffered from a serious form of neurasthenia, with attacks of anxiety and crises of angina pectoris. They have left me a walking dead man. [...] The cause of my illness is clear. In the vast field of activity that opens before Russian writers, I was the only wolf. I've been advised to change my skin. Idiotic advice: a wolf is not a puppy dog that can change its skin or have itself shorn. For years I have been treated as one treats a wolf: they put me behind a closed barrier, according to the best rules that men of letters have devised for persecuting a man.

In the end the ferocious beast let it be known that he was not a wolf but a man. Let us be honest: that too is cowardice. A writer who is silent ceases to exist. This is how it is: from the moment he closes his mouth he ceases to be a true writer. And if a true writer grows silent, he is condemned to die.

The causes of my illness must be sought in the persecution to which I have been subjected, in the silence in which I have been constrained."

The greatest Russian prose writer in the country was not invited to the ceremonial parade of the First Congress of Soviet Writers in 1934. Two years later, desperate, ill, and exhausted, he accepted a commission which for many years we did not want to believe: the creation of a theatrical work on Stalin, the dramatization of certain events from his early life, entitled *The Shepherd* (one of Stalin's first pseudonyms), a piece that would be based on the insurrection of Kutai, of which Dzhugashvili had been one of the principal instigators, a bloodbath of the beginning of the century, which began at Batum and spread throughout Transcaucasia.

But there is unfortunately no doubt that Bulgakov worked on this piece. In the diary of Yelena Sergeevna Bulgakov (the writer's third wife), in the entry under February 7, 1936, it is written in black and white that Mikhail Afanasevich had finally "decided to write a work on Stalin." Three years later, Yelena Sergeevna notes (on August 19, 1939) that the work is "nearly finished." When it was read at The Moscow Art Theater, the author was near death. (I have not been able to discover his exact diagnosis: some speak of "malignant hypertension," others of "a sort of uremia.")

Throughout this period Bulgakov was desperately working on the manuscript of *The Master and Margarita*, revising it day in and day out, copying it over God knows how many times. He requested new "documents" and supplementary "materials" for the development of *The Shepherd*. Perhaps in this manner (and indeed how else could he have managed it?) he put off finishing the work: first, like Scheherazade, he continued the story in order to prolong his life; then, like "Monsieur de Molière," who was so dear to him, he died playing a role that he could no longer play. That is how I see the end of his life.

Just before his death, at the beginning of 1940, he received a visit from Boris Leonidovich Pasternak. The sick man was overjoyed, says Vitaly Vilenkin, one of the few men of the theater to stick by him to the very end. What might they have said to each other then, these two great writers of Stalin's Russia? Perhaps something of great importance that even Pasternak did not dare to transmit to us in writing. Or perhaps just the sorts of banalities that are usually uttered at the end of a life.

Some details should be added to this portrait of the writer. Bulgakov paid special attention to his appearance and clothing. According to Valentin Kataev, who knew him since his youth, "Blue eyes" (as he was called) wanted to maintain the characteristics of a provincial intellectual: "He wore shoes with buttons and with satin tips," a vest with a pocket watch, a bow-tie, a monocle, and sometimes a flower in his buttonhole. This was not merely the style of a theater man. He wanted to be different in his attitude and dress. Difference would become one of the principal signs of the dissident. "Bulgakov," writes Kataev, "had great respect for all the pre-revolutionary authorities," but did not like the "commander" (Mayakovsky), or Meyerhold, or Tatlin, or others like them.

How much more bearable than all this, dear Danilo, are the first and last sorrows of *A Tomb for Boris Davidovich*? At least we don't have to ask permission to emigrate. And that is something.

POSTSCRIPT – *When I wrote this letter, we did not yet know of Bulgakov's diary, which, along with "The Heart of a Dog," had been confiscated by the GPU in the course of a search of the writer's home in 1926. Maksim Gorky intervened on the writer's behalf to have the texts restored. They were given back in 1929, but after the episode Bulgakov destroyed his journal, contradicting the famous line from his novel according to which "manuscripts don't burn." But the author of* The Master and Margarita *was partly right. In 1990, upon the collapse of the KGB, the part of the diary that had been confiscated (1922–1925) — the copy made by the police, which had not burned — was published in the journal* Oktiabr'.

While Bulgakov was writing letters to Stalin and the Soviet government, he knew very well that they were aware of his opinions. The notes seized by the GPU bore the subtitle Pod piatoi *(Under the Heel). Molotov once confided to Ushakov, at the end of the 1960s, that "the entire Politburo had read Bulgakov's diary." They had determined that "the writer had anti-Bolshevik sentiments."*

What else could they have concluded, having read these lines, written on the night of December 18, 1924: "I am afraid they want to send me to 'one of those territories not so far away' to compensate me for my exploits." The writer did not hide his displeasure at having to collaborate with that "muddy journalistic cesspool which Soviet press has turned into" (January 3, 1925). He complains, "It is hard to write literature today. And for me, with these thoughts that pierce through what I write whether I like it or not, it's equally hard to publish and to live" (October 24, 1923).

One finds current ideas expressed by this "conservative to the marrow," as Bulgakov defined himself, who thought that politics was "always the same, always rotten and contrary to nature." In 1923 he predicted that "perhaps the world would be divided into two camps, communist and fascist." The entry is dated September 30, 1923; September 17, according to the old calendar."

In those times and under that regime it was dangerous to keep a diary.

Diaries could be used against one as proof of accusations, as evidence in trials. Letters to friends could be used in the same way. Only those who had lost everything and had nothing more to lose wrote open letters. Few have been preserved.

The theater piece on which Bulgakov was working at the end of his life initially bore the title The Shepherd; *then it was changed to* Batum. *As far as we know, Stalin read the manuscript and did not approve its production for the stage.*

Probably he did not find the text apologetic enough.

Nadezhda Mandelshtam

Memoirs most often make mediocre books, even when they are interesting. The books of Nadezhda Mandelshtam are more than memoirs: they bring to life before our eyes not only one of the greatest Russian poets of the twentieth century but the century itself and the fate of poetry within it.

One must avoid pathos when speaking of Nadezhda Mandelshtam and her works. This is not always easy. The fate of Russia's twentieth-century poets was tragic. Yesenin, Mayakovsky, and Tsvetaeva committed suicide; Gumilyov was executed; Mandelshtam was killed by the gulag, Khlebnikov by "homelessness"; Akhmatova and Pasternak died as internal émigrés.

The literary rehabilitation of Osip Mandelshtam began, along with that of many others, after Khrushchev's speech to the Twentieth Party Congress. I emphasize *literary* rehabilitation because at the moment of this writing there has been no political or legal rehabilitation of the man, despite numerous proposals to do so. In the journal *Moskva* (no. 8, 1964), Nikolai Chukovsky managed to publish a form of introduction to nine poems of Mandelshtam, noting that "the poet had greeted the October Revolution," had desired "to stay in the Soviet Union" at all costs, but had been exiled to Voronezh, disappearing "in the troubled times that followed." In the same journal of 1967, Mandelshtam's *Conversation about Dante* was published. That year in Yerevan, the journal *Literaturnaia Armenia* published his *Journey to Armenia*, which in its time had been condemned by *Pravda* (August 30, 1933), an event that marked the beginning of the end for Mandelshtam. An excerpt from Nadezhda Mandelshtam's memoirs was published as a preface to this text, one of her rare appearances in print in her own country. In 1968 the journal *Voprosy literatury* (no. 4) published extracts from Mandeshtam's *Notebooks*. Finally, the poet's name entered the literary lexicon of encyclopedias, although the manner in which his life ended was still omitted. A special volume of selected poems appeared in 1973 in the *Biblioteka poetov* series founded by Gorky. Its publication had been postponed several times due to the publication of Nadezhda Mandelshtam's memoirs abroad. In another context, this list of data might constitute a kind of bibliography. Here they are stages in a rehabilitation, the "defense and exemplification" of Mandelshtam.

Nadezhda Mandelshtam's opinions are extremely harsh and subjective, both towards the world of the 1920s that she depicts, which certainly contained more potential for good than for what subsequently took place, and towards the numerous Russian and non-Russian writers she encountered, the Russian formalists, for instance—who did only what they could—or Eliot or Sartre, whose "liberty" she refers to as "sadism." Such are *"les chemins de la liberté,"* as Sartre would say. Nadezhda Mandelshtam was a victim of intellectual exile, imposed on her by an "internal emigration." It is perhaps natural that, after all she went through, she considered things in the light that she did. But opinions are not the most important thing in the memoirs of Nadezhda Mandelshtam.

She reveals to us, as no one before her or since, how the great twentieth-century Russian poets, with whom her fate was crossed, lived and suffered. She tells us of what we could not even imagine: of Anyuta Gorenka, who took the Tatar pseudonym Akhmatova, of her passion and vanity; of the people Anna loved and those she despised, of her worry for her son, Lev Gumilyov; of Marina Tsvetaeva ("the most tragic fate I have ever known") and her love for Pasternak; of Pasternak's reserved nature; of Khlebnikov, who sank into himself but for whom there was no salvation; of Mandelshtam and their common fate, and of the poet's love for other women more beautiful than she. "Perhaps it was not love but destiny that united us."

All this cannot be summarized in a letter of this nature: the *fear* that is stronger "than both love and jealousy"; sleepless nights that were "times of terror" ("and we had reason to be afraid"); "the class of literary bureaucrats that is far more terrible than the non-literary, for it betrays freedom of thought in good conscience"; the "I" that is easy to lose and so hard to find again; the masks people wore, which for many came to replace their actual face; the fate of the Jews, who are special also "because they share the fate of their own people as well as that of the people on whose territory they are encamped" ("I sometimes think that every true intellectual is in some measure a Jew"); the price that we paid in our time by "listening to wise men and geniuses"; that time itself, which favored "those incapable of thinking their own thoughts"; the death that she awaits without fear, now that she has finished her mission, "hoping against hope." "All is finished. I am ready."

POSTSCRIPT – *After Nadezhda Mandelshtam's death, Joseph Brodsky offered a key to reading her works. Russian prose of the second half of the nineteenth century was based on the poetry that had preceded it. "The great majority of Dostoevsky's characters," said Akhmatova, "are nothing but Pushkin's characters grown old." This phenomenon was repeated in the twentieth century. Nadezhda Mandelshtam was most influenced in this regard by two poets, Osip Mandelshtam and Anna Akhmatova. She memorized their verses, kept watch over that which they did not dare put down on paper. "And all this grew inside her because, if there is one thing that can take the place of love, it is memory."*

The verses of the two great poets, Brodsky recalled, became "her conscience and her personality." They constituted for her "a linguistic norm. When she sat down to write, she was destined to compare her words against theirs. Her works, in their content and in the style are a 'Postscript' to the nobler form of language that is poetry."

It is a beautiful theory, but I do not believe it. Writers don't merely grow out of the work of other writers, not even the very best. Nadezhda Yakovlevna had what is most essential for writing inside her. Otherwise she would not have become what she was.

Ariadna Efron
For Evgenia Ginzburg

Russia, undated

During my various journeys I attempted to piece together what Marina Tsvetaeva left behind in Russia: poetry, letters, and memoirs. Some facts are clearer than others.

Marina hanged herself in Yelabuga during the evacuation of 1941. The location of her grave is uncertain. Her husband, Sergei Yakovlevich Efron, was killed later that same year as an "enemy of the Party." Their son Georgy, "Mura," volunteered for the Red Army and died in World War II. Their daughter Ariadna, "Alya," fought for the republicans in the Spanish Civil War. In Paris she took part in the activities of leftist circles. She believed that the Soviet Union was building socialism. Filled with enthusiasm, she was the first member of the family to return to Moscow, at the beginning of 1937. Two years later she was arrested as "an imperialist agent." She spent sixteen years in the gulag. She was rehabilitated in 1955.

I met her through the help of friends. I promised her "not to write anything about our meeting" while she was still living, a promise I kept. She was diffident and reserved. There was great suffering in her blue eyes. "I lived not my life but the life of someone else." She was not yet an old woman. From her mother's biography, I knew that she had been born in 1912. She seemed to have lived several lives without experiencing youth in any one. She had been in correspondence with Boris Pasternak. From the camps she wrote him long, passionate letters of the sort that her mother probably did not dare write when she had been in love with him. Pasternak responded with brief messages of encouragement and sometimes sent her money. Their correspondence has been preserved. It is said to resemble an epistolary novel. The brave woman director of the post office in the Siberian town of Turachansk allowed these letters to "pass through." She neither confiscated them nor denounced the correspondents, as she was required to do. The circumstance is like a Russian novel: some brave individual appears suddenly, a secondary character whose actions become decisive.

Pasternak sent Ariadna chapters from *Doctor Zhivago*. She read them several times over, responding at length with pertinent comments written in a beautiful style. Like so much else at the time, the letters could not be published. But nor were they lost. Before his death, Pasternak gave them back to Ariadna. I have heard that a Slavic scholar managed to photograph them at the poet's dacha in Peredelkino. Another manuscript that did not burn. Yelizaveta Yakovlevna Efron, "Liliya," Sergei's beautiful sister, whom Marina called "the light of our family," read me one of the letters she had received from Ariadna in the camps. Misfortune can sometimes be beautiful.

After being set free, Ariadna devoted herself to preserving her mother's works. She collected nearly all that remained. Despite the odds, a great deal had remained. Part she gave to Yelizaveta Yakovlevna, part to the *zaum* (transense) poet Kruchonykh: scattered works and manuscripts, unfinished notes, unpublished, unpublishable. Thus was the literary bequest of Marina Tsvetaeva salvaged. Marina's younger sister Anastasiya lived in Vologda. I wanted to visit her but was unable. I asked my friend Sveto Masleša to find and help her. Without him I would not have met Ariadna, Marina Tsvetaeva's unfortunate daughter.

POSTSCRIPT – *I wrote this letter and dedicated it to Evgenia Ginzburg at the moment when I learned of Sveto Masleša's suicide in Sarajevo.*

Kruzhok

Paris, April 4, 1990

I finally made the acquaintance of Andrei Sinyavsky. We met through Yevgeniya Berg, who for years taught Russian literature at the School of Oriental Languages in Paris, where I also gave lectures for a time. The *Russkii kruzhok* (Russian Circle) still meets in her small salon. In its day, when the distinguished emigré slavicist Gleb Struve was living, it enjoyed moments of brilliance. The list of those who visited it included Dmitry Merezhkovsky, Bunin, Tsvetaeva, perhaps Shestov, Berdyaev, Vladimir Lossky, probably Nabokov just after he fled Nazi Germany, Nina Berberova, and many others. Zamyatin, being of the Left, avoided emigré organizations. Pasternak did not dare to make contact when he visited Paris in the 1930s. He knew he was being watched. But he visited Marina Tsvetaeva and was shocked by the poverty in which she was living. Akhmatova did not stop in Paris on her way to London, where, near the end of her life, she was awarded a poetry prize.

Yevgeniya Berg has invited the Russian actress Olga Obuchovskaya, newly arrived from Leningrad, who reads to the *kruzhok* materials collected by friends of Nikolai Gumilyov for his definitive rehabilitation: the stories told about the Tagantsev affair, in which the poet was implicated, are utterly false. Gorky's intervention came too late. The quick and summary inquest did not take into consideration Lenin's order that the matter be looked into "attentively." I believe I can get a translation of the text published in the Belgrade journal *Književnost* and have already written a brief preface.

Sinyavsky speaks openly about "Russian nationalism" and the publications of the organization *Pamiat'* (Memory), which he calls "*chernostentsy*" (ultra-nationalist). He criticizes Shafarovich's study *Russophobia*, which he considers "fascist, akin to *Mein Kampf*." He is reserved towards Solzhenitsyn: *The Gulag Archipelago* is a grand work, but *The Red Wheel* is worthless. I agree with him. We talk about emigration, how it deforms people, especially writers. He didn't know about the letters with which I tried to get him and Daniel released from the gulag twenty years before. There is another I wrote, protesting the fact that in Yugoslavia his works were not published for fear of an intervention by Soviet diplomats, and proposing the translation of his new book on Russia and the Soviet Union.

Sinyavsky reminds one of a pre-Revolutionary intellectual. He is discrete and unpredictable, gentle and impulsive. He smokes a lot. He rises and politely asks permission to go into the other room in order to light his pipe. In Paris he and his wife publish, with a great deal of effort, the journal *Syntaxis*. They recently visited Russia. "It's completely changed." Perhaps they'll go back for good.

POSTSCRIPT – *Yevgeniya Berg died in the spring of 1992. With her Paris's Russian Circle passed away too, at the very moment when Russia appeared to be rising from its ashes. Perhaps someone will write its history.*

The diaspora of Russian culture lived modestly and died in silence.

Portraits of Stalin

Zagreb, 1985

Books on Stalin and Stalinism are becoming ever more numerous. Each corroborates or corrects the others. Many facts and opinions are repeated. Perhaps this is inevitable: the subject itself requires that we return to it.

One of the most recent books on Stalin is worthy of attention. It is entitled *A Portrait of Stalin* and is the work of Anton Antonov-Ovseenko (it came out in Russian in the USA). This author, too, repeats things that have been noted elsewhere, but he also says things that have not been known before now.

Antonov-Ovseenko's position is unique. He is the son of the well-known revolutionary Vladimir Antonov-Ovseenko, who led the 1917 assault on the Winter Palace, one of Lenin's closest collaborators and friends, a member of the Party since 1903. After Lenin's death, he allied himself with Trotsky. He was one of the signatories of the famous "Letter of Forty-six" (from the end of 1923) against "the dictatorial regime instituted by an internal faction of the Party." Stalin got him off his hands by sending him on diplomatic missions (to Czechoslovakia, Lithuania, Poland, and Spain during the Civil War). He called him back to the USSR in 1937 and then eliminated him. Vladimir Antonov-Ovseenko was a journalist, poet, and critic. He was one of the first to be rehabilitated by the Soviets, in 1956.

His son Anton is a historian. He was born in Moscow in 1920. After his father's death, he spent more than ten years in the camps, with brief periods of liberty, between 1940 and 1953. His mother was killed in prison in 1937. Today he lives in Moscow, almost completely blind. (The Union of the Blind is the only organization to which he belongs.) He wrote his book "from the inside," with the experience of a man who passed through the camps and has nothing more to lose. For this reason his expressions are direct and decisive. He makes statements rather than arguments, accusations rather than interpretations. "The consequences of the Stalinist terror were tragic. We must speak about them openly and loudly." His book seems more like a chronicle than a history. It is a worthwhile testimonial, which, as a historical study, is mediocre.

Works of this sort present event after event, enumerating crime after crime, describing one case behind another. They are characterized by a particular form of cumulative discourse (*The Gulag Archipelago* and Roy Medvedev's *For a Judgment of History* are constructed in this manner as well). Preoccupation over content pushes concerns for form and care over method to a secondary plane. The historical methodology developed and imposed by the Stalinist system is of no use in explaining what (in this book) is defined as Stalinism. While Medvedev is interested in the social phenomenon of Stalinism, Antonov-Ovseenko considers only Stalin at the center of the system. This move changes the proportions of individual events in relation to history as a whole but does not permit the "portrait" to be reconciled with "objective conditions," "historical necessities," or some other "dialectical" laws.

Faced with the fact that the witnesses are old or dead, that the documents are in large part inaccessible or lost, and that both have been falsified, Antonov-Ovseenko makes use of everything that is still available in order to preserve and renovate *memory*. Numerous friends helped him in his research, but he took the entire responsibility for what was written on himself. The unedited memoirs of old Bolsheviks, unknown testimonials of victims of the terror, declarations by their parents and friends—all this he had at hand. He does not cite the names of those who, as Nadezhda Mandelshtam writes, "want nothing but to be left in peace." He avoids including a hagiography of his father, who enters the book only when he is needed for parts of the argument. He writes about himself rarely. It is only through marginal comments that we learn he was in the "camp complex of Pechora" and he "served his sentence at Vorkuta," in the extreme east of the far north. He experienced "an ocean of pain before opening [his] eyes." He was a Stalinist, even after the death of his father. "Nearly all of us were."

This book is not merely a settling of scores. It poses instead questions about responsibility and complicity. "It is beyond dispute that Stalin bears a historical responsibility. But this does not remove any blame from those who helped him. [...] The executioners of Ravensbrück, Auschwitz, and Dachau received the punishment they deserved. Why have the executioners of the Solovetsky Islands, of Kolyma, and of Bamlag never even been named? I am not asking that they be punished, only that their names be released. [...] O you, great tribe of Party secretaries whose services have not yet been immortalized! A Shakespeare is needed to render unto you your just deserts!"

Antonov-Ovseenko does not show how Stalin derived from Lenin, or Lenin from Marx, or Marx from Hegel, as is often done today. He maintains that the "dictatorship of the proletariat" facilitated the dictator's seizure of power. He faults Lenin for not having stopped Stalin immediately, once he had realized what the latter was. He faults the "heroes of the Revolution," including his father, for not having had the strength to question Party orthodoxy and "unite against the usurper." He faults those of his compatriots who, after all and despite all, are prepared to rehabilitate the greatest criminal in the history of Russia. "Stalin did not become Stalin merely because of historical circumstances."

The portrait of Stalin Ovseenko offers us is clear and decisive. It allows no concessions or justifications. The "merits" of Stalin, which others have sought and discovered, appear insignificant and unlikely to the author. He contests equally the statesman, the theoretician, and the commander-in-chief. He recognizes a certain "adroitness" only in the head of the Party, the Party that he himself constructed. "There isn't a tyrant from Nero to Hitler, who could measure up to him," especially in terms of the number of people killed: tens of millions during collectivization, tens of millions in the purges, still more tens of millions, largely because of his faulty leadership, in the war. The numbers presented by Ovseenko cannot be verified.

Stalinism put its seal on the very ideas on which it was based. "In exterminating millions of people, it subjected the population to blind, absolute obedience." The regime managed to produce a "layer of glorious idiots." It brought on a profound "crisis in Marxism: thousands of books were written in opposition to Marx."

To those events that are relatively well known Ovseenko adds new details. "Khrushchev's speech revealed much but concealed still more." A separate *shameless history* (more historical illustration than historiography in the true sense of the word), in which numerous "engineers of the human soul" took part, may be glimpsed behind the scenes: the poet Aleksandr Bezimensky exalts processions and executions (of Pyatnikov and Serebryakov) in occasional verse; the Azerbaijani bard Samud Vurgan recites an ode, kneeling before Stalin and gazing into the sky; Leonid Leonov proposes a calendar for the new era, which will begin with Stalin's birth; the academician Mitin publishes the manuscript of an executed rival colleague under his own name; hundreds of painters organize a monstrous exhibit entitled *Stalin in Soviet Fine Art*; at the ceremonial celebration of the chief's sixtieth birthday, at the Bolshoi Theater in 1939, "the two thousand people in attendance applaud the honoree for a half an hour."

"Ivan the Terrible and Peter the Great did not cut off enough heads," cynically declares the General Secretary to the director Sergei Eisenstein.

Ovseenko tries to find answers to numerous enigmas: why Ehrenburg's books were "arrested" while nothing ever happened to Ehrenburg; why the dictator took pity on Paustovsky; why Maxim Gorky was poisoned; why the death of Nadezhda Krupskaya, Lenin's widow, resembled an "execution." The iron curtain of history has covered a portion of the stage, perhaps forever. The political education of the new generation could not have been more gruesome. "Young people, the witness of these pogroms, learned just one lesson well: everything is permitted."

Ovseenko cites several works from the enormous bibliography on Stalin and Stalinism (those of Souvarine, Bazanov, Hingley, Tucker, Trotsky, Cohen, and so on), most of which are unavailable to scholars in the USSR. After the appearance of his book, he has remained in Russia. What might have happened to people who wrote such books previously has not happened to him. There are several possible reasons for this: he is the son of Vladimir Antonov-Ovseenko; Vladimir Antonov-Ovseenko has been rehabilitated; Anton Antonov-Ovseenko has also been rehabilitated. In Stalin's time all these together would not have been sufficient. Something then has changed.

Antonov-Ovseenko overcomes the commonplaces that often characterize books of this sort. His book is too sincere to be cynical, too burdened by bitterness to be prudent, too tragic to be libelous: its author knew the gulag; he is motivated by the desire to say everything and more, to remember and help others to remember: "It is the duty of every honest man to write the truth about Stalin. This is a debt before those who died at his hands, those who endured that dark night, those who will come after us."

"We haven't the strength to forget," wrote Aleksandr Blok just after the Revolution, on the eve of his death. One wonders, after reading this book, what sort of history is this that so depends on memory. "To dominate history" appears more difficult than ever. Prehistory lasts longer than could have ever been foreseen.

Zagreb, 1984

Many people even among the most knowledgeable specialists on the Soviet Union have been surprised by the extraordinary richness of information wielded by Roy Medvedev. In the Khrushchev era he was able to conduct research in some of the most restricted archives. He is familiar with the notes and unedited memoirs of the most eminent personages of contemporary Soviet history. He managed to obtain taped conversations with several of those who had not had the opportunity to write down their experiences. Certain politicians and academics obtained materials for him that were inaccessible to everyone else. During the Brezhnev years, when his brother Jaurès was committed to a psychiatric hospital, it seemed that Roy would be prevented from continuing his work. But this, fortunately, did not happen.

The book *For a Judgment of History* was written over a long period of time, during which it was continually augmented and deepened. It is not easy to characterize. It's a work of history but not only that. Placed before a range of historical data, for which he attempts to find adequate articulation, the author does not adopt the tone of the historical lecture (especially where he works only with facts, attempting to accumulate them and translate them into the discourse of accusation). In the French review *Les Temps modernes*, Bulat Okudzhava recently declared that the work "is not only about the image of Stalin but about our history, about us. It must be spoken about; we want it to be known." These words define the best way of understanding Medvedev's undertaking.

Medvedev differs from most Soviet dissidents in the fact that he has remained an adherent of socialism. He considers himself a Leninist and does not question the October Revolution. (For this reason his work has provoked serious reservations in some dissident circles.) But the richness of factual information he offers us confers on the work extraordinary force and credibility. One has the impression at times that Medvedev wrote this text as an inversion of Stalin's *Short Course*: a long historical or anti-historical line of Stalinist deformations parades before us, replete with violence, terror, labor camps, the "betrayal of the revolution."

At this moment, when the Soviet Union has begun to speak openly about Stalin's misdeeds and Medvedev's position has become easier to defend internally, it seems time that *For a Judgment of History* (or better *Let History Be the Judge*) should be published at last. How much longer shall we have to wait?

On the Perestroika of Writers

Maastricht, May 12, 1989

Maastricht is located some halfway along the road between Brussels and Amsterdam. This ancient lowland village on the river Maas, which the French in the highlands call Meuse, is nearly as beautiful and picturesque as Bruges (Brugge). From the fifth to twelfth of May, the fifty-third Congress of the International PEN Club was held there. Sixty-eight years after the romantic Dawson-Scott and the realist John Galsworthy founded it in 1921, this initially English and later cosmopolitan organization accepted its first Soviet members. It was they who asked to join, while their request was unanimously approved.

Anatoly Rybakov, Andrei Bitov, Fazil Iskander, and Igor Vinogradov traveled to Maastricht as representatives of the newly created Russian chapter. There were arguments in Moscow and Leningrad regarding who did and who did not have the right to join PEN. The Russians exaggerated the organization's importance, many members of which are minor writers, just as they exaggerated many other things in the West. The dispute made its way across the Soviet border. Joseph Brodsky let it be known from New York that he would resign from the organization if certain compromised members of the USSR Writers' Union were accepted into it.

In the end approximately fifty names were entered into the Russian chapter, including those of Aitmatov, Akhmadulina, Astafyev, Bogomolov, Dombrovsky, Dudintsev, Granin, Karpov, Kim, Korotich, Likhachev, Okudzhava, Rasputin, Rozov, Rozhdestvensky, Voznesensky and Yevtushenko. These names were read at Maastricht by Anatoly Rybakov, who recalled, in addition to all the other misfortunes, "the immense spiritual losses" experienced by the Soviet people and its literature. He expressed the hope of finally seeing Soviet and émigré writers reunited.

On this occasion I delivered a welcoming address in Russian to the writers from the USSR, and after our meeting published the letter whose contents are reprinted here.

"We are witnessing an important event in the history of this organization, in the history of the relations among writers and writers' organizations, and perhaps even in the history of literature. It is important first of all because the Russian writers, thanks to the changes that have taken place in their country—changes in which they are taking part and to which they are providing the impulse, which are designated by the all too generic and perhaps banal terms *perestroika* and *glasnost'*—have accepted and satisfied the conditions stipulated in the statutes of PEN International. It is also important because without them we would be poorer and incomplete. It is important, finally, because this meeting is the result of our joint efforts and because it can take place without the consequences that in the past would have surely plagued those of you who have come and spoken so openly.

I would like to emphasize the unofficial, that is, non-governmental, non-ideological character of this undertaking. I have in mind the decision of free writers to become part of an organization that defends their freedom. We know—those of you from the Soviet Union know best of all—the kinds of harm brought against writers and writing by literary organizations with apparatchiks and a *nomenklatura* at their head. They intruded not only on ideology and direction but on the very content and form of expression, dictating literary 'resolutions,' handing down 'decisions' in the name of literature. Leaving questions of theory and practice to the writer himself, to his competence and capacity to resolve them in and by the work of literature, let us keep watch together over the rights of the author, over the inalienable right to his own choice and the form of expression that is demanded by the work itself, over the right to be different in that choice and expression, just as in life itself.

One of the essential characteristics of the Russian literary tradition is its profound aspiration to truth. There was a time when we expected a great deal from Russian and Soviet writers, perhaps more indeed than they were capable of giving (we Slavs perhaps expected even more than others). Then came a time when we stopped expecting anything at all, rejecting in disdain whatever was offered or imposed on us by the USSR. We all remember that in the most difficult of those times, ruinous not just for authors and for literature, there were those who never stopped thirsting for truth, if only in silence. Their silence was eloquent.

In your country today the right to speak openly has at last been re-conquered. I am convinced that, rejecting conformism and violence, you will help us all to defend together the rights of authors, the rights of man, and to protect the freedom of literature, the freedom of man. I am happy to see at last writers and not their substitutes among us and to shake the hands of true literary creators, not the literati of power."

POSTSCRIPT – *Igor Vinogradov spoke for the Russian writers. His speech was surprising to many. The authors collected here, he said, were of modest talents. There were greater writers beyond the boundaries of the USSR. He cited their names: Solzhenitsyn, Brodsky, Aksyonov, Maksimov, Voinovich, Etkind, Kopelev, Sinyavsky... In a country that had never known democratic institutions, he said, repeating Rybakov's thought, there will be much to do for everyone. It will be necessary to defend writers in difficulty, along with the high place of literature, and the rights and dignity of human beings. He declared his opposition to those who would, in his own country, introduce a law prohibiting the "discrediting" of persons in positions of power. We applauded him, without forgetting who it was that occupied such positions.*

At the same time, in Amsterdam, the largest exhibition ever of the works of Kazimir Malevich had been organized. Many of his unknown pieces had finally resurfaced from the gallery vaults of Moscow and Leningrad. I went to see them almost as a form of pilgrimage. Among the last canvases painted in his life, in the first half of the 1930s, is an extraordinary self-portrait of the artist in avant-garde Harlequin dress. With a pathetic gesture of the hand, he seems to be justifying or defending himself. A canvas entitled "Complex Forebodings," painted between 1928 and 1932, portends the terror of the gulag in a style similar to that of the artist's famous "Red Cavalry." Beside a pale, undifferentiated human figure stands a red house with a black roof but without doors or windows. On a third canvas I see a running man before a red house and a white house, both without doors or windows, both equally cheerless. Between them, stuck in the ground, rises an object that could be a sword or, perhaps, a cross.

For Mikhail Sergeevich Gorbachev

Paris–Zagreb, December 1991

With the end of 1991 the Soviet Union ceased to exist. On December 26 its president, Mikhail Gorbachev, resigned and left the Kremlin, an action unprecedented in Soviet history. It was the last act in a drama that had lasted for seventy years.

The USSR was simultaneously a great power and an underdeveloped country. History has shown that such a contradiction must be resolved sooner or later. We have just witnessed its resolution. Other empires have crumbled from external pressure; this one fell from the inside out. Other states have been destroyed by war; this one dismantled itself in peace. Other upheavals of this magnitude have been accompanied by great bloodshed; in this one, until the moment of Gorbachev's exit, there was almost no bloodshed at all. Colonial powers amassed great riches; with the end of the USSR, Russia was left in poverty. Nations of great power have taken care to ensure a better life for their future generations; in the USSR the nation of greatest power lived worse off than those who accused it of oppressing them. These are problems of history but also of destiny.

Perestroika changed the history of the world but could not alter the destiny of the USSR. Mikhail Gorbachev was better loved abroad than in his homeland. It is naive to think that one love can replace the other. Even the staunchest enemies of the USSR before Gorbachev's arrival tried to help him save it once he was in power. The custodians of the old regime declared him a traitor. In dismantling the regime he inherited, he found himself left among its ruins. The economy overturned his political program the moment the latter had become most positive. It was in essence life itself that accomplished this overturning, the life of people constrained to live every day insulted and injured by poverty and uncertainty. Gorbachev had the courage to recognize this and accept the consequences: it was not possible to continue in this way.

He used no force against the other peoples seeking freedom, even though an array of terrifying weapons was at his disposal. In this manner he saved his own people from the disdain and hatred of others. Any true statesman would have tried to change the poor organization of his regime and the horrendous conditions in which it found itself. No one could have done any more than he: the President of the Supreme Soviet denounced the Soviet Union. It was Gorbachev in fact who overturned Gorbachev.

I watch him during his farewell speech, at the moment when he is leaving power, and he appears neither sad nor discouraged. He does not present himself as victorious or defeated. He appeals to "hope and faith," "wisdom and spirit," (the word "spirit," *dukh*, was long avoided in this sense, in this country). It seems to me that I see a red flag beside him, symbol of the Party that, with him at its head, has just fought its last battle in a lost war. He speaks sincerely and with the clarity that has always characterized his words: "It was no longer possible to live as we have lived until now. Everything had to be radically changed. There was no other choice... What has been done is of historical significance. Society has become free. It has been politically and spiritually liberated. The totalitarian system has been abolished. Free elections, freedom of the press, freedom of religious worship, popular representation, and Party pluralism have become realities. Human rights are now recognized as a supreme principle. The Cold War is over. The threat of world war has been avoided, while the arms race and absurd militarization that destroyed our industry and our social and moral conscience have been ended. The peoples and nations have realized a true liberty, opening the way to self-determination."

None of these undertakings has been completed. The majority have not even gone half way. A state in decomposition, an economy in ruins, a growing impoverishment of the people, interethnic conflicts, anarchy. One has the impression that Gorbachev, at his departure, feels that he has been misunderstood. He himself has not understood everything that's happened. Many things came about unexpectedly, surprising even him. Nevertheless, in a totalitarian regime little happens that is not, in some manner, expected. Gorbachev softened totalitarianism just enough to allow to happen what he himself, perhaps, did not want.

Six years ago, when the extraordinary man from Stavropol assumed the leadership of his country at the head of the Party that governed it, no one could have imagined that so many things would change so rapidly. No one should be surprised therefore by "the resistance of dying forces of the past, of old structures of the Party, the state, and the economic apparatus"—other departing words of Gorbachev. But all his actions were not enough to allow the creator of *perestroika* and *glasnost'* to remain in power, even if he will certainly remain an important figure in history. It seems almost that history took it upon itself to remove him from power in order to preserve him for itself and keep his image pure. Given the nature of his inheritance, it was impossible for Gorbachev to accomplish even a part of what he desired: to bring into accord such diverse entities as central planning and the market, collective and private property, the "guiding role" of the Communist Party and a multiparty system, the state apparatus and a state of law, centralized and decentralized management, bureaucracy and entrepreneurship, "people's democracy" and democratic freedoms, "real socialism" and socialism "with a human face." On more than one occasion Gorbachev had recourse to compromises, but in some cases, against all expectations, he managed to find radical solutions. He committed errors of judgment: in attempting to bring an end to totalitarian (Stalinist) communism but remain a communist himself; in hoping, especially at the beginning, to use the power of the Party against the country's ills, the very Party that had created those ills; in long believing (or so it seemed at least) that the Soviet system could save itself through simple corrective measures.

But he realized the limits of the possibilities before him, some of which he had created, sometimes involuntarily. He retired from the scene as a reformer who could no longer carry the weight of the reforms he had undertaken on his shoulders. At the moment of his departure, some see in him only an actor in a drama that had to come to an end, others see a hero, still others a saint. Mikhail Gorbachev's role was none of these, although elements of them all were part of his character. In the Commonwealth of Independent States, whose preliminary conditions he created, it became clear that there was no position for him: this is perhaps the last paradox of his political destiny, which could not do without paradoxes. His successor, whom he himself had brought onto the political scene, arrogantly chased him from the Kremlin stage. The man who has replaced Gorbachev is closer, in language and culture, to the people on the street. In theater of this sort, the case is not unique.

I leave for some other occasion conjectures about what the new Russian state will be like: national and traditional or democratic and modern, Orthodox or schismatic, "saintly" and mystical or secular and "populist," white or red, Slavophile or westernizing, Asiatic or European, a Russia that "cannot be understood with the intellect" and in which "one must simply believe" (Tyuchev) or the "hard," "great-assed" (*tolstozadaia*) Russia sung by Aleksandr Blok, "with Christ" or "without cross." Whatever form it assumes it will need to take store of what remains after the Soviet Union, and of what has been irretrievably lost. Fallen empires are not mourned.

Few indeed will mourn the fallen order or the ideology that sustained it. But the idea of human emancipation remains nevertheless, an idea over which the "first socialist country" threw its enormous shadow, as do the will and energy, faith and hope that that idea inspired and sustained, not only in the USSR but in our century as a whole. Russia cannot adequately evaluate its history if it skips over or undervalues this fact.

Humanity will continue to work towards its own emancipation, very likely with greater prudence and less utopianism. We are entering a time in which secular eschatologies will perhaps long be suppressed: this is the price for having tried to create "a better world and a more just society" (I write these words without bitterness or irony). Russia itself paid the greatest part of this price. The geniuses of Russia's past spoke of its mission in the world, of the desire to save humanity without divine aid. One must avoid pathos when speaking of their words, for they did much more harm than good.

POSTSCRIPT – *Gorbachev did not leave happy. "I know no happy reformers," he declared. In today's political world sometimes one must leave in order to be believed, and remain silent in order to be listened to. This is what Gorbachev is faced with.*

To a group of believers and priests who visited him on the eve of his departure he confessed that he did not share their faith but understood those who pray. "My mission is to make this country more humane by civil means, for the first time in the course of its history... This is my prayer." He did all he could to fulfill such a mission. Perhaps history will answer his prayer.

The support accorded to the addressee in these lines is not unconditional. It is premised on the assumption that he will not return to the office he has abandoned. Such a return could reduce or distort the importance of his historical role. His task in history was greater than he himself was.

Archives and Memory
To Boris Yeltsin, President of the Russian Federation

Zagreb, Spring 1992

It was impossible to hide the crimes, but many of the guilty escaped punishment. *Glasnost'* did not open the archives of the Cheka, the GPU, the NKVD, the KGB, the Comintern, or the Supreme Soviet. But despite that fact, a portion of the dossiers they contained made their way into the light of day. "Every dossier is a living destiny," wrote a Russian poet.

Some of those guilty of crimes have destroyed the documents in which they were compromised. Others continue to do so. The names of the victims are being forgotten, those of their executioners erased. What remains in the archives must be saved. This, at the present moment, is one of the great duties of culture, all the more so since contemporary politics in Russia and the former USSR have shown themselves incapable of accomplishing tasks of this nature.

A young writer recently read the following words at the Moscow Writers' House: "Meyerhold was shot. I have seen his dossier. It also contains a letter that, after the death sentence had been read, Meyerhold sent to Vishinksy. It is a striking document. In it the director lists 'the illegal methods of interrogation' to which he was subjected by the judge. He had broken Meyerhold's left arm (not his right, which he needed for signing his confession) and forced him to drink his own urine. Meyerhold had cried, fallen to his knees, crawled. But in the end he had been forced to sign."

However painful it might be, we desire to know the contents of other such dossiers. Especially those who lost their families and close friends in the gulag have a right to the truth. I have a right to know how my grandfather Nikolai and my uncle behaved at their trials, what the accusations laid against them by their interrogating judges were, what they were constrained to sign.

After the collapse of the Soviet system, documents from the archives have begun to circulate in Moscow, Leningrad-Petersburg, Kiev, Odessa, and various other cities. Many expected to see great dissident works of literature emerge from their hiding places in boxes and basements, but nothing of the sort happened. *Perestroika* and *glasnost'* did not give birth to a literature of their own. In any case, that is not how literature works. Bulgakov's sequestered diary was retrieved from the police archives, not Babel's sequestered novel. It is less than what we expected but, paradoxically, more than what has emerged from the boxes and basements.

In Moscow and St. Petersburg today one may acquire, for a modest sum, a copy of a dossier; for a greater sum, one can even obtain an original document that has no copies. Since the installation of the new government, the question of archives, that is, of the memory preserved inside them, has been neglected. People who are devoid of cultural and historical understanding have no idea of the importance of such testimonials for culture and for history. Some are afraid of them. It has been reported that you are planning to sell the archives of the Comintern, which contain a portion of the memory of Europe and of the world.

The issue of rehabilitation has likewise not been examined, as it ought to be. Since the change of regime, in the former Soviet states it is easier to rehabilitate a tsarist ultra-nationalist *chernostenets* than a liberal once condemned as "Trotskyite." History will make decisions to the extent that it has a basis on which to make judgments. The new bureaucracy is as devoid of historical consciousness as the old was. In questions of rehabilitation, one must also consider questions of memory.

The past must not be forgotten, most of all so that it will not be repeated. Russia's past has been tragic. I would ask you, Mr. President, to please reflect on this and do everything in your power to avoid new tragedies.

For a New Dissidence
To Adam Michnik
and György Konrád

Paris–Zagreb, 1992

Both the place and role of the intelligentsia and the dissident movement of Eastern Europe have changed. Criticism of the government today unfolds on the public square, in the parliament, in the press. Literature is no longer needed for this work. All the better for literature.

Government and ideological censorship has ceased to operate, or, where it still exists, now works for another kind of government, a different ideology. This is also the case with self-censorship, which has been relegated to a personal responsibility.

Dissidents are no longer the most useful figures for literature (tomorrow this will not be the case, but that is another question). Democracy has taken dissidence upon itself. This does not go without saying. "Democratic praxis" develops poorly in post-totalitarian society: most often what we find is that hybrid of democracy and dictatorship— "democraship." We should distinguish *transitional* phases from actual *transformations*, which are overdue or have not yet even begun. The writer who wants to be a dissident in the old manner, at whatever price, is dubious as a writer.

Very few have managed to turn dissidence into literature. It is easier to admit that today than it was yesterday. The author who distinguishes himself more through his positions than through his work can attain in literature only the place he deserves as an author. This is not the case in politics, but that too is another question. The customers are no longer the same, but the demands of literature itself have not changed. Writers who do not wish to accept that they have learned nothing from what came before.

The language in which today's changes are being discussed is rather more journalistic than literary. One must come to terms with this. It could have been anticipated. The role of the author as one who incites the nation belongs to the past. Under totalitarianism the intellectual could serve as a hostage to the truth (as I referred to Sakharov in one of these letters), but the price for this was high. We were offered the opportunity to defend the insulted and the injured, to align ourselves with the minority against the majority, to protect even those with whom we disagreed. Today's scenario furnishes few such roles. In the relationship of politics to literature, one must not hope that the author will be given an important place. All the better for the author. Therein lies the greatest opportunity for literature, and for art as a whole.

Following the changes at the end of the 1980s and beginning of the 1990s, some authors and intellectuals distinguished themselves in politics and attained positions in government, thanks to their services under the old regime, in conflict with it. How to be of service under the new conditions is a question to which we do not yet have an answer. There is more than enough work to go around, but one must first of all establish what is expected of the author: what obligations, what risks, how much freedom or madness? Let us hope that the most courageous of authors will greet with irony the ignorance and vanity of new rulers, the egotistical worm of chauvinism, primitive populism and false messianism, the bad taste of new slogans and political performances, the inflation of signs and symbols. If national (national-governmental) and religious (clerical) ideologies are exclusive and manage to impose themselves upon culture, then the new dissident movements will be antinationalistic and secular. This will be neither easy nor without danger, and not merely in the domain of literature: to ridicule those who imitate the rituals of past centuries, laugh at those who try to prove through petty party politics that others are to blame for everything, and oppose the ideologues who offer their services to clueless leaders. "No One writes to the Colonel" wrote one Latin American author in the title of his book. Some are prepared for this. Authors' associations, academies, the "honest intelligentsia" did it before and, if need be, will do it again. This, we have said, is the inflation of signs and symbols in action.

The new dissidents (let us call them that conditionally, until they find a better name on their own) will once more come face to face with the understanding that true transformations are rare and difficult, sometimes grotesquely so. Western Europe followed its own path, not optimal but much more efficient. Emulating it in everything would be hard; I don't know whether doing so would be worth it. We Easterners have shown Europe where it should not go, saving it from the strain and sacrifices of one of the most enthralling utopias humanity has known, one of the most tragic adventures in all history.

Perhaps it is also our misfortune that we haven't the right to seek compensation or gratitude from anyone. We can defend ourselves from derision, justify ourselves: it is impossible to underestimate the idea of emancipation, and that idea will sooner or later come back to life. That idea, however, in its original form, remains alien to the greater part of the intelligentsia of Eastern Europe, especially to the conservative, traditionalist part, which in the West is called the Right while in the East I don't know what they could call it.

I realize that I speak as though there were still two sides. A third way is obviously harder to find than we thought. The new dissidence will most likely confront this search.

I don't know when that will be.

An Interrogation
The following letter was written before my native city of Mostar was destroyed. To the Secretary of Internal Affairs, Mostar, Bosnia-Herzegovina

Zagreb, June 30, 1991

My father, Vsevolod Matvejević, died in May of 1989 in Mostar. Several years before his death he was interrogated by the Internal Affairs Police of the city. A friend of his, Vladimir Timofeev, a Russian by nationality, had been charged with collaborating with the Soviet intelligence services: among the relatives and friends who had visited him from the USSR, someone had spied in Mostar and taken information back to Moscow.

Timofeev, an engineer by training, was sentenced to a year in prison, but because of his age and poor health he was released early. Russian books were found in his apartment, along with issues of *The Russian Idea*, which Timofeev had received from my father and loaned to two or three other friends. This was defined as "dissemination of enemy propaganda." Timofeev had been a mineral engineer, hardworking and cultured. Born in Moscow at the beginning of the century, he had emigrated in his early youth, just after the October Revolution. Yugoslavia had become his second homeland. He spent his working life in Bosnia-Herzegovina and was considered one of the most highly qualified specialists in his field. The trial and sentence affected him terribly, and he died soon after.

My father was interrogated during the investigation. He was already an old man (more than eighty) and had undergone an operation for cancer of the larynx. He spoke with difficulty, in a painful whisper, a cannula inserted in his throat. He wanted to defend Timofeev but was afraid for himself, torn between friendship and fear. I find it difficult to imagine the two old Russians standing before their Yugoslav accusers, all the more so since the greatest blame was mine in having sent my father the incriminating texts.

In the desire to understand all the details of this investigation, I would ask you please, considering the change of regime, to allow me access to the dossier in question.

POSTSCRIPT – *Despite the change of regime, I received no response to this letter.*

On the eve of the Yugoslav war, I witnessed an especially revelatory event on the occasion of my father's death. After his departure from Odessa, he had met Nikolai Berdyaev and adopted his ideas on Christianity. In rejection of the "folly of the schism," Vsevolod Nikolaevich Matveevich had requested an "ecumenical funeral," which would combine the prayers of a Catholic priest, an Orthodox priest, and a Protestant pastor. The religious authorities forbid their subordinates to conduct such a "metic" ceremony and allowed only the Protestant pastor to participate, who had come from far away. A Muslim sage declared, "The misfortune fell upon a city where one cannot even say a prayer together."

These words were circling in my mind when, in my native city, I saw the Orthodox church destroyed along with many mosques, while the Catholic church in which I had kneeled as a boy was irreparably damaged. In my father's house, which was also destroyed, at the bottom of an old wooden trunk, tied together by a dark green string, were the few letters that Berdyaev had sent to his young pupil, my father. My only hope is that, in the course of the interminable looting, a thief might have carried away that thin packet before our house was burned down. In an "ex-world" where so many things have been overturned and distorted, even a thief can sometimes be a good thing.

Our Disappointments
To Brodsky

Paris, March 1991

Many things have happened since our last meeting. We lost a friend—Danilo Kiš. Vasko Popa also died recently. It was just a few years ago that the three of us were in New York and tried to pay you a visit, but you were ill and it wasn't possible. Danilo sent you our warm regards from the podium of the PEN Club meeting and wished you a speedy recovery. Soon after that he too fell ill.

His illness actually began at the time of his "case" (yes, that's what they call it). It's said that ugly experiences cause ugly illnesses, and I am beginning to believe it. I told you about it at our first meeting, in Rio in the seventies, in that old colonial style hotel when you were working on the preface for the American edition of *A Tomb for Boris Davidovich*. We were drinking something strong, you more than I, standing and talking at length and at full voice, in Russian. Pretty girls were hovering nearby (we were younger then). Danilo was extremely grateful to you for your support. He was on trial at the time, in the press and the courts. I had tried to defend him and ended up being accused as well. We wanted the affair to be given attention abroad. You helped us, and not only through your preface to *A Tomb for Boris Davidovich*.

The invitation to come to the US, which I received thanks to your help and that of Susan Sontag, was especially important to me. Danilo too was happy to come to New York, though unfortunately it was there that his illness was diagnosed. The last time I saw him, before he became seriously ill, he was seated at his desk in Paris, translating your poetry. He had found some wonderful phrasing solutions and was reading them aloud. He was as happy as a baby that you had received the Nobel Prize, even though he too had been a candidate.

This is all now "literary history." How different it might have been. After all that happened in the meantime in so-called Eastern Europe, I too find myself in a sort of emigration. I'm teaching at the Sorbonne Nouvelle, as you once did at Columbia. One must do something. I talk about the "Other Europe," its cultures and literatures during this transition from totalitarianism to post-totalitarianism, and so on, amidst the quagmire in which people historically often find themselves after a whirlwind of events. Many things appear to me in the form of paradoxes and contradictions that it's easier to state than explain. I wrote these thoughts down for Danilo over the last few years. I reproduce them here from my notes.

We wanted our borders with Europe to be opened. Now Europe is afraid of opening its borders to us.

We sought the freedom of all nations. Now nationalism is erupting everywhere.

We demanded the recognition of the free profession of religious faith. Now we face clericalism and fundamentalism that know nothing of freedom or tolerance.

We believed we were defeating Bolshevism and Stalinism, which created the gulag and Kolyma. Now they have ceded their place to the ideology of nationalism, which caused two world wars and made Auschwitz possible.

Democracy is proclaimed but without the creation of a democratic society: we find only a mixture of democracy and dictatorship—"democraship"—in more than one new regime of the "Other Europe."

Free markets and the market economy are touted as the remedy for all ills, while so many of these countries lack even the most elementary goods.

We demanded a measure of dignity in the relations between people and peoples (how pathetic these words sound to me now!) and find instead the disdain of the western world for the poverty of the eastern, and the humiliation of the East asking for western aid.

We did everything we could to defend and promote dissident literature (a symbolic example), and now that we find that literature confronted with critical appraisals in its own languages it is clear, with rare exceptions, that most often there was more dissidence than literature (we saw it before, did we not, but most often were hypocritically silent on this point).

This litany could easily be extended in equally paradoxical variations, especially with regard to Russia or, let's say, the Soviet Union. That horrifying system does not fall as we wished but crumbles more quickly than we had hoped. Still, despite all its faults, it was a system; what remains now—chaos, poverty, humiliation—is worse than what was there before, at least in Russia. And what will happen if to this is added what Pasternak called "the Russian tendency toward excess"? So much is expected from *perestroika*, but what kind of "reconstruction" was ever possible in the Soviet system? People believe more in *perestroika* outside than inside the USSR, and, as far as it's possible to judge, *perestroika* will be more important for Europe than for Russia. Gorbachev himself is thought of as more reliable outside his country than in it, and he has perhaps done more for other peoples than for his own. His country can be thankful to him most of all for not having again covered it in shame by denying the rights and freedoms of other peoples. I feel true sympathy for him but realize he cannot continue to play the role he has played until now: one cannot long remain conserver and reformer, hero and victim, the Pope and Luther. It's impossible to continue such a role for long, especially in a country where for centuries not laws but the men in power, their passions and transgressions, have been the rule.

It's also impossible to make an instrument of renewal out of a party in power, in a single-party system, which has been one of the principal causes of the disaster to begin with. One of our young philosophers encourages the Soviet Communists not to hurl themselves into an empty pool (and it really is empty). But many do so out of habit—it's been going on for so long. Solzhenitsyn's recent letter on the "reorganization of our Russia" demonstrates the poverty of political culture in the author of *The Gulag Archipelago*. What could bringing back nineteenth-century *narodnichestvo* (populism) or the old *zemstvo* (land council) possibly accomplish? They should adopt the ideas of Gogol, Dostoevsky, and Solovyov, but reject Pushkin, Chekhov, and Herzen? Create an Orthodox Russia in a Russian manner? Such an attitude borders on obscurantism. After a Sakharov we had the right to expect a Montesquieu. But our expectations have betrayed us.

I suspect that in the greater part of the countries we're discussing, despite all the differences among them, one would not find that minimum of experience of secular culture that makes the creation of a national community and modern society possible. For some time now I have been telling believers, in Yugoslavia and elsewhere, that, according to the teachings of Christ, they should first be Christians and only after that Orthodox or Catholic: I enjoin them not to be, first of all, Russian, Serbian, or Bulgarian Orthodox; or Polish, Croatian, or Slovakian Catholics; and then, second, Orthodox or Catholics; and then, finally, at the end, Christians. Christianity is overturned in such a manner, just as some "comrades" managed to do with Marxism. The individuality of the nation is counterpoised to that of the citizen, and this view corresponds to collectivism more than to a state of law capable of truly guaranteeing individual freedom.

Republicanism is foreign to the greater part of Central and Eastern Europe, where the *identity of being* (accompanied by nostalgia for one's past and history) prevails over *identity of fact* (with plans for today, real and attainable). The right to be different is one of the major conquests of this century of delusions, but particularism in and of itself is not a value. It becomes a value only when one holds it as such. Anthropophagy is, I have often said, grinding my teeth, one way of being different. I am tired of repeating such banalities.

I am tired of writing "open letters" to governments and people in power these last twenty years. How much time I have wasted in this senseless work! What good has it done anyone? What has changed as a result of it? Not I, indeed. But that has little importance in regard to all the rest. I am still sorry to see the idea of human emancipation and a more just society disappear from the horizon. I know how naive it sounds to say such things today, after all that has happened. I'm not talking about the disappearance of utopia (to hell with that) but the disappearance of hope. This is the most important thing for us, who no longer have a god. In the end, in the face of what's happening, I would like to find a role for myself other than that of gravedigger.

But today's script appears to offer no better role than that.

Final Letters

POSTSCRIPT – *As in a novel, certain personages have appeared more than once in this epistolary. At the very start Karlo Štajner and his* Seven Thousand Days in Siberia *made their appearance, along with Sinyavsky and his friends and compatriots in the gulag, Joseph Brodsky in his exile, Bulat Okudzhava and his nostalgia for song, Danilo Kiš... We have crossed their path on several occasions in this story. Their fate can in a manner be understood as its conclusion.*

I met Andrei Sinyavsky again at the Sorbonne after a trip to Russia, from which he had just returned at the end of 1992. I found him profoundly disappointed by the changes that he had seen. He appeared resigned and visibly older. I listened to his presentation on the parallels between Lenin and Stalin. He was helping himself to doses of alcohol too large for someone whose health had been ruined by such experiences as his. He spoke in Russian, not without difficulty, about things that no longer existed and in a manner in which one could no longer really speak about them. I was shaken.

I saw in him not the most gifted writer of the emigration but a perfect example of the Russian intelligentsia, its virtues and contradictions. I had written him a long letter from Geneva about dissidence in the Other Europe, more particularly, a fragment about what seemed to me to be our fate after the fall of the empire. I include here some of its lines. Yet another "litany."

Heirs without Heritage
To Andrei Sinyavsky
The Home of Denis de Rougemont

December 1992

A portion of today's Europe resembles the third world of yesterday: remains of the Soviet Union, especially Russia, Belarus, and Ukraine, regions in former Yugoslavia and the Balkan peninsula, Bulgaria, Albania, Romania, perhaps Greece. Since the revolution that took place on this continent at the end of the 1980s, the concepts of west and east correspond to more parts of the world than ever. The terms "Eastern Europe" and "Central Europe" again mean what they meant before the Cold War. We could be reassured by the corrected usage of the terms if things themselves were in better order.

Rhetoric adapts to the events of which we are witnesses. Political speech continues to form and direct them. Literature defines itself in relation to them, "taking its distance" or "engaging" them, most often to its own detriment. One must be on guard against how to avoid the traps in which words that do not correspond to things can catch us, emblems that obfuscate rather than reveal content: Chernobyl, the Moscow putsch, the Berlin Wall, Christianity "before the wall," "war in the wilderness," the "Balkan powder keg," and so on. Rhetorical figures, unavoidable in these situations, are capable of altering the dimensions of events, decreasing or increasing, depending on how they are used, their importance. Judges often have little patience for metaphor; they prefer direct speech.

It isn't just that the system collapsed in the countries of the Other Europe. Society itself exploded.

The totalitarian regimes were defeated, but we remain obsessed by totalitarianism.

We believe we can conquer the present but are unable to take control of the past.

We watch freedoms being born and either abuse them or are unsure what to do with them.

We denounced history but continue to be pervaded by historicism.

We condemned utopianism, but the best among us are nostalgic for a utopia that might save us.

We defended national heritage, against which we must now defend ourselves.

We wanted to "preserve memory," which now hinders and punishes us.

Partitions are being imposed, but there is very little left to partition.

Every day we declare that things can get no worse, and every day they continue to do so.

We based our hopes on culture, but culture itself has found no basis.

We congratulated ourselves on finally breaking free from misfortune, but misfortune follows us like a shadow.

Many of us nursed a blind faith in Europe, in which the greatest European minds have never ceased to doubt.

In this manner our horizon appears in broken lines and dark shades. I exaggerate little. We lack guiding ideas. Positive thoughts are few; tried values and probative examples are lacking altogether. Ideologies have betrayed us; politics have given out. Faith has been misused in a variety of ways. Uncertainty oppresses us, disorder surrounds us, while we ourselves sometimes appear as heirs whose inheritance has fallen into dispute or been snatched away.

*Emigration and Dissidence**
TO A FRIEND WHO IS STILL
AFRAID OF BEING NAMED

                                                        Paris–Moscow, 1993

POSTSCRIPT – *I took a brief trip to Russia and saw there what I had not wanted to see. That's the way it is. I have nothing to add to the previous part of this epistolary, to the instances of disillusionment already enumerated. The catastrophe appears even more serious than I had imagined, not only on the political and social planes but on the moral and spiritual as well.*

I spent very little time in Moscow, a stopover on my way to Pskov and St. Petersburg. The latter city had just changed its name. I would have preferred that it take Petrograd instead. I looked for several friends, émigrés or dissidents of before, but could not find anyone. I still admire and respect all their abnegation and suffering. I noted, however, the following lines in my travel journal. I am sending them to a friend who is still afraid of being named in a letter that—at last I can hope—will not be censored.

I have observed emigration from the standpoint of the child of an émigré. I have known its hopes and its chimeras. I remember a Cossack in an old fashion black caftan, who once stopped by our house to have tea, which my father had prepared in the samovar. He did not drink coffee and could not understand how others could. He and his friends were announcing every day the imminence of decisive events that would change the course of things. He was preparing to return to Russia the following spring, when he would be seventy years old. He died at ninety, on the eve of the Soviet Union's collapse. If he could have returned to the Kuban, what would he have found there from before?

Over the years, traveling around the world, I met many émigrés of this sort. I myself became one. I saw how excluded and dispersed they were—in a word, how alone. The country to which they return is not

---

* The present chapter does not appear in the 1994 Croatian edition of the *Epistolary*. This translation is based on the 1995 French edition and the Italian edition of 1998. [– Translator's note.]

their homeland. The one they left no longer exists. Their vision doubles between "us" and "them," "back home" and "here." Every emigration is a function of necessity or misfortune, of unanticipated events or historical injustice. Émigrés are split between the life "before" and the life "after," between rupture and nostalgia. This eschatology is aggravated by external obstacles and internal divisions. Émigrés react against one another without being able to do without one another. Their quarrels are for the most part small-minded and sterile, incited by rivalry or envy. A certain number of them find refuge in a kind of subculture and live according to the criteria it imposes. Their capacity to make judgments suffers from it; their works often show traces of it; their lives remain affected by it.

The fate of those who emigrate depends, among other things, on the baggage they bring with them on their narrow rafts. Nevertheless, some nations owe the defense and preservation of their heritage to émigrés, especially when they have been in danger. This is why émigrés believe that their merits, real or imagined, confer on them the right to decide the destiny of the nation. Their propositions seem unacceptable in the countries they have left, incomprehensible in the countries where they have settled.

Under totalitarian regimes we find, in addition, an "internal emigration." Its cultural ties are stronger but its freedom of expression is more limited. Despite this, in the course of the century such internal exile yielded works of the greatest importance. Some of its traits distinguish it from dissidence per se. Often condemned to silence, its silence can at times be eloquent.

As for Russia, dissidents had no precise notions of their objectives. They expressed themselves best through attitudes rather than ideas. They did not constitute an opposition in the European sense of the term: the regime in which they found themselves did not tolerate opposition. Nor did they represent an alternative to the power in place, for the power of the regime prohibited any alternative to itself. Dissidents had no common program, excluding perhaps that of opposing the programs of the power in place.

When today, after the sudden changes, the old dissidents (or what remains of them in Russia and elsewhere) form projects, they show to what extent they were accustomed to contest rather than affirm, to destroy rather than create. While under the Soviet regime it was difficult to contest, it was impossible to create.

Those who return to their countries after having been away tend to apply what they have seen in the old world to the reality before them, not realizing that they have lost any link they might have once had with that reality. A good number of dissidents have decided to put off their return. This is perhaps not a bad decision.

The Collapse of the Intelligentsia
To Bulat Okudzhava

Paris–Zagreb, December 1993

At our brief meeting in Paris in 1991 we barely had time to shake hands. I heard that you were ill. I'm happy to learn that you're doing better. It seems you're no longer singing, which is too bad.

I'm writing under the influence of the latest news from Russia. I remember your words at our meeting in Moscow in 1976: "Anything can happen if they only start…" I don't know anymore where things start and where they end. Perhaps you're not surprised by what's been happening in the former USSR, but I am, even if I didn't expect much better. Who could have imagined that in the first free elections in Russia half the population would refuse the liberty being offered to them? That Russia would be opposed to "the choice of Russia"? The "choice," it's true, is Yeltsin, and he isn't worth much, not more than the man himself. If the West supports such a president, it's for fear of someone worse. But the "lesser evil" is still an evil.

Those responsible for the worst of Soviet politics are returning to political life. The very men recently chased from the "White House" amidst cannon fire are being elected to the parliament. The former single party system is being transformed into a caricature of a multiparty one. They stop governing "in the name of the people" and install an anonymous populism. They agree to reform the constitution and show the reformers the door. The red dictatorship is replaced by one that's brown and black. They turn away the nationalists and it is *chernosotentsy*, ultra-nationalism that enters the scene. Such contradictions are possible only in Russia.

A variety of charlatans have always been part of the country's history. But no one expected the appearance of a Zhirinovsky. I myself could not have imagined that the majority of the country's citizens would vote for the "liberal democracy" that he promises, for the fascist ideology on which his words are predicated, for the folly he incarnates. This, too, demonstrates the poor state in which Russia finds itself. Nor is it just Russia but rather the entire Soviet Union that has now renounced the

"Soviet," the communist state that has abandoned communism. The very existence of the Russian people is in ruins, and its moral losses are still greater than its material losses.

I have the impression that in such a situation the intelligentsia once again does not know what to do. Things have gone further than anyone expected. No one sees a way to stop them and make sense of them. On neither the Right nor the Left are there solid proposals, and who even knows what is Right and Left in this situation? Soviet intellectuals remained relatively reserved toward *perestroika*. I have been briefed on the speeches at the recent Writers' Union assemblies in Moscow and ex-Leningrad: those who mounted the podium were, for the most part, of mediocre (Soviet) education and, in the majority of cases, were even ignorant of true Russian culture. (The former "dissident" writer Eduard Limonov recently went to Bosnia in order to shoot, "from the heights of the Serb positions" in Pale, at the inhabitants of Sarajevo. He really did it, and boasted about it, and even had himself captured on film.) Vladimir Volfovich Zhirinovsky did not appear *ex nihilo*: he is simply a caricature of what was already there.

At the end of 1993, following the defeat of freedom in the "first free elections," it seems to me that the best elements of the intelligentsia have made the decision to keep their distance or remain silent. Is it possible that they feel guilty? Or do they want to avoid being dragged into some kind of ongoing machinations? Is there in this attitude something of the ancient desire for rupture, the *otshchepenstvo* (nay-saying) to which the noblest spirits of Russia aspired at the end of the last century and beginning of the present? Or did "Soviet practice" manage to suffocate such a tradition? Perhaps writers, so often forced to "conform" or "take a position," according to the official slogans of the regime, have chosen of their own initiative to no longer remain in tow? I would like to believe it. But I fear this is not the case. We await the appearance of a new dissident movement, intellectual and moral, worthy of the values and ideals of Russian culture. It is nowhere in sight. Perhaps we wait in vain.

Russia is one of the rare countries of Europe, perhaps the only one, where the majority of intellectuals refused to take part in elaborating a national project per se. They "went to the people." They refused the state. In tsarist Russia there was no national state in the European sense of the term. The empire was something else. Defining a nation and creating a state depend on work that, in this case, was left only half done. It's dangerous to try and compensate for being behind after the fact (remember Italy and Germany of the 1920s and 1930s), especially when those who undertake the task are clowns or charlatans.

Despite all its defects, or perhaps, in a certain measure, thanks to them, the Soviet Union brought the history of Russia into world history. This brought little advantage to the Russian people, who today find themselves on the brink of great poverty. Russia is in the process of returning to its own history, which is less ambitious but more congruent with its calling. Perhaps we are at the end of one "time of troubles" (*smutnoe vremia*) and at the beginning of an epoch in which the nation will confront itself. I repeat that I no longer know where things start and where they end. These are questions that obsess me.

In my country an indescribable war has begun, national, civil, religious, I don't know what else—fratricidal. Could a similar misfortune overtake Russia, made graver by the "Russian tendency to excess" and by the means at the country's disposal? The thought fills me with anguish. It made me write these lines and made me suddenly feel like leaving for Moscow, St. Petersburg, Prague, Budapest, Warsaw, and anywhere else I could think of just to talk with writers and friends. I changed my mind, paralyzed by a feeling of powerlessness.

I often listen to your song-poems, dear Bulat, and am disconcerted that you have lost your voice. (Is this, too, symbolic?) I wonder what meaning such works have for young people of today in Russia. Is there anyone who sings like this today in Moscow or *Piter*? Does anyone still need songs like yours?

A few days ago in Paris, where I share the fate of a new emigration, I met a group of young Russians in faded jeans in the metro, singing the old romance *Svecha gorela, svecha gorela* (A Candle Burned). One youngster distanced himself from the rest to sing *Yevrei, Yevrei* (Jew, Jew). Yesterday we were all German Jews. Then we became Russian Jews. Who knows what kind of Judaism we'll share tomorrow. I have described our encounters in Moscow, Ohrid, and Zagreb in my epistolary. I hope to send you a selection in Russian translation soon.

Okudzhava's Reponse

Moscow, Spring 1994

Dear Predrag,

I was very happy to receive your letter. What you're doing in rendering clear our uncertainties, even our despair at what is happening in Russia, is important work. I understand you well. I spent a great deal of time in a similar state. I thank God that, because I am a student of Russian history and especially because I find myself in this shit hole of today, none of what's been happening manages to surprise me. Of course I suffer and torment myself. But there is no surprise.

I'll try to explain my thoughts in a few words.

For centuries Russia has lived under the blows of clubs. These blows (tsarist and especially communist) contributed to the creation of an illusion of well-being, integration, and good will. No sooner have the clubs been lowered than society and its people begin to show their true face.

Here is how I see that face.

Russia has never experienced democratic institutions. It was a society with a slave psychology that served the prince (*kniaz'*) or the tsar, the great leader or the general secretary. Russia never lived freedom. It knew a kind of anarchy (*volia*) but not true freedom. Human dignity has never been respected here. Respect was reserved for abstractions, the idea of the fatherland or of one's heritage, but not for the human personality... I would also add this: there has never been, in Russia, respect for the law.

This is why I think one can expect nothing good until Russia has democratic institutions, until it has them in its blood. This will take a long time, many generations. And much suffering.

I don't mean to say that all of Russian society is like this. But there are very few righteous men here, and those there are have little influence on the life of society.

Bulat Okudzhava

POSTSCRIPT – *For some time I received no news from Okudzhava. Mutual friends let me know that he had fallen ill. In the meantime I changed homes and countries more than once. My life had begun to appear to me as some-*

thing "between exile and asylum." At last I managed to telephone Bulat from Rome to invite him to read, along with several friends, one of his works at Campidoglio. His voice was faint and lower than before when he replied that he no longer traveled by air and it would be too far by train. Even to Vladivostok he planned to take the train. We talked for some fifteen minutes as I tried to convince him to come. I cited a fragment of "The Third Rome," which he'd written long ago in Moscow in opposition to the Stalinist Moscow rhetoric:

> The monk Filofei wrote to the Tsar:
> "The first Rome lost its faith.
> The second was taken by the infidels.
> The third Rome must be built in your empire."
> The Tsar received the message in silence:
> "How can one build an Eternal City
> In a precarious world?"

I think Bulat was smiling as he listened to me: "The Eternal City is still far off, while the end of the comedy is close at hand." That was the response I understood. He seemed to want to finish certain things but was having difficulty doing so. It reminded me of one of the last songs he wrote, which he sang on the occasion of Vladimir Vysotsky's death: "But his hand shook and the refrain does not fit the verses" (No drozhala ruka, i motiv sa stikhom ne skhodilsia). I stopped insisting. But we made an appointment to see each other soon, at the beginning of summer in Paris. "Poka!" (See you!).

I took the Rome–Paris flight on the fifteenth or sixteenth of June. According to my usual habit, I watched the planet's surface from the air: the Tyrrhenian Sea, the Gulf of Genoa, the still white Alps, and some lakes in the mountains, rivers, the Île-de-France. As we approached Paris, I opened my copy of Le Monde: Bulat Okudzhava had died in Paris the day before.

I stayed at the airport for several hours, just enough time to get a return flight. Land and water, plains and mountains—I saw nothing more, only a few clouds. Bulat Shalsovich—as some of his friends called him—leaves a great absence.

Several days later the Moscow journal Novoe vremia published Okudzhava's letter that I cited above. It was perhaps the last letter he ever wrote. I had given it to a friend, a correspondent for the Russian press in

Rome. It had been placed on the page next to an In Memoriam entitled, "God of Moscow Dead in Paris." Bulat would have smiled at such a title. I see that smile even now, like that of an adolescent prematurely old, half melancholic, half resigned.

On the very same page of the same journal appeared an obituary for the actor Yevgeny Lebedev: "National treasure, actor of the century, patriarch of the Petersburg stage, theatrical genius." Bulat had respected him a great deal. I had had occasion to see him during a tour in Zagreb, where he'd played the role of the horse Kholstomer in an adaptation of Tolstoy's short story, under the extraordinary direction of Tovstonogov. When he'd trembled on stage, the entire audience had trembled with him. In Leningrad he'd asked me not to publish the text of our conversation after the debate organized by the journal Neva.

They departed quietly, one after another. They were much more than "fellow travelers" on the road of dissidence; they were, despite themselves, idols who despised every form of idolatry: Varlam Shalamov, Nadezhda Mandelshtam, Sinyavsky, Brodsky and Kiš, Vysotsky, Aleksandr Galich and Bulat Okudzhava. There were once so many...

They've left behind an empty space no one and nothing will ever fill.

A Perverted Slavicism

Rome, Summer 1994

Of late things are going poorly in Yugoslavia, now "ex," in a war that is simultaneously national, civil, religious, and memorial. I emigrated from the country, just as my father emigrated from his native Russia in the 1920s. Sometimes—I must say it once more—destinies repeat themselves.

From Paris and from Rome, the cities in which I now live, I leave sometimes for Zagreb or venture as far as besieged Sarajevo. I am growing accustomed, not without a sense of resignation, to this situation. Of what use is all that I've tried to do until now? What good have all these open letters of my Epistolary *done, in which I thought I was defending not only values and principles but real people in danger, in order to change and perhaps improve the world? Even while writing them, however, I suppose I was conscious of my naiveté.*

I lost numerous friends, first from among the Serbs, those who supported the paranoid politics of their "national leader," then from among the Croats, those who detested my "cosmopolitanism." I fell in with the losing Bosnians. I loved the Yugoslavia that was lost.

The evolution of things in Russia frightens me and fills me with pain. There it is still worse than before, alas, and impossible to turn back. I don't dare return to Odessa anymore. A brief stay in Pskov and St. Petersburg made me feel sick inside. I will not go to Moscow soon. Some time ago, many of my French and Italian friends had reproached me for criticizing Boris Yeltsin, who was for them "providential," the "only democratic alternative" to totalitarianism in Russia. Subsequent events have made it clear who he is in truth.

I see that the Russian intelligentsia, what remained of it, has tumbled as I feared. The Association of Russian Writers has disappointed me even more than the politicians... I write once again to the new leaders in that old institution at its headquarters: 52 ulitsa Vorovskogo, Moscow. Thus closes the circle.

To the New Administration of the Writers' Union of Russia

Recently in Moscow the Writers' Union of Russia, under the direction of Yury Bondarev, awarded the Mikhail Sholokhov prize to Radovan Karadžić, tiring poet, psychiatrist at the service of Milošević paranoia, leader of the nationalists for a Greater Serbia, which besieged and bombarded Sarajevo, practiced "ethnic cleansing," established concentration camps, raped, and murdered. A Stalinist like Mikhail Sholokhov deserved to have the shameful prize that bears his name given to a person compromised to such an extent as Radovan Karadžić.

The Russian Writers' Union has become the reference point for the worst of nationalists. The fault is not that of the great Russian literary tradition, for it too is a victim. Yury Bondarev is a holdover of the Stalinist *nomenklatura*.

When the war criminal came to Moscow to receive his prize, not a single writer worthy of the name shook his hand. So few true writers are left in any case. The jury had decided to compensate Karadžić for his commitment to "the Slavic cause." What is this cause in the name of which the Bosnian Slavs, Islamicized long ago, are being led to the slaughterhouse?

I dream of what the Slavicism, the *slavianstvo*, of yesterday represented, the hope of humiliated, insulted, impoverished peoples who wanted to unite together in order to subsist, as well as that of certain naive, generous Slavophiles of nineteenth-century Russia: the Slavic sentiment at the base of the national idea proposed by men such as Strossmayer and Masaryk, in which the elevated spirits of Janáček and Hašek believed; the Yugoslavism that served as a calling for Croatian poets like Krleža and Ujević in their youth, and for Ivo Andrić all his life; the spiritual attitude of so many of our Serb brothers, which, despite my cosmopolitan skepticism, became mine as well. What we see now becoming clearer day by day is an archaic and perverse Slavicism prepared to oppress the weak and unarmed, a demented and retrograde ideology that has been, and remains—except perhaps when it is suicidal—the sister of fascism and daughter of the hysteria now afflicting our countries.

These two must not be confused. It is time to put an end to the confusion. I will continue to cry out in the wilderness.

POSTSCRIPT – *Behind the simultaneously tragic and comic figure of Radovan Karadžić hovers the shadow of a monster of genius: Slobodan Milošević. He is the beneficiary, alas, of sinister support from among the ex-nomenklatura of Russia, which Europe fears.*

Of this I am ashamed.

The Gulag So Long Ago

This epistolary is not chronologically consistent. The story is divided according to its own calendar. It ends two or three years before its final letters, with the death of its hero Karlo Štajner. We met Štajner at the beginning of this book. He was in the gulag with my uncle Vladimir. He became friends with my father and with me. After the fall of the communist regime, the postman delivered to his home, at 91 Jordanovačka cesta, the decision of the Croatian Parliament depriving him of his pension. I had little respect for the President of Croatia. His political agenda of attempting to "reconcile all Croats," extending a hand in this manner to the old Ustashe, was one of the reasons for my emigration. But I had defended him when he was in prison under the old regime. I decided to write to him on Štajner's behalf.

To Franjo Tuđman
PRESIDENT OF
THE REPUBLIC OF CROATIA

Paris, May 4, 1991

I have learned that the Parliament has suspended the pension of Karlo Štajner, who spent twenty years in the gulag and wrote the book *Seven Thousand Days in Siberia*. The person who informed me was his wife, Sofya Yefimovna, who waited for him in Moscow for those twenty years and now helps him in his old age.

Štajner will soon be ninety years old. He is weak from prostate cancer and has lost his eyesight. His book helped to unmask the misdeeds of Stalinism. It was awarded the Goran Prize as a work of the resistance. This work and these accomplishments deserve to be recognized.

As far as I understand, Štajner received his pension through the direct intervention of Tito. If the commission that removed it desired to demonstrate in this manner its position with regard to former communists, it made a grave error: Štajner was a victim of Stalinist communism.

I assure you that I would never ask a favor for me personally. I only ask you to help a ninety-year-old man who spent twenty years in Siberia and left one of the most convincing testimonials of the gulag.

I thank you in advance.

POSTSCRIPT – (Zagreb, 1991–92). *A letter from the Cabinet of the President of Croatia found me at my Parisian address. Karlo Štajner's pension had been reinstated. Only McCarthyist extremism could have prevented it. In the meantime, the elderly Štajner had passed through a difficult period. He had been awarded his pension in Tito's time. Was he to lose it amidst what was happening in Europe today? How would Sonya live without it? To whom could he entrust her?*

Štajner first lost his smile, then his memory, then his reason. Once again he is being fired at from behind on the Hoerlgasse in Vienna. They torture him, shove a cigarette into one of his eyes. The partisans rescue him, send him abroad. Now he's searching for a taxi; he must get to a secret meeting with an important personage. He repeats disparate words: Zona, zek, nary, razvod, kipiatok, makhorka, Maklakovka—*nightmares of the gulag.**

The doctor to whom we took him decided to have him transferred temporarily to the geriatric ward, near the psychiatric hospital at Vrapče, near Zagreb. The other hospitals were full of wounded. The war's ferocity was growing more intense.

In May of 1991 I accompany him, in the car with Sonya, to the psikhushka, *as the Russians say. We don't want to leave him with the dying old people. Sonya barely manages to hold back her tears. His reason has come back: he understands where he is. We return two or three days later because Sonya wants to take him home. "A few days more in here and I would die," he says. He is weak but in good spirits. I recall Varlam Shalamov, removed from a home for the elderly in the winter of 1982 and installed in a psychiatric hospital. He caught cold en route and died.* Psikhushka *and* gulag.

Štajner lived several months more. I spoke at his gravesite in Zagreb's Mirogoj Cemetery, on a quiet spring day, before a small group of former comrades, survivors of the camps and elderly, superstitious Jews, of whom so few remain in Central Europe that the Other Europe itself seems to be disappearing. Beside me stood Sofya Yefimovna, accustomed to patience, strong from suffering. Perhaps this open letter is the best epilogue to this story, Russian and European.

Karlo Štajner fell gravely ill in the winter of 1991. The expression of his face grew more distant. He looked at the walls of his room as at those of a prison. He seemed to want to go away somewhere or return. Winter, distance, departures, and returns are sketched across the surface of his existence. They appear to me now like metaphors of his life and work: the cold of Norilsk and the Solovetsky Islands, the distance between the White Sea and the Sea of Okhotsk, the gulag, *Seven Thousand Days in Siberia, Return from the Gulag, A Hand from the Grave*—titles of his books. Whenever I met him in his final years I had the impression that it

---

* Zona is the portion of the gulag in which the prisoners are confined; *zek* is a detainee; *nary* are the wooden planks that make up the beds of the prisoners in the barracks; *razvod* is the word the prisoners use to denote the changing of the prison guards; *kipiatok* is a boiling kettle; *makhorka* is a camp cigarette; *Maklakovka* is the name of the Siberian village where Štajner spent his last year of exile. [– Translator's note.]

was all passing constantly before his eyes. Of all that he left us his testament.

He lost his boyhood friends long ago, first among them being those who shared his fate in the purges and the camps. Some simply grew old and died. Some did not want to believe what he had lived through and written about. Others reproached him for remaining faithful, despite everything that had happened to him, to the ideas for which he had suffered. There were ever fewer of us who came to see him. He was more and more alone. That had to be, it seems.

Štajner lived a long life. But it was divided into before and after the camps. He tried to reconcile one with the other. In a sense he lived both one life and another: humble and honorable at the same time, tragic and full of dignity. He lived on, it would seem, in large part because the desire to bear witness to what had happened to him and to his comrades gave him strength. He often wrote and spoke about this salutary desire.

The book *Seven Thousand Days in Siberia* waited a long time to be published. Its author managed to bring it forth in spite of the opposition of his old comrades. When it did finally appear in print, it changed his life. He came into contact with numerous readers, who greeted him with trust. Hundreds of thousands of copies of his work have contributed to a definitive coming to terms with Stalinist depravity. Karlo Štajner is one of the most important protagonists and witnesses of the events of contemporary history. In battles in which only the losers prevail, he was a hero of our time. More than this: he helped us to a new understanding of heroism itself.

In this connection, let me repeat my words of some twenty years ago.

Today there are fewer and fewer of those who are prepared to confront the reasons that induced Štajner's generation to take positions such as the one Štajner himself took. One day in 1917 news from the front arrived: in the trenches of Galicia, in the settling of scores of the Great Powers, his father had perished. The boy was left a poor orphan in a large Jewish family on the outskirts of Vienna. He protested against poverty and oppression, joining the labor movement and the Communist youth organization. When, at twenty years old, he nearly bled to death on the steps of the Hoerlgasse, wounded by a police bullet, his friends proposed to send him abroad so that he could take refuge in Yugoslavia. He came to Zagreb to help those who, like him, had joined the fight against injustice. He first met the writer August Cesarec at Zrinjevac. They spoke in

German. He adapted to his new environment and learned the language. Then he met Josip Broz, who was not yet called Tito, and attracted the attention of the comrades to his abilities. He met Miroslav Krleža and read his *Journey to Russia*. When the police again uncovered his tracks he went to Russia, full of enthusiasm, to put his experience "at the service of the world revolution." In Moscow his enthusiasm waned, but he continued to hope. In the purges that convulsed the "first socialist country" he abandoned all hope. We bury his illusions but not the ideals of his youth. We bury Karlo Štajner, rendering honor unto him and his ideals.

In Russia Štajner lived through many unhappy years, but he never blamed the Russian people for his unhappiness. He saw well the unhappiness that those same very people endured. He returned from the gulag thanks to the intervention of Tito and the understanding of Khrushchev. He lived modestly. He worked hard to see that his testimonial, *Seven Thousand Days in Siberia*, should be published. It has seen twenty editions and been translated into more languages still. He was awaiting the Russian translation, which friends there had told him was being prepared. It was, I'm convinced, his last wish. But those are the kinds of wishes that are often not granted.

He asked for no privileges for himself and was angered by those who did. Perhaps in the end, from us, he would hope for just one favor: that we should look after his wife, Sofya Yefimovna Moiseeva, who did so much for him, waiting for him those seven thousand days with the certainty that she would one day see him again. It is the least we can promise to Karlo Fridrikhovich, as his closest friends called him, and probably the last thing we can do for him.

Afterword
An Open Letter to the Reader

St. Petersburg, Spring 1995

These letters were written in the course of a quarter century. In this period the world changed immeasurably. It became easier in some countries to write open letters than in others. Where freedom was greater, they were published without impediment. Under authoritarian regimes there was resistance. On the part of some there was little surprise. Others considered them a provocation.

Letters of this sort become "open" only when they are published. They are not written only for those to whom they are addressed. Authors of such letters, moreover, are not well received. One of my books, which comprised seventy-five "open letters," was published in Belgrade in 1985 in a *samizdat* edition. Its distribution was obstructed in Zagreb where it was listed among "pornographic works." It bore the subtitle *Exercises in Morality*. The epoch did not at all lend itself to "exercises in style."

Nevertheless, the situation in Yugoslavia was more favorable than in other "eastern" countries. There the risks were small compared to those in the countries under Soviet domination. The authorities were extremely hostile to nationalist separatism, but I was no national separatist. Pro-Soviets were considered dangerous, but I was unlikely to be considered in such a light since my father was a "white" émigré from Russia. The Titoist regime displayed its differences from Stalinism ostentatiously, and I made efforts to defend the right of difference. The party in power proclaimed itself leftist, while I tried to place the values of the Left in opposition to it. The Yugoslav Communist League was accused of being dissident; I was dissident in relation to the Yugoslav Communist League. Its leaders were attacked for "revisionism"; I became a revisionist of the revisionists.

These letters were not published without difficulty. Some of them had to wait a long time and were subject to omissions, sometimes to the point of mutilation. The attacks they occasioned got me expelled from the Communist League, with which I ended up breaking completely. The Party functionaries turned against me when, in one such letter, I allowed myself to propose that Tito should resign. My ideas on Yugoslavia attracted the hostility of the nationalists, who were powerful in cultural spheres. The secularism I professed earned me the disdain of the clerics, who are influential in that part of Europe. In June of 1968 I spoke at an assembly at the Student Center of Zagreb, then surrounded by a police cordon. On the request of the Attorney General of the Republic, my speech was banned, while the journal I published was confiscated. The Supreme Court later upheld these sanctions.

During the 1970s I had to face up to the consequences of the gulag. I made four journeys to the USSR and learned of the fate of some of the closest members of my family. These discoveries reinforced my convictions, encouraging me in my refusal to comply. Not wanting to align myself with either the official government line or a program of national particularism, I was drawn to the philosophers of the Korčula School, united around the Zagreb journal *Praxis*, who critiqued both the Stalinists and the nationalists, the distortions of "theory" and "practice" in the USSR as well as in Yugoslavia. In 1971 the organizers of this heretical school asked me to become part of its advisory council. It was at that moment being subjected to the worst kinds of bullying attacks from both the bureaucrats in power and the nationalists who lorded it over the cultural sphere. I found myself among intellectuals who, like me, were searching for salvation. I have written about this in various other books: I am indebted to them. They are nearly all dead now.

I met there, among others, the elderly Ernst Bloch, marked by his forced passage from East to West Germany, Herbert Marcuse, then at the height of his fame, Henri Lefèbvre with his sixty-eighters of Nanterre, Erich Fromm in all his maturity, Jürgen Habermas, still a young man, Eugen Fink, Lucien Goldman, Pierre Naville, Lombardo Radice, Mario Spinella, as well as numerous philosophers and sociologists from all the nations of Yugoslavia, among them Rudi Supek and Gaio Petrović. Leszek Kolakowski, who had been expelled from the Communist Party of Poland, and Karel Kosik, who would later be expelled from that of Czechoslovakia, also attended the first meetings. We read together various passages from the "Letter of 2,000 words" and discussed it in detail before its distribution in Prague. Other attendees included Kostas Axelos and other contributors to the Parisian journals *Arguments* and *Socialisme ou Barbarie*; Ágnes Heller, Ferenc Fehér and György Márkus from

Budapest, still linked at the time to Lukács. We welcomed several friends of Sartre as well, along with members of the Gramsci Institute of Rome (the only Western participants associated with communism before the term "Euro-communism" began to be used in Italy). Followers of Trotsky, organized around Ernest Mandel, showed themselves in turn, as did certain anarchists, among whom figured Daniel Guérin and several of his friends, along with free thinkers like Lelio Basso and certain of his disciples. Max Horkheimer and Theodor Adorno, founders of the Frankfurt School, sympathized with the members of this "school of heterodoxy." The Soviet leaders never allowed philosophers from their country to meet with us.

We counterpoised Marx and the vulgate Marxist, Kautsky to Lenin, Lenin to the Stalinized Leninist, the February Revolution to that of October, the October to the Thermidor, revolutionary ideals to the revolution "betrayed," the New Left to the old leftism, utopia to utopianism, the single party system to party pluralism, self-management to state authoritarianism, a culture of criticism to "revolutionary culture," socialism "with a human face," however vague, to the supposed "real socialism" and, further, to a faceless capitalism. I saw in intellectual liberalism a condition of independence; in a kind of anarchism a counterweight to party-mindedness; in our dissidence a possible catharsis; in freedom of expression, so often vain, an expression of freedom. I was certainly aware of the danger that the form of writing called "journalism" based on social criticism might pose for literature. I also sensed aspects of intolerance among certain members. I wondered how, being a man of the Left, one becomes a free man.

The School of Korčula, which was interrupted by force, remains insufficiently known in Europe. In the USSR it was considered "the worst form of revisionism"; its members were called "traitors" and "slanderers" of communism and socialism. Yugoslavia's Communist League reproached it for slipping into a "critique of everything existing." Following a discussion on charisma in politics and on certain charismatic personalities in power, the school and the journal *Praxis* were practically buried in 1974. That same year I sent my letter to Tito, naively suggesting that he resign. While I continued to respect the best of his achievements, the manner in which, in 1972 and 1973, certain Croat, Serb and other leaders, were ousted from their positions, the autocratic, Bolshevik methods employed on such occasions, along with the condemnations inflicted on numerous intellectuals at the time, incited me to write many of these letters and furnished me with arguments.

This was not simply a spontaneous expression of dissatisfaction. I had reflected on the habit, or mania, of writing open letters. I was inclined towards epistolary literature and had models before me, ancient and modern. In the Slavic tradition such missives, addressed simultaneously to friends and to the public, were common practice. As a young man I was especially interested in Herzen's *Letters to an Old Companion*. Later I grew enthusiastic over Gogol's *Selected Passages from a Correspondence with Friends*. In this century that sees too much written and more than necessary published I decided to make a selection of epistolary fragments, addressed not solely to friends but also to those on whom their fate depended.

Numerous letters of this sort are still circulating the world. Some were sent long ago and may still be en route. Others have been lost without anyone's knowledge of how or where. Still others were tossed into the sea, sealed in bottles. We shall happen upon them some day. Someone will undertake to write their story and perhaps it will help us to reconstruct the history of our time: requests and laments addressed to tribunals and institutions, to parties and political leaders; demands for retrials or reductions of sentences; missives in which innocence is proclaimed or hope for rehabilitation espoused; denunciations concealed inside archives or sought out for purposes of destruction; letters sent from concentration camps, written no one knows how or when, copies of which were hidden in the most secret recesses of barracks, in the space between two bricks, in garbage dumps. Responses received, or new sanctions—such as, for instance, the suspension of the right to correspondence, sometimes the equivalent of a death sentence; letters that arrived from the place of exile and made those who received them ill at ease; those from an "internal emigration," marked by reticence and circumspection because of censorship and fear. Whoever their authors might have been, simple people or famous writers, one would have to include them all, organize them according to God knows what criteria, in order to make them—an idea that would have appealed to certain writers I'm fond of—a great epistolary novel, historical or epic, a work more moving than any that the literature of dissidence has ever given us, a work beyond literature.

I exaggerate, but only slightly. Few indeed are the works of literature worthy of the name—novels, biographies, diaries, memoirs, travel narratives, or genealogies—that do not include letters within them. The letter is certainly the first, and perhaps also the last, literary genre.

Authors of open letters are more often comic than sublime. Few of them have avoided the fate of Moses, the unhappy professor protagonist of Saul Bellow's *Herzog*, who have not, like him, known this "mania for writing to important personages, to friends, even to the dead." Moses knew it was ridiculous to act this way, but it didn't depend solely on his will. There comes a moment when one can go on no more, when the only exit, it seems, is to take up a pen and write to someone, write "to them," as fast as possible, before one has a chance to think twice, no matter what may happen.

Occasionally a great deal of time passes before a letter of this sort is published, before it becomes an "open letter," which is when the author atones for his gesture. The mail sent to those in power is opened by subordinates, and it is they who decide whether it will be passed on to the addressees. One must not believe it is the prince who retrieves the glove tossed at his feet. His valet takes charge of the challenge, accepting it or not, according to his mood and convenience. If a duel were actually fought, there would be nothing chivalric about it. One does not obtain satisfaction except in the future, generally too late.

Those who copied and dispersed these missives were, for the most part, anonymous and alone. The risks they ran are barely imaginable. How can we express to them our gratitude? If they survived, they have nothing more to do with it.

The author of open letters usually receives no responses. Joseph Brodsky compared him to the "heroides" of Ovid: "It's as if he were writing to the dead or on their behalf." One reads such letters, nevertheless, before witnesses. One puts them forth in diverse locations. One reproduces them, lets them circulate, and, in the end, publishes them. At an extreme, one keeps the receipt, unique proof attesting to the fact that a letter was indeed sent, specifying the date and the name of the addressee. I have kept the receipts of the greater part of the letters collected here. I don't know if they prove more my distrust of others or my personal weakness.

In this chronicle I have collected only those letters that touched on Russia, the country in which my father was born and in which so many members of my family disappeared. The book therefore differs in its composition and organization—by what was omitted and what added—from my previous *Epistolaire de l'autre Europe* (Paris, 1993), to the point that it becomes another and, in a sense, parallel work. The difference is due to a sometimes uncertain experiment in form and appropriated narration in the present work. I was tempted by the idea of a kind of epistolary *Bildungsroman*, which would reflect, at one and the same time, the apprenticeship and growth of awareness that has marked my experience, avoiding as much as possible the stereotypes of "historical" testimonials and "fictionalized" biographies.

That the author of these letters has at times been ingenuous, the present story has taken upon itself to demonstrate. I championed the Yugoslav idea: at this very moment an army pretending to belong to Yugoslavia is pulverizing the villages of Bosnia with cannon fire. The old bridge across the Neretva in my native town has been destroyed. Yugoslavia does not exist, let alone the idea of it. I defended the "insulted and injured" from various national groups, some of whom are responsible for the war among nationalities that is devouring my country. I hoped for the installation of democracy in Eastern Europe, while all we have obtained as a result is what I called, in one of my final letters, "democraship." The changes we dreamed of—this is one of my "historical experiences,"—in coming into existence, frequently take on grotesque form.

The last of these letters were sent from Paris and Rome, the first from Eastern Europe and Zagreb. I no longer knew to which city I belonged or where I would return. I desired, at one and the same time, to remain present in order to witness, and to distance myself in order to preserve my independence. Living between one's homeland and the place of emigration, simultaneously between exile and asylum, is not the worst situation for a writer to be in. Perhaps the same can be said, without exaggeration about the role of critical minds in the old democracies of the West. Our fates seem gradually to converge the more we leave behind the Cold War.

I end this afterword in Saint Petersburg a quarter century after the first letter of my epistolary. I observe the unbearable disorder that reigns in this harmoniously constructed city—thus it is in all of Russia—and invoke once more Pushkin's lament: "My God, how sad our Russia is!"

I have already noted the instances of my disillusionment. I have nothing more to add. I refuse to make predictions: they are too often the prerogative of charlatans.

Name Index

Achour, Mouloud, 74
Aćimović, Tihomir, 45
Adorno, Theodor, 215
Aitmatov, Chingiz, 71, 174
Akhmadulina, Bela, 33, 34, 174
Akhmatova, Anna (Gorenka, Anyuta), 18, 30, 42, 62, 68, 71, 87, 134, 142, 161, 162, 163
Aksyonov, 176
Amalrik, Andrei, 28
Andreev, Leonid, 81
Andreev, Yury, 97, 100
Andrić, Ivo, 205
Antić, Miroslav, 96, 107
Antonov-Ovseenko, Anton, 155, 168, 169, 170, 171
Antonov-Ovseenko, Vladimir, 168, 171
Antonovich, Olga, 22, 23, 43, 47, 48
Apollinaire, Guillaume, 72
Astafyev, Viktor, 174
Averintsev, Sergei, 36, 108
Axelos, Kostas, 214

Babel, Isaak, 19, 20, 41, 52, 73, 182
Babitsky, Konstantin, 67
Bakunin, Mikhail, 137
Barbieri, Frane, 24

Basso, Lelio, 215
Bazanov, 171
Bazarov, Vladimir, 140
Beckett, Samuel, 140
Belinsky, Vissarion, 87
Bellow, Saul, 217
Belozerskaya, Lyuba, 156, 157
Belyi, Andrei, 87
Berberova, Nina, 166
Berdyaev, Christian, 116
Berdyaev, Nikolai, 15, 16, 36, 37, 44, 88, 109, 110, 166, 187
Berg, Yevgeniya, 166, 167
Bergolts, Olga, 95
Bergson, Henri, 116
Bezimensky, Aleksandr, 170
Bitov, Andrei, 174
Bitov, Oleg, 139
Bloch, Ernst, 123, 214
Blok, Aleksandr, 15, 172, 180
Blucher, Vasily, 47, 97
Bogdanov, Aleksandr, 141
Bogomolov, Vladimir, 174
Bogoraz, Larisa, 28, 67
Bonch-Bruevich, Vladimir, 136
Bondarev, Yury, 205
Bonner, Helena, 112
Borges, Jorge Louis, 119

Borisova, Alla, 18, 99
Bortnyansky, 107
Böll, Heinrich, 79
Brezhnev, Leonid, 19, 24, 27, 30, 35, 51, 63, 66, 68, 71, 76, 78, 81, 106, 127, 172
Brik, Lili, 87
Brodsky, Joseph, 12, 18, 29, 30, 33, 95, 122, 163, 174, 176, 188, 192, 203, 217
Broué, Pierre, 147
Bryusov, Valery, 52
Buber-Neumann, Margarete, 26
Bukharin, Nikolai, 17, 52, 61, 82, 88, 101, 120, 127, 131, 132, 133, 134, 135, 142, 145
Bukovsky, Vladimir, 28, 67
Bulchis, Algimantas, 97
Bulgakov, Mikhail, 33, 42, 87, 115, 119, 156, 157, 158, 159, 160, 182
Bulgakov, Sergei, 37
Bulgakov, Yelena, 158
Bunin, Ivan, 12, 32, 166
Bursov, Boris, 97

Camara, Djigui, 74
Carillo, Santiago, 101
Ceaușescu, Nikolae, 120

NAME INDEX

Cesarec, August, 100, 210
Ciliga, Antun, 26
Chaadaev, Pyotr, 32, 87
Chagall, Marc, 19, 87
Chekhov, Anton, 4, 7, 103, 109, 116, 190
Chernyshevsky, Nikolai, 109
Chkalov, 6
Chukovsky, Nikolai, 161
Churchill, Winston, 69
Cohen, 171
Custine, Astolphe, 4
Cvijić, Duka, 70
Cvijić, Štef, 70

Dal, 26
Daniel, Yury (Arzhak, Nikolai), 9, 27, 28, 61, 166
Dashevskaya, Lyudmila, 110
da Silva Carozo, Bonaventura, 74
Dawson-Scott, Catherine, 174
de Gaulle, Charles, 69
Deloné, Vadim, 67
del Río Mercador, Ramon, 145
Demichov, Pyotr, 105
Denikin, Anton, 56
Desnitsky, Vasily, 140
Deutcher, Isaac, 26, 146, 147
Đilas, Milovan, 41
Dombrovsky, Yury, 81, 174
Dostoevsky, Fyodor, 7, 12, 13, 15, 17, 37, 44, 48, 64, 77, 86, 95, 163, 190

Dreyfus, Alfred, 127
Drmljuga, Vladimir, 67
Dubček, Alexander, 145
Dudintsev, Vladimir, 174
Dudko, Sergei, 108
Dzherzhinsky, Feliks, 145

Efron, Ariadna, 130, 164, 165
Efron, Sergei, 164
Efron, Yelizaveta, 165
Ehrenburg, Ilya, 57, 171
Eisenstein, Sergei, 39, 42, 69, 171
Eliot, T. S., 162
Erdman, Nikolai, 157
Erenburg, Ilya, 57
Etkind, Yefin, 18, 176

Fainberg, Viktor, 67
Father Gennady, 108, 109
Father Vladimir, 108
Fehér, Ferenc, 214
Filofei, 16
Fink, Eugen, 214
Florovsky, George, 13
Fonvizin, Denis, 87
France, Anatole, 87
Franco, Francisco, 69
Frank, Sigismund, 111
Fromm, Erich, 214
Fučík, Julius, 100
Fyodorenko, Nikolai, 8, 9

Gabiskiria, Amiran, 40
Galich, Aleksandr, 105, 203
Galilei, Galileo, 128
Galsworthy, John, 174
Gershenzon, Mikhail, 87
Gide, André, 77

Ginzburg, Aleksandr, 28
Ginzburg, Evgenia, 58, 164, 165
Gladkov, Fyodor, 41
Glan, Bety, 106
Gogol, Nikolai, 7, 87, 190, 216
Goldman, Lucien, 214
Gončar, Oleš, 51
Gorbachev, Mikhail, 88, 127, 133, 144, 177, 178, 179, 180, 190
Gorbanevskaya, Nataliya, 28, 67
Gorkić, Milan, 70, 106, 145
Gorky, Maxim, 42, 57, 87, 96, 137, 139, 140, 141, 142, 143, 162, 166, 171
Gramsci, Antonio, 134
Granin, Daniil, 174
Grigorashenko, Konstantin (Uncle Kostya), 19, 20, 21
Grigoroshenko, Mikhail (Uncle Misha), 21
Grigorashenko, Nikolai (Grandfather), 47
Grigorashenko, Nikolai (Uncle Nikolai), 20, 21, 22
Grigorashenko, Nataliya (Meshkova, Aunt Tusya), 20, 21, 22, 23, 43, 48, 49, 54, 64
Grigorashenko, Neonila, 21
Grigorashenko, Vladimir (Uncle Vladimir, Volodya), 20, 21, 24, 47, 48, 49, 70, 119, 207

Name Index

Grigorashenko, Yelena, 19
Grigorenko, Pyotr, 28, 105
Grujić, Nikola, 45, 46, 47
Guérin, Daniel, 215
Gumilyov, Nikolai, 18, 32, 134, 161, 162, 166
Gur-Emir, Timur, 76

Habermas, Jürgen, 214
Hašek, Jaroslav, 205
Havel, Václav, 28, 88
Hebrang, Andrija, 145
Hegel, Georg Wilhelm Friedrich, 170
Heidegger, Martin, 116
Heifetz, Jascha, 20
Heller, Ágnes, 214
Herzen, Aleksandr, 36, 87, 109, 137, 190, 216
Hingley, Ronald, 171
Hitler, Adolf, 69, 98, 170
Hoffman, Branko, 151
Horkheimer, Max, 215
Horvatin, Kamilo, 70
Hugo, Victor, 102
Husák, Gustav, 120, 155

Ibarruri, Dolores, 81
Ilyina, Galyna, 106
Iskander, Fazil, 174
Ivan III, 16, 171
Ivanov, Ivan, 33, 34, 50, 52
Ivanov, Vsevolod, 81
Ivanov, Vyacheslav, 87
Isaković, Antonije, 150
Izewbaye, Dan, 74

Jakobson, Roman, 87
Janáček, Leoš, 205
Jankelević, Vladimir, 116

Jeremić, Dragan, 115, 116, 117, 118, 119
Jighida, Baba, 74
John Paul II, 128

Karadžić, Radovan, 205, 206
Karamzin, Nikolai, 87
Karataev, Platon, 7
Karpov, Vladimir, 174
Kaštelan, Jure, 46
Kataev, Valentin, 19, 146, 158
Kautsky, Karl, 215
Kazakova, Rimma, 72, 84
Kazimirov, Igor, 50
Kharitonov, Ivan, 4, 8, 61, 62, 63, 78
Khlebnikov, Velimir, 161, 162
Khrushchev, Nikita, 10, 11, 40, 41, 88, 131, 146, 161, 170, 172, 211
Kidrich, Boris, 133
Kim, Yuliy, 174
Kirov, Sergei, 145
Kiš, Danilo, 3, 8, 25, 31, 41, 42, 47, 70, 72, 114, 117, 118, 119, 120, 148, 155, 156, 159, 188, 189, 192, 203
Kiselev, Nikolai (Kolya), 31, 34, 35, 36, 38, 39, 47, 50, 66, 72, 107, 108, 111
Kleptikov, 105
Kohout, Pavel, 28
Kolakowski, Leszek, 214
Konrád, György, 183
Konwicki, Tadeusz, 28
Kopelev, Lev, 176

Korneichuk, 97, 100
Korolenko, Vladimir, 7
Korotich, Vitaly, 174
Kosik, Karel, 214
Kotkin, Valentin, 72, 74, 77, 79, 83
Kovačić, Ivan Goran, 24
Kozmaš, Ciril, 8
Kravchenko, Viktor, 26, 114
Krupskaya, Nadezhda, 171
Kuprin, Aleksandr, 87
Kuron, Jacek, 88
Krleža, Miroslav, 3, 9, 10, 31, 66, 70, 81, 86, 97, 100, 122, 139, 140, 156, 205, 211
Kropotkin, Pyotr, 120, 136, 138, 155
Kruchonykh, Aleksei, 165
Kundera, Milan, 28, 155
Kuznetsov, Eduard, 28

Larin, Yury, 61, 131
Larina, Anya, 61, 88, 135
Lashko, Vera, 28
Lazarev, Ivan, 36, 108, 109
Lefèbvre, Henri, 214
Lebedev, Yevgeny, 203
Lenin, Vladimir, 17, 36, 52, 56, 68, 69, 71, 78, 80, 84, 107, 109, 134, 136, 137, 140, 145, 166, 168, 170, 192
Leonov, Leonid, 86, 171
Leontev, 36, 37, 109
Lermontov, Mikhail, 6, 12, 134
Leskov, Nikolai, 62, 103
Levin, Lev, 142

Name Index

Levitansky, Yury, 33, 34
Libedinsky, Yury, 87
Liberman, Yevsei, 133
Likhachev, Dmitry, 174
Litvinov, Pavel, 67
Lisiansky, 34
Lomakina, Antoniya, 71
London, Artur, 121, 145
Lossky, Vladimir, 166
Lukács, György, 215
Lukić, Sveta, 96, 106, 107
Lukin, Vladimir, 106
Lunacharsky, Anatoly, 17, 52, 80, 82, 87, 134, 141
Luther, Martin, 190
Lvovna, Miriam, 73

Maksimov, Vladimir, 79, 176
Malevich, Kazimir, 18, 176
Mandel Ernest, 215
Mandelshtam, Nadezhda, 8, 42, 68, 71, 116, 134, 142, 155, 161, 162, 163, 169, 203
Mandelshtam, Osip, 8, 12, 30, 32, 35, 41, 68, 90, 104, 134, 142, 161, 162, 163
Malraux, André, 82, 122, 137
Mao Tse Tung, 69
Marchenko, Anatoly, 28
Marcuse, Herbert, 123, 214
Markovna, Ida, 97, 100, 101, 102
Márkus, György, 214
Marx, Karl, 37, 146, 170, 215
Masaryk, Jan, 205

Masleša, Sveto, 76, 104, 105, 106, 111, 156, 165
Matveevich, Nikolai, 119, 181
Matveevich, Vsevolod, 3, 19–20, 31, 48, 99, 119, 186, 187
Matvejević, Predrag, 119, 120, 121, 201
Mayakovsky, Vladimir, 33, 52, 57, 100, 157, 159, 161
Medvedev, Roy, 88, 114, 155, 169, 172, 173
Merezhkovsky, Dmitry, 166
Metakse, 38, 39, 50
Meyerhold, Vsevolod, 100, 159, 181
Michnik, Adam, 88, 183
Mihailov, Mihajlo, 31, 80
Miller, Arthur, 11
Milošević, Slobodan, 205, 206
Mitin, Mark, 171
Modzelewski, Karol, 88
Moiseeva, Sofya, 26
Molière, 44, 158
Molotov, Vyacheslav, 159
Montesquieu, Baron de, Charles-Louis Secondat, 190
Motorin, 104
Mounier, Emmanuel, 137
Mukhtabarov, Omon (Aman), 74, 75
Mussolini, Benito, 69
Mussorgsky, Modest, 108

Nabokov, Vladimir, 12, 75, 166

Nagy, Imre, 120, 145
Nalbandyan, Dmitry, 66
Napoleon, Bonaparte, 102
Nassidze, Sulkhan, 42
Naville, Pierre, 147, 214
Neizvestny, Ernst, 11
Nekrasov, Nikolai, 134
Nekrich, Aleksandr, 97
Nero, 170
Nikolaevsky, 26
Nikolsky, Boris, 97
Nixon, Richard, 94

Obuchovskaya, Olga, 166
Okudzhava, Bulat, 33, 61, 78, 79, 80, 81, 82, 89, 172, 174, 192, 198, 201, 202, 203
Ordzhonikidze, Grigory, 145
Ovid, Publius Naso, 86, 217
Orwell, George, 137
Ozerov, 78

Palevsky, 8
Pasternak, Boris, 7, 33, 42, 80, 87, 88, 130, 134, 158, 161, 162, 164, 165, 166, 190
Patriarch Nikon, 56
Patriarch Pimen, 109
Paustovsky, Konstantin, 19, 171
Pavlović, Živojin, 26, 145
Pavlovsky, Aleksei, 98
Peshkov, Aleksei, 142
Peter the Great, 15, 56, 94, 171
Petlyura, 56

Name Index

Petrović, Brana, 14
Petrović, Gaio, 214
Pilnyak, Boris, 52, 87
Pisarev, Dmitry, 133
Plato, 141
Platonov, Andrei, 81
Plekhanov, Georgy, 109
Pokrovsky, Mikhail, 141
Popa, Vasko, 67, 188
Popov, Anton, 66, 96, 99
Pozner, Pavel, 74
Prohić, Kasim, 7, 8
Prokofiev, Sergei, 62
Proudhon, Pierre-Joseph, 141
Proust, Marcel, 80
Pushkin, Aleksandr, 4, 6, 7, 12, 13, 18, 32, 134, 163, 190, 218
Pyatnikov, 170

Radek, Karl, 80
Radice, Lombardo, 214
Radvolina, Ida, 100
Rakoczy, 81
Rashidov, 71
Rasputin, Valentin, 81, 116, 174
Razin, Stenka, 106
Registan, 33, 34
Repin, Ilya, 65, 70
Richtman, Zvonimir, 145
Rozanov, Vasily, 53, 81
Rozhdestvensky, Robert, 73, 79, 174
Rozov, Viktor, 174
Rublev, Andrei, 65
Russell, Bertrand, 116, 137
Rustaveli, Shota, 42
Rybakov, Anatoly, 81, 174, 176

Sahi, 38
Sakharov, Andrei, 56, 88, 105, 109, 112, 120, 183
Sanguineti, Edoardo, 67, 68, 69, 70, 71, 72, 78, 79, 81, 82, 83, 84, 85
Sappho, 12
Sartre, Jean-Paul, 50, 116, 162, 215
Ščepanović, Branimir, 118
Scriabin, Aleksandr, 99
Seifulina, Lidiya, 52
Serebryakov, Leonid, 171
Sergei (Sergius) of Radonezh, 56, 93
Semyonovich, Leonid, 61, 78, 83
Shafarovich, Igor, 166
Shakespeare, William, 44, 170
Shalamov, Varlam, 10, 58, 90, 91, 92, 104, 120, 203
Shao Chi, Liu, 129
Shaw, Bernard, 137
Shchedrin, Rodion, 52
Sheskin, 4
Shestov, Lev, 51, 102, 116, 166
Shklovsky, Viktor, 86, 87, 88, 89
Sholokhov, Mikhail, 42, 106, 205
Shostakovich, Dmitry, 18, 30, 42, 62
Sidur, Vadim, 104, 105, 106
Šik, Ota, 133
Sinyavsky, Andrei (Terts, Avram), 9, 12, 27, 28, 61, 88, 166, 167, 176, 192, 193, 203

Škvorecký, Josef, 28
Slezberg, Olga, 58
Smirnov, Vladimir, 66
Soloukhin, Vladimir, 10
Solovyov, Sergei, 102, 105
Solovyov, Vladimir, 7, 15, 36, 44, 109, 110, 190
Solzhenitsyn, Aleksandr, 25, 26, 34, 55, 56, 57, 58, 66, 76, 79, 80, 88, 90, 93, 106, 108, 109, 111, 120, 166, 176, 190
Sontag, Susan, 122, 188
Sorsky, Nil, 56, 93
Souvarine, Boris, 171
Spinella, Mario, 214
Springer, Axel, 80
Stadnyuk, Ivan, 97
Štajner, Karlo, 24, 25, 26, 70, 92, 114, 130, 155, 192, 207, 208, 209, 210, 211
Štajner, Sofya, 208, 209, 211
Stalin, Yosif (Dzhugashvili), 5, 35, 40, 41, 42, 47, 63, 68, 69, 72, 75, 76, 77, 80, 81, 87, 97, 98, 100, 111, 116, 120, 128, 131, 132, 145, 146, 147, 150, 156, 157, 158, 159, 160, 168, 169, 170, 171, 172, 173, 192
Stardelov, Georgy, 96, 100
Steiner, George, 146
Stepanov, Vladimir, 81
Stolypin, Pyotr, 56, 141
Stravinsky, Igor, 42, 53
Strossmayer, Josip, 205
Struve, Gleb, 166

Sukhanov, Nikolai, 140
Supek, Rudi, 214
Surovtsev, Yury, 61, 62
Sverdlov, Yakov, 87

Tatlin, Vladimir, 159
Tchaikovsky, Pyotr, 99
Telemann, 81
Tikhonov, Aleksandr, 140
Timofeev, Vladimir, 186
Tito (Josif Broz), 24, 35, 63, 69, 106, 120, 122, 148, 208, 211, 214, 215
Togliatti, Palmiro, 101
Tolstoy, Lev, 6, 7, 13, 16, 44, 109, 203
Tomashevsky, Boris, 32, 81
Topadze, David, 42
Tretyakov, Sergei, 65, 100
Triolet, Elsa, 87
Trotsky, Lev (Bronshtein), 17, 26, 52, 62, 69, 101, 120, 134, 144, 145, 146, 147, 168, 171, 215
Tsvetaeva, Anastasiya, 165
Tsvetaeva, Marina, 130, 161, 162, 164, 165, 166
Tucker, Robert, 171
Tuđman, Franjo, 208

Tukhachevsky, Mikhail, 47, 97, 100
Turgenev, Ivan, 6, 62
Tvardovsky, Aleksandr, 32, 33, 157
Tyutchev, Fyodor, 44, 180
Ujević, Tin, 205
Ushakov, 159

Vagapova, Nataliya, 106
Varga, Yevgeny, 133
Vekhov, Aleksandr Alekseyevich, 66, 67, 110
Veseletsky, Afanasy, 71, 77, 83
Vilenkin, Vitaly, 158
Villon, François, 34
Vinogradov, Igor, 174, 176
Vishinsky, A. 120, 123, 131, 142, 143, 181
Vitkovsky, Dmitry, 58
Vlady, Marina, 61
Voinovich, Vladimir, 176
Voznesensky, Andrei, 33, 174
Vrangel, Pyotr, 56
Vronsky, 52
Vujović, brothers, 70

Vulević, Čedo, 148
Vurgan, Samud, 171
Vysotsky, Vladimir, 33, 61, 95, 104, 202, 203

Wilde, Oscar, 137

Yagotkin, 105, 106
Yakir, Iona, 47, 97, 100
Yakovleva, Nataliya, 106
Yashvili, Marina, 42
Yeltsin, Boris, 127, 181, 204
Yesenin, Sergei, 33, 52, 134, 161
Yevtushenko, Yevgeny, 33, 82, 174
Yezuvitov, Andrei, 97
Yudenich, 56

Zamyatin, Yevgeny, 13, 87, 142, 166
Zhdanov, Andrei, 27, 53, 62, 64, 66, 106, 120, 134, 141
Zhirinovsky, Vladimir, 198, 199
Zhivkov, Todor, 120
Zoshchenko, Mikhail, 28, 42, 62, 84, 87

Also available from CEU Press

WRITING EUROPE

Edited by
Ursula Keller, publicist, film-maker, dramaturg
and program director at the Literaturhaus Hamburg and
Ilma Rakusa, writer, publicist and literary scholar

What do we mean by Europe? Thirty-three renowned authors from 33 European countries attempt an answer—in serious, ironic, skeptical, or optimistic tones. Their essays, written for the symposium held at the Literaturhaus Hamburg in 2003, reflect the astonishing diversity of European cultures. Not only are the style and experience of the individual authors remarkable for their distinctiveness, but their perspectives and views also appear to have little in common—at first glance.

The editors have created a unique literary project, a milestone in the vitally necessary cultural discourse about Europe.

Contributors
Ursula Keller GERMANY • *Ilma Rakusa* SWITZERLAND
Guðbergur Bergsson ISLAND • *Andrei Bitov* RUSSIA • *Hans Maarten van den Brink* THE NETHERLANDS • *Mircea Cărtărescu* ROMANIA • *Stefan Chwin* POLAND • *Aleš Debeljak* SLOVENIA • *Jörn Donner* FINLAND
Mario Fortunato ITALY • *Eugenio Fuentes* SPAIN • *Jans Christian Grøndahl* DENMARK • *Durs Grünbein* GERMANY • *Daniela Hodrová* CZECH REPUBLIC
Panos Ioannides CYPRUS • *Mirela Ivanova* BULGARIA • *Lídia Jorge* PORTUGAL • *Dževad Karahasan* BOSNIA • *Fatos Lubonja* ALBANIA • *Adolf Muschg* SWITZERLAND • *Péter Nádas* HUNGARY • *Emine Sevgi Özdamar* TURKEY • *Geir Pollen* NORWAY • *Jean Rouaud* FRANCE • *Robert Schindel* AUSTRIA • *Ivan Štrpka* SLOVAKIA • *Richard Swartz* SWEDEN • *Nikos Themelis* GREECE • *Emil Tode* ESTONIA • *Colm Tóibín* IRELAND
Jean-Philippe Toussaint BELGIUM • *Dubravka Ugrešić* CROATIA • *Dragan Velikić* SERBIA • *Tomas Venclova* LITHUANIA • *Māra Zālīte* LATVIA

2004, 372 pages
ISBN 963-9241-89-x cloth $/€ 43.95 / £25.95
ISBN 963-9241-90-3 paperback $/€ 22.95 / £12.95

AVAILABLE TO ORDER AT ALL GOOD BOOKSHOPS OR
CHECK OUT OUR WEBSITE www.ceupress.com
FOR FULL ORDERING DETAILS.